Corpora, Language, Teaching, and Resources:
From Theory to Practice

EC Vol. 12
Etudes contrastives

La collection *Etudes contrastives* propose des travaux qui confrontent les langues les plus diverses dans leurs usages multiples, apportant des éclairages inédits sur des phénomènes d'équivalence, d'interférence ou de non-coïncidence. Elle offre une ouverture sur la traduction en tant que contact de langues et pratique de réexpression à implications sociales et culturelles.

Collection placée sous la direction de
Anne-Marie Laurian et Thomas Szende

Natalie Kübler (ed.)

Corpora, Language, Teaching, and Resources: From Theory to Practice

PETER LANG
Bern · Berlin · Bruxelles · Frankfurt am Main · New York · Oxford · Wien

Bibliographic information published by die Deutsche Nationalbibliothek
Die Deutsche Nationalbibliothek lists this publication in the Deutsche Nationalbibliografie; detailed bibliographic data is available on the Internet at ‹http://dnb.d-nb.de›.

British Library Cataloguing-in-Publication Data: A catalogue record for this book is available from The British Library, Great Britain

Library of Congress Cataloging-in-Publication Data

Corpora, language, teaching, and resources : from theory to practice / Natalie Kübler (ed.).
p. cm. – (Etudes contrastives; 12)
ISBN 978-3-0343-0054-4
1. Language and languages–Study and teaching. 2. Corpora (Linguistics)
I. Kübler, Natalie.
P51.C65 2011
407.1–dc23

2011020104

Cover design: Thomas Jaberg, Peter Lang SA

ISBN 978-3-0343-0054-4
ISSN 1424-3563

Hochfeldstrasse 32, CH-3012 Bern, Switzerland
info@peterlang.com, www.peterlang.com, www.peterlang.net

Printed in Switzerland

Contents

NATALIE KÜBLER

Introduction

The first Teaching and Language Corpora conference started in 1994 in Oxford and took place every two years in the UK until the year 2000 when TaLC first moved to another European country, namely Graz in Austria. Since then, the TaLC conference has appeared in Italy (Bertinoro, 2002), Spain (Granada, 2004) and France (Paris) in 2006. The Paris conference was thus number seven.

TaLC has evolved since the first one and has developed in many different directions. Three main directions can be highlighted. The first one deals with the numerous resources that have been created to use corpora in different teaching settings. The second one is more theoretically bent and proposes to analyse specific characteristics in the language in order to evaluate how they could be taught; this part also deals with the place of corpora among other teaching resources, such as dictionaries, grammars and the Internet. The third one is closer to more classical approaches in applied linguistics and has become more and more important as this approach deals with the concrete use of corpora in teaching and its impact on the learner's motivation, knowledge, and skills in the field of languages.

This volume is a continuation of the TaLC tradition which takes into account the huge increase in computer facilities for language teaching and the teaching of language-related fields, such as translation, linguistics, terminology, or even literature and cultural studies. The papers presented here also deal with the use of more theoretical corpus linguistics concepts that can be applied in the classroom, and with the growing possibility of using more user-friendly tools and programmes to create resources that can be applied in language-related teaching.

Another very important factor that must be taken into account in this context is the way universities all over Europe have started applying the Bologna Agreement reform, which makes it compulsory for all students in Europe to learn at least one second language, whatever their field of study is. Most European students however have to learn at least English as a second language, as it has been for several decades now the lingua franca of world communication, not only in business and exchanges, but also in scientific communication, be it in hard sciences, life sciences, social sciences, or humanities. This factor shows a dramatic increase in the need for new resources and new approaches in teaching English and namely, English for specific purposes. Corpora can provide learners, teachers and other trainers or practitioners with new approaches and resources, as long as some guidance goes along discovery and resource creation and use.

The present volume has therefore been divided into five chapters which each put together different approaches related to language, teaching and corpora.

1. Bringing corpus use to effective practice

In the first chapter "Bringing corpus use to effective practice", Bernhard Kettemann and Georg Marko deal with the issue of using the advantages of data-driven learning in the teaching of Critical Discourse Analysis. Applying an original approach, the authors first describe the project they assigned their student, namely using corpus linguistics tools and data-driven learning to explore texts on Creative intelligence from a Critical discourse Analysis Theory. To then evaluate the DDL approach on students they assessed the students' research diaries, answers to a questionnaire and papers. The research diaries were mainly analysed from a qualitative point of view, but also as a sort of "learner corpus" from a corpus linguistics point of view. Results showed that although corpus linguistics tools enhanced students motivation to search further and use more corpora, they still show some hesitation which is mainly due to the lack of competence and confidence in using corpora. This supports the assumption made above that there is still a gap between corpus linguists and their audience, such as students or teachers for example.

Fear of using corpora is also a point that is underlined by Gil Philip who reports on a comparative study in the teaching of phraseology to different groups of students using corpora, dictionaries, Google, or a mix of the above. Her results prove that corpora have a positive effect on language production, but that the qualitative improvements students who use corpora show in their command of the language, also depends on the fact that they add corpora to an already existing set of effective tools. In the next two papers, the authors are trying to meet the needs for a more effective use of corpora by students and teachers. Alex Boulton focuses on the problem of changing traditional and cultural habits of learning among students and teachers. Being in favour of a user-friendly approach to corpora, he demonstrates how using existing, free, resources can lead learners to explore a variety of questions related to language learning and other areas. In the analysis of an experiment led with 30 students, he shows that a corpus linguistics approach for language students leads them to learn not only linguistic concepts, but also a way of learning and skills that can be adapted to various subjects.

The second part of this chapter illustrates how corpus linguistics is playing the role of keystone in a variety of approaches and needs. The communicative approach to language teaching recommends to focus on discourse analysis, and thus use genuine text. It is difficult however to dispose of any grammatical examples. In her study of the French verb jouer in a French journalistic corpus, Angela Chambers shows how corpus use can provide useful examples of grammatical patterns, but also useful examples of literal vs metaphorical meaning of the verb. It is argued that the rich variety of examples provided by corpora do not undermine the focus on studying genuine texts, but complete this approach. Corpora also prove to be appropriate in the learning and teaching of academic and specialised English. In another study based on contrastive adverbs in two corpora of theses in two quite different and specialised subject areas (Politics and Materials Science), Maggie Charles shows how corpora can help non native speakers of English in writing scientific papers. By studying the specific rhetorical functions of contrastive adverbs, students understand the rhetorical purposes of the writer and are thus enabled to use contrastive adverbs in their writing in an appropriate way. By comparing the analysis of the adjectives little and few in the academic writing sub-corpus of the BNC and in a small corpus of social science in the light of genre analysis and critical discourse analysis, Josta Van Rij-Heyliger shows how a corpus-based approach combined with those two types of analysis can help learners understand the social functions of different genres and the linguistic characteristics of those. Classical concepts of corpus linguistics, such as semantic preference and semantic prosody, can find a place in language teaching. By analysing those concepts in a specialised corpus, Sylvana Krausse indicates how they could be dealt with in a specialist language class.

Corpora in the classroom can have other applications than language teaching and learning. In an analysis of multilingual corpora, Josef Schmied shows how contrastive analysis can represent a basic resource for contrastive analysis. He illustrates this in analysing a multilingual translation corpus in English, German, French and Spanish and showing that a multilingual corpus can help learners become more autonomous than by using a bilingual corpus.

2. Learner corpora

Learner corpora represent a type of corpus of which the study has thrived during the last decade. The analysis of such corpora casts light in the learners' process and evolution, be it first language learners or second language learners. Juan Pablo Jimenez-Caicedo and Meg Gebhard show how learners' corpus analysis can help identify the way learners develop their writing skills and also what are the features that characterise this type of learner writing. In studying the use of prepositions by Spanish learners of English, Maria Belen Diez Bedmar has collected a four-year longitudinal corpus of leaners at the University of Jaen. Her results show which type of prepositions pose problems to this specific type of learners and how they evolve during their four-year study. Results can then be used to improve the learning process by focussing on specific difficulties. A second type of learner corpus, which is quite new in the domain, is the corpus of a translation learner. Castagnoli et al. present the development of the MeLLANGE corpus, which has been aligned and annotated at various levels, namely PoS-tagged, annotated with metadata concerning the learner and the translation situation, and annotated with an error-typology. They show how this learner corpus can be analysed and used from a corpus-driven and a corpus-based perspective in order to teach translation. This leads us to the fourth chapter, which deals with the creation of corpus-based resources and tools for language-related learning and teaching.

3. Resources and tools: creation

Corpora have been used for a long time for the creation of resources in various domains; "paper" corpora were already used in lexicography, terminology or language teaching. Since computerised corpora have appeared, the increase in the creation of corpus-based resources has been dramatic. Mojca Pecman presents a model for analysing collocations in scientific discourse that allowed her to create phraseological corpus-based data that can be used either for teaching the phraseology of scientific articles in English, or as a help for non-native speakers scientists who have to write in English. Olympia Tsaknakis suggests how a natural language processing tool developed to recognise proverbs in Greek can be used to provide corpus-based resources for foreign language teaching and learning. At the border between resource and tool creation, Olivier Kraif and Agnès Tutin describe the creation of a parallel corpus of academic papers in English and French, which ahs been annotated for 'semi-frozen expressions'. Using a corpus query tool that allows them to retrieve words or expressions from the parallel corpus, they explain how this corpus is used in the same way as a bilingual dictionary, but with more precise information, leading the learner to discover how semi-frozen expressions can be translated from French into English. Finally, Philippe Martin introduces a tool, WinPitch Corpus, which is dedicated to the teaching of spoken second language, using audio examples of spontaneous speech. WinPitch includes assisted speech to transcription alignment and a variety of functionalities that enable the teacher to present learners with genuine speech segments; it also allows learners to create their own speech segments and let the teacher correct the prosody for example. Before actually using the tools and resources in the classroom, some evaluation can be done to see what is the most appropriate way of adapting those resources to language-related learning and teaching. This is the subject of the fourth and last chapter.

4. Resources: evaluation

Two types of evaluations are presented here: first the assessment of a variety of corpora for different pedagogical aims, second the comparison of corpus use and dictionary use. Isabella Chiari explores the way language variations are presented in two written corpora of Italian (CORIS/CODIS and COLFIS) and two corpora of spoken Italian (LIP and C-ORAL-ROM). The issue of divergences in representing and classifying language variations is highlighted and she makes recommendations for the use of those corpora for teaching language variations. Although they can be extremely useful in this respect, it is necessary to pay attention to the differences in typologies and presentations of variations, and sometimes to the inconsistencies that can be found. In the last paper of this book, Geoffrey Williams analyses the lacks current electronic dictionaries present as far as a specific group of users is concerned: the ESP/EAP learner. He compares how scientific usage is described in three major learner's dictionaries and suggests using a corpus-based solution that uses prototype theory. He shows that this approach brings to the learner the information that cannot be found (or not completely be found) in dictionaries.

This book widely covers the relationship between corpora and language-related learning and teaching. It is hoped that the reader will find some ideas, advices, and useful suggestions in the diversity presented here.

References

Botley Simon et al. (eds) (1996) *Proceedings of Teaching and Language Corpora.* University of Lancaster: University Centre for Computer Corpus Research on Language.

Burnard L. & T. McEnnery (eds) (2000) *Rethinking Language Pedagogy: Papers from the third international conference on language and teaching*. Franfurt am Main: Peter Lang.

Kettemann B. & G. Marko (eds) (2002) *Teaching and learning by doing corpus analysis*. Amsterdam: Rodopi.

Wichmann, A., S. Fligelstone, Ennery & G. Knowles (eds) (2002) *Teaching and Language Corpora*. London and New York: Longman.

Part one

Bringing corpus use to effective practice

BERNHARD KETTEMANN & GEORG MARKO

Data-driving Critical Discourse Analysis

Learning about language and ideology by autonomously exploring a corpus (of creationist literature)

Abstract

The basic question behind this article is whether it is possible to use all the advantages of data-driven learning not only for foreign language teaching, but also in the teaching of discourse analysis or, more precisely, of Critical Discourse Analysis. We report on a small-scale project cum study we conducted to find out about the potential of this approach.

1. Corpus-driven exploratory learning

Generally speaking, discovery learning, which owes its intellectual foundation to pedagogical constructivism (cf. Wikipedia, "Constructivism learning theories"), is "an approach to instruction through which students interact with their environment – by exploring and manipulating objects, wrestling with questions and controversies, or performing experiments" (Ormrod 1995: 442, cit. in Conway 1997). New technologies provide the environments in which such self-determined and active learning can flourish (cf. Conway 1997); it therefore does not come as a surprise that there has been a desire to draw upon electronic corpora and concordancing software for discovery learning.

The basic idea of corpus-based discovery learning is that if learners – with some guidance and instructions from their teachers – work freely and independently with data in the form of language corpora, this can have positive effects on the depth as well as the range of what they become aware of, of what they observe and of what they understand. Intellectually, the approach owes a lot to constructivist pedagogy. This strategy has been shown to work quite successfully in learning a foreign language, especially at higher proficiency levels (see especially the work of Tim Johns (2002; Johns & King 1991) and of Silvia Bernardini (2000, 2002)). Bernardini calls her approach *corpus-based discovery learning*, while Johns prefers to term it *data-driven learning*. We personally like the expression (*corpus-driven*) *exploratory learning*. However, all these just function as flag terms, because learning (and teaching) in the way intended rests on a package of six interconnected didactic principles. The approach is:

a. *Data-driven*: The starting point for any language-related questions as well as the motivating force for seeking answers to them lies in the linguistic data. This means that students, rather than trying to find general rules and statements illustrated in the data, look at the latter to draw their own inductive conclusions.
b. *Corpus-based*: Enabling students to prepare and view textual data with the help of corpus linguistic tools (especially concordances and word lists), and the concomitant uncommon perspectives on texts, makes inductive reasoning easier.
c. *Autonomous*: Students can examine the data at their own pace and according to their own preferences and learning styles.
d. *Explorative*: Students are encouraged to simply dive into the data and to allow it to inspire their creativity rather than to examine pre-given issues systematically and exhaustively. In other words, they are supposed to search and look around rather than to re-search and examine.
e. *Process-oriented*: It follows from d. that the process of exploration is presented as the most important aspect, which – or so we hope – will heighten the pleasure of doing linguistics and boost students' confidence in their own research skills.
f. *Non-target-oriented*: It follows from d. and e. that students are not given specific tasks, and no specific results are expected of them. This should encourage them to pursue momentary whims, hopefully increasing the number of serendipitous findings. The teacher consequently acts as a guide and as an advisor, not as a mediator of knowledge nor as a judge of the students' performance.

These principles – most of them actually requirements of the learning environment – implicate certain didactic goals. Most of these have already been mentioned, but just to summarize them again:

i. *Inductive reasoning*: Students should draw their own conclusions from the data.
ii. *Awareness*: Students should come away with a sensitivity to and semi-conscious[1] awareness of linguistic and discursive phenomena rather than explicit foolproof knowledge.
iii. *Intrinsic motivation*: Students' general motivation should increase. This is closely linked with the next two goals.
iv. *Self-esteem and self-confidence*: Students should develop a positive view of themselves as language learners and language researchers.
v. *Pleasure factor*: Students should enjoy the process of exploring language and discourse.
vi. *Meta-cognitive reflection*: Students should be made to critically reflect upon their own reasoning and learning.

2. What is the use of exploratory learning in Critical Discourse Analysis?

When we discuss the benefits of an exploratory approach to learning and teaching, we must bear in mind that all the six goals just mentioned might play a more immediate role in the learning *of* a language than in the learning *about* a language. To be sure, prominent targets in the didactics of linguistics include:

- explicit knowledge of concepts and theories
- systematicity in the analysis of a phenomenon
- scientific soundness of argumentation
- coherence in presentation

1 By *semi-conscious* we mean that we do not necessarily have the explicit knowledge of concepts and terminology ready, but have at least a vague idea of the concepts.

which are not directly subsumable under any of the six goals listed. But it is probably safe to say that without a learning environment promoting these six goals, any attempt to achieve the last four is bound to fail.

2.1 Why CDA?

The main focus of our current research and most of our teaching is on Critical Discourse Analysis. This is also the preferred approach in the majority of the Master's and Doctoral theses that we supervise. Critical Discourse Analysis – usually abbreviated as CDA – looks at the role that language plays in creating and maintaining views of the world – sometimes called ideologies – and social relationships that are considered to form the fundament of socio-political problems and struggles.

In its research practice, CDA – to put it bluntly – interprets the meanings that particular forms may have, trying to find out about these meanings' social, political and/or cultural significance. This can be graphically represented as follows:

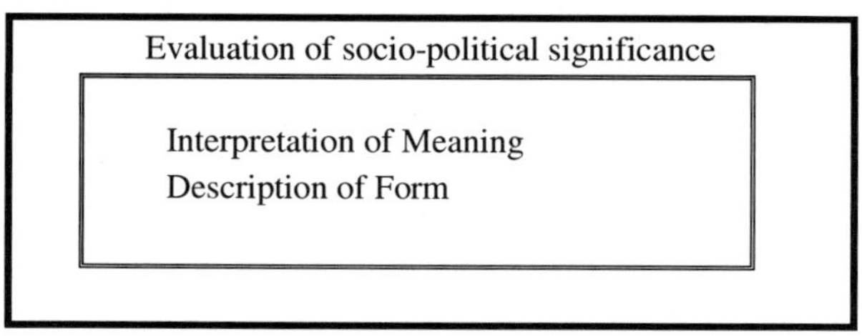

Fig. 1: The three levels of discourse.

A major problem for students is that when they are doing their own analyses within the framework of CDA, they find it difficult to cover all these three steps, i.e. describe forms, interpret meanings, and evaluate socio-political significances. They either describe the linguistic details of the texts they examine, or they resort to socio-philosophical speculations without making any references to concrete linguistic details. The consequence is uninspired (and uninspiring) lacklustre presentations, papers and theses.

Part of the problem certainly lies in CDA's tendency not to assign equal weight to the three levels itself, preferring, as it were, socio-political significance. There is a deplorable lack of data-oriented studies within CDA, especially with a corpus linguistic emphasis. However, the problem also seems related to the low levels – from our point of view – of our students' intrinsic motivation with respect to research, and our didactic inability to raise these.

Are there then any remedies for this set of interconnected problems? In a course involving Critical Discourse Analysis, we decided to adopt the approach of corpus-based exploratory learning and put it to the test at the same time. This was the purpose of the small-scale study whose design and results we describe here.

3. The study

3.1 Research question

What objective and subjective effects (if any) does exploratory learning based on a large corpus of a particular discourse type have on students' understanding of the connections between language and the construction and dissemination of world views, and on their ability to translate this into a systematic approach to discourse analytical research?

3.2 Context

The subjects of the study were the 17 students attending a seminar entitled *The Language of American Christian Fundamentalism*, held in the summer term of 2006. We chose this course as it took a Critical Discourse Analytical approach to the study of fundamentalist language. This meant that any effect that exploration of the corpus might have should immediately become visible in the research that students were required to undertake themselves (an oral presentation and a written term paper). Integrating the project into the course also allowed us to provide guidance in the normal course of classes: exploratory learning does not mean that students are completely left to their own devices.

3.3 Corpus

The exploratory learning sessions were supposed to focus on one large corpus provided by us. This corpus was thematically limited to a major issue raised by American Christian fundamentalism, viz. Intelligent Design (ID), the most recent version of Creationism. Proponents of this theory argue that there is substantial scientific evidence suggesting that the universe and in particular nature could not have evolved itself, without having been planned by an intervening intelligence. The approach meticulously avoids reference to religious concepts, which would a priori exclude it from any science curriculum (cf. Scott 2004: 116–131, Shanks 2004).

After featuring in an op-ed article in the *New York Times* by the Austrian Cardinal Christoph Schönborn (2005), the topic of Intelligent Design had been mentioned extensively in the Austrian media. As, however, it was never discussed in any depth, we expected students to be at least mildly interested in and curious about the topic.

For the corpus, we selected eight major works promoting Intelligent Design (see References for details). These were OCR-scanned to make them computer-readable. The size of the corpus was 633,876 word tokens (23,067 word types). Theoretically, students were not restricted to this ID-corpus, but we were expecting them to do most of their work with it.

It is important to mention that the topics that students had to deal with for their presentations and papers were not connected to Intelligent Design. This was to avoid giving an advantage to particular groups.

3.4 Procedure

In the first two sessions of the course, we introduced the participants of the seminar to the theory and practice of Critical Discourse Analysis and of corpus analysis (we primarily used *WordSmith Tools 3.0*: Scott 1999). They were also given extra material on these two topics – an extensive handout on CDA and a shortish manual for the most important functions of WordSmith. Then students got access to the programme and the corpus.

They were required to spend at least one hour per week (over a six week period) exploring the corpus according to their own interests. They were encouraged to follow intuitions and whims, cursorily or systematically looking at concordances or word lists, possibly also going beyond the corpus (e. g. considering further fundamentalist corpora provided by us, using WebCorp at <http://www.webcorp.org.uk/>, doing advanced Web or library searches). To document what they had been doing and to make the progression of their inquiries trackable, they had to keep research diaries. We provided occasional (though not regular) incentive questions, either content-related ("What is Intelligent Design's attitude towards non-human nature?") or language-related ("What is the role of adjectives in the texts? Which semantic domains predominate in adjectives?"). As the course was partly conducted via an e-learning platform (WebCT at <http://xanthippe.edu.uni-graz.at>) and the diaries were uploaded there, the students' creativity was supposed to be further stimulated by reading each others' contributions. Our tutor Christian Blinzer provided technical and other help on the platform.

3.5 Search types

In class, we carried out a variety of searches designed to encourage students to make use of the wide range of research options possible with WordSmith. With respect to word listing, for instance, we demonstrated how to use stop lists to eliminate function words (Table 1),

N	*Word*	*Frequency*
1.	design	2377
2.	evolution	1933
3.	theory	1554
4.	natural	1416
5.	science	1345
6.	life	1295
7.	intelligent	1154
8.	scientific	1138
9.	evidence	1115
10.	complexity	1000

Table 1. The 10 most frequent content words in the ID corpus or how to produce lists of multi-word clusters (Table 2).

N	Cluster	Freq
1.	the origin of life	146
2.	on the other hand	100
3.	the origin of species	73
4.	on the basis of	60
5.	in the fossil record	56
6.	the theory of evolution	56
7.	the origin of the	52
8.	for the origin of	51
9.	in the case of	50
10.	in the first place	50

Table 2. The 10 most frequent 4-word clusters in the ID corpus.

We also demonstrated how to employ the Keywords tool to identify the lexical forms most significantly deviating from 'ordinary' language (as represented by the BNC: Table 3[2]).

2 This was done using the wordlist at <http://www.lexically.net/downloads/version4/downloading%20BNC.htm> (we only later learned that it was not possible to use this list with WordSmith Tools 3.0).

design	2377
evolution	1933
theory	1554
science	1345
intelligent	1154
natural	1416
scientific	1138
of	23041
complexity	1000
is	11397

Table 3. 10 words occurring significantly more often in the ID corpus than in the BNC.

In connection with the Concordance function, we particularly highlighted the possibility of finding collocates, such as the most common nouns premodified by the word *intelligent* (Table 4):

N	Word	Freq.	*N*	Word	Freq.
1.	design	844	*8.*	direction	4
2.	cause	111	*9.*	activity	3
3.	agent	81	*10.*	creator	3
4.	agency	50	*11.*	intervention	3
5.	designer	18	*12.*	purpose	3
6.	causation	9	*13.*	uncertainty	3
7.	source	6			

Table 4. The 13 most frequent nouns premodified by *intelligent* in the ID corpus.

In addition, we drew students' attention to the possibility of also investigating more grammatical questions, such as which words are most likely to form adjectival compounds with *like* (table 5),

ape(-)like	10	bowel-like	1	matrix-like	1
bird-like	9	bulblike	1	miracle-like	1
hair(-)like	8	bush-like	1	monster-like	1
machine(-)like	7	button-like	1	mouse-like	1
mammal-like	7	cadaver-like	1	needle-like	1
law(-)like	6	cakelike	1	net-like	1
gill-like	5	cellophane-like	1	paddlelike	1
human-like	4	code-like	1	phoenix-like	1
life(-)like	4	computer-like	1	pressurelike	1
whip(-)like	4	detergent-like	1	rhinoceros-like	1
fish-like	3	disclike	1	rodentlike	1
reptile-like	3	domino-like	1	rod-like	1
watch-like	3	English-like	1	serpent-like	1
cell-like	2	fin-like	1	serum-like	1
clock-like	2	gamelike	1	snakelike	1
fingerlike	2	gorilla-like	1	sonar-like	1
force-like	2	horse-like	1	soul-like	1
goldberg-like	2	hydraulic-like	1	TPA-like	1
torpedolike	2	jointlike	1	tubelike	1
trough(-)like	2	keylike	1	velcro-like	1
amoeba-like	1	lattice-like	1	wars-like	1
artifact-like	1	lens-like	1	whale-like	1
barrel-like	1	lizard-like	1		
biochemical-like	1	man-like	1		

Table 5. Compounds with – like in the ID corpus.

or the negative prefix *non* (table 6):

nonnegotiable	2	Nondeterminism	1	non-mammalian	1
non-question-begging	2	nondigestible	1	non-massive	1
nonreductive	2	nondiplomats	1	nonmolecular	1
nonrepeating	2	nondividing	1	non-moral	1
nonrepetitive	2	nondogmatic	1	nonnegotiable	1
non-slaves	2	nondominant	1	non-optimal	1
nonsupernaturalist	2	nondualistic	1	non-organic	1
non-swimmer	2	non-elite	1	nonpartisan	1
non-visual	2	non-energetic	1	nonpeptide	1
non-ad hoc	1	nonentity	1	nonpositivistic	1
non-adjacent	1	nonenzymes	1	nonproductive	1
nonadvantageous	1	non-estrus	1	nonpurposive	1
non-american	1	nonevidence	1	nonregular	1
nonbalanced	1	non-eye	1	nonselective	1
nonbeing	1	nonfiction	1	nonself	1
non-believer	1	non-fictional	1	nonsexual	1
nonbinding	1	non-flying	1	nonspecialized	1
nonbiologist	1	nonfused	1	nonstarter	1
nonbrittle	1	non-gradualistic	1	nonsterile	1
non-chemical	1	non-gravitational	1	nontechnical	1
non-Christian	1	Nonindependent	1	nonteleologically	1
noncomplex	1	nonindexed	1	nontheists	1
nonconforming	1	non-industrial	1	nontoxic	1
nonconformist	1	nonlactating	1	non-trivial	1
non-conscious	1	non-lawyers	1	nonverbal	1
non-contracting	1	nonlethal	1	nonviable	1
nonconvergent	1	non-literal	1	nonvolatile	1
non-descended	1	nonliteralist	1	non-webbed	1
nondesigners	1	nonlocality	1	nonwhite	1
nondeterminacy	1	nonlogical	1	nonzero	1

Table 6. Words with the prefix non- in the ID-corpus.

All these types of searches were supposed to show the students what is possible, and to spark a fascination with corpus analysis, thus serving as a springboard for new ‘expeditions’.

3.6 Evaluation

To examine our research question, we analysed three types of data allowing insights into the students' exploration of the corpus:

- *Research diaries*: These should provide information about the process of research as well as about students' subjective experiences.
- *Evaluative questionnaire*: At the end of the course, all participants had to complete a questionnaire intended to reveal how they judged the project's usefulness in general, and with regard to their ensuing course work.
- *Papers*: We also examined students' written papers to assess the project's effect on their quality.

4. Results and discussion

The main body of data for the evaluation are the research diaries, which we first analysed qualitatively and then additionally subjected to a corpus linguistic examination.

4.1 Qualitative analysis of the research diaries

4.1.1 Method

By qualitative analysis we mean that we sought to identify the most salient tendencies noticeable in what the students wrote in their research diaries. For this purpose, we made a profile for each entry – an entry being what one student wrote and handed in for one week of the project. A profile is a matrix of categories into which we entered a verbal description.

This looks as follows:

Name	Johanna SECHSER	Week 1
Queries	Corpus	Corpora from the ICAME-CD, esp. Frown and Wellington C. of Spoken NZ Engl.
	Function	Wordlist (esp. statistics)
	Content	Statistics, comparison between spoken and written language (e.g. T/T ratio higher in the latter, or more longer words)
Approach	Descr./Interpret.	Detailed description. In addition, interpreting the results with respect to the difference between spoken and written, not content-related though.
Other activities	Related	–
	Unrelated	–
Metacomments	Technical	No problems with installing
	Procedural	–
	Approach	Comments on the scientific nature of the programme
	Material	–

Table 7. Profile for the qualitative analysis of the research diaries.

As can be seen, each profile contained information on the:

– *Queries*: Which corpora were searched? Which programme tools were used? Which specific aspects were examined?

In addition, we also described:

– *Other activities:* Which activities going beyond corpus searches were carried out, e.g. reading in the corpus, looking for background material and information, looking up words in dictionaries, etc.? Are they related to the corpus searches or not?
– *Metacomments*: Did the student comment on technical problems, on the approach of corpus linguistics or Critical Discourse Analysis, on her or his own proceeding, on the material, etc.?

These, however, turned out to be of less importance as they occurred relatively rarely and very inconsistently.

The profiles of each student were summarized in a person profile. From these we then tried to distil the basic tendencies of the whole group. As we ended up with only 17 students, any idea of creating a database (with a programme such as MS Access) was discarded. We have to admit that some of the students did not produce six entries, partly as a result of technical problems or miscommunication on our part concerning deadlines within the Easter break, but partly also a consequence of growing laxness on their part. Oddly enough, four students dropped the course after taking part in the project. All these are signs that it was not a complete success.

4.1.2 Results

– *Corpora used*

The instructions for the project centred almost exclusively on the Intelligent Design corpus, merely mentioning the possibility of using and/or compiling other corpora. Nevertheless, none of the participants spent all of the six weeks with the main corpus: on the contrary, the great majority used more than half their time examining other sources.

At the top of the list were texts by Christian Fundamentalist groups provided on the e-learning platform. Contrary to our intentions, these texts were regarded as a representative reference corpus of American Christian Fundamentalism. Especially after week 3, when students were assigned topics for their presentations and papers, they almost exclusively focused on texts from this collection, usually selected according to content criteria (i.e. if our topic is "Fundamentalist views on abortion," then we just take into accounts texts dealing with abortion).

Why did students so easily stray away from the main corpus? Firstly, we may have underestimated the degree of attraction the topic and thus also the corpus held for our students. In its attempt to engage in scientific argumentation about the impossibility of evolution and the possibility of creation, the discourse of the Intelligent Design movement does not feature ostentatively and (to most European minds) exaggeratedly religious outcries. This may be the reason why students found the potpourri of Fundamentalist texts much more stimulating, because there they very quickly found those elements they were expecting, e.g. *God, sin, homosexuality, abortion, Satan*, etc.

Secondly, students went for quick results and did not – at least in this initial phase of working with corpora – really appreciate the quantitative dimension of corpus research, and its potential to make repeated patterns of language visible. This also became manifest from the fact that for some of them it made no difference whether they examined individual texts of 300 words or a collection of 600,000 words, and from some of the metacomments we got ("Without reading the text, I do not know what to do with the data."). This suggests that a relatively large and homogeneous corpus may have less to offer than a heterogeneous one, no matter what the size.

A third reason was that many participants felt uncomfortable with the ID corpus because it was only vaguely related to their paper and presentation topics. Some commented that they did not know why they were supposed to deal with it, merely that it was expected of them as far as marking was concerned (this is, of course, not completely true because we marked according to effort and enthusiasm or the lack of them, and this was also announced). This means there was a certain pragmatic and utilitaristic attitude in students, an aspect which we had also underestimated or which we had hoped the approach would override.

– *Tools used*

WordSmith has two main tools that differ in function and use, namely *Wordlist* and *Concord*, ignoring the various subtools for the moment. Interestingly, students showed a strong preference for Wordlist, producing lists of all kinds (comparisons, keywords, with and without stoplists, multi-word clusters, etc.). Concord was principally used with a complementary function to Wordlist, namely to find out how often a certain word or word component was used in a corpus. It also featured in the search for extraordinary examples. Its potential for making ordinary, commonly appearing textual patterns visible was well-nigh ignored.

The first reason for this preference for Wordlist over Concord is that wordlists can be produced immediately without profound preconsiderations – unlike concordances, for which you have to formulate searches. As already mentioned, students seemed to go for quick solutions and results, and as wordlists show something at once they served this objective. The frequent use of Wordlist additionally suggests that students feel more comfortable when working on the lexical level of discourse analysis. They may not see too clearly how aspects of grammar and vocabulary interact and they may not see how grammar and lexicogrammar contribute to meaning and to the construction of worldviews.

– *Approaches taken*

The research diaries suggest that students took different paths in their corpus analyses. Some spent the first weeks describing data, preferably those aspects easily read off from wordlists (word frequencies, total word numbers, type/token-ratios, etc.). From week 2 or 3 onwards, they began to interpret the results, usually with reference to the content of the texts in the corpus ("*Bible, Genesis and God* do not occur in the ID corpus because Intelligent Design seems to avoid speaking about theological aspects of creation"). This usually went hand-in-hand with specific content-related searches in Concord ("Does *music* occur in the context of *sin* or *evil*? If so, this would suggest an association of music with a negative moral judgement"). While approaching the corpus in such a way agrees perfectly with the guidelines of the project, it poses a problem for exploratory learning because the possibilities are limited and quickly exhausted – this is maybe why many students changed corpora almost every week. But it also implies that the motivation-enhancing potential of autonomous corpus work is impeded or suspended.

The second (smaller) group combined descriptions with interpretations right from the beginning – in intelligent and original ways, if such judgment is permitted. Most of the time they had a specific question which they then examined with the help of the data. This meant that they actually proceeded very systematically – from the point of view of exploratory learning, perhaps too systematically. In their structured and organized approach, they did not allow themselves to explore the corpora freely and aimlessly, on the wings of saltationist associations. However, we also have to bear in mind that a research diary is not necessarily a precise documentation of what students really did. Being aware of what was normally required of them and being able to cope with these requirements, the students of this second group may have unconsciously construed their experience with corpus analysis as more systematic than it actually had been. Still, working with the corpus did not seem to completely free them from the constraints they were familiar with in academia.

– *Development*

There was clear progress regarding the technical side of work with corpora. Up to week 3, almost all the students added new methods of analysis or refined those they had already used. This, of course, also increased the depth of interpretation (if included). And generally speaking, they quickly became relatively competent WordSmith users.

However, almost all developments came to a halt from week 3 onwards. This was the point when the students got their presentation topics and left behind the ID corpus. It was also the point where they had developed certain patterns which they then used quasi-automatically with any new corpus (e.g. produce a wordlist minus function words with Wordlist, look for religiously-relevant terms with Concord, and then draw conclusions about the content of the corpus texts). Many students forgot about the research diary guidelines and just reported on what they had done for their presentations and papers – mostly concerned with the collection of texts and the search for background information – quitting corpus work for good.

4.2 Corpus analysis

To complement the qualitative analysis of the research diaries, we decided to do a corpus analysis too.

4.2.1 Method

We changed all the diary entries, in whatever electronic form we had received them, into TXT files to analyse them with WordSmith. This yielded a corpus of 44,304 word tokens (4,090 word types).

We primarily concentrated on the semantic domains of some of the most salient words and structures because they provided insights into what students actually described in the diaries. As this study was supposed to complement the qualitative data described above, we did not carry out a detailed, let alone exhaustive analysis.

4.2.2 Results

As a first step, we produced a wordlist of the most important content words used by students in their research diaries. We concentrated on the top 250 words and manually lemmatised this reduced list, merging different forms of the same word (or closely related words) into single entries. A closer look at the semantic domains that are represented by both large numbers of types as well as tokens supports the tendencies already noted above[3].

The largest group covers words (or concepts[4]) searched for, found and/or discussed in the analyses. This suggests a strong preoccupation with the description of data.

God	*138*	*man*	*51*	*Genesis*	*19*
intelligent/	*126*	*mock*	*50*	*Satan*	*18*
intelligence		*family*	*32*		
design	*119*	*evangelical*	*31*	*pill*	*18*
science/scientific	*98*	*sex*	*29*	*Darwinism*	*18*
theory	*96*	*religious*	*29*	*religion*	*17*
fundamentalism/	*95*	*pro*	*29*	*honour*	*17*
fundamentalist		*origin*	*28*	*species*	*16*
Christian	*94*	*natural*	*28*	*homosexuality*	*16*
Bible/Biblical	*86*	*contraception*	*28*	*designer*	*16*
music	*85*	*church*	*26*	*Christians*	*16*
abortion	*76*	*evil*	*23*	*amino*	*16*
evolution	*72*	*anti*	*22*	*war*	*15*
woman	*60*	*sin*	*21*	*neo*	*15*
ID	*58*	*marriage*	*21*	*capitalism*	*15*
Darwin	*57*	*children*	*21*		

Table 8. Lexemes for search words/concepts in the Research Diary corpus.

3 The following lists only contain lexemes (or lemmata) occurring at least 15 times.

4 The difference cannot be recognized in the list, e. g. whether students looked for the word God or simply talked about God's role for Christian Fundamentalism.

There are other groups which add to this impression, e.g. descriptive terms of linguistics:

word	*599*	*noun*	*37*	*title*	*18*
text	*51*	*language*	*36*	*plural*	*16*
quote	*54*	*negative*	*30*	*article*	*16*
context	*53*	*author*	*28*	*written*	*15*
book	*53*	*page*	*27*	*content*	*15*
term	*38*	*discourse*	*20*		

Table 9. Lexemes for linguistic descriptions in the Research Diary corpus. (Negative here is not evaluative, but for the description of (negative) connotations of expressions).

and also terms that are used for referring to results in a very general sense.

occur/occurrence	*264*	*type*	*54*	*key word/keyword*	*32*
list	*160*	*concordance*	*53*	*combination*	*29*
wordlist	*79*	*cluster*	*48*	*class*	*27*
result	*78*	*token*	*47*		
example	*60*	*view*	*34*		

Table 10. Lexemes concerned with results in the Research Diary corpus.

This group also includes a lot of quantifying expressions (in this context, it should be noted that many quantifiers qualify – pun intended! – as function words and therefore do not even figure in our wordlist).

frequent	*104*	*common*	*28*	*mainly*	*19*
frequency	*63*	*ratio*	*28*	*lot*	*18*
order	*43*	*least*	*27*	*high*	*18*
number	*42*	*little*	*21*	*various*	*16*
top	*29*	*several*	*20*	*percent*	*16*

Table 11. Quantifying lexemes in the Research Diary corpus.

Lexemes concerned with the processing of data, i.e. with interpretation, evaluation and argumentation, also figure prominently, even though they are still less frequent and less varied than those dealing with description[5].

fact	*41*	*point*	*22*	*evidence*	*16*
topic (~theme)	*31*	*information*	*22*	*reason*	*15*
idea	*25*	*role*	*21*	*mean*	*15*
question	*23*	*argument*	*18*		
case	*23*	*show*	*17*		

Table 12. Lexemes concerned with data processing in the Research Diary corpus.

This imbalance remains, even if we include other elements which also point to the process of data interpretation, namely

– mental process verbs:

want	*64*	*see*	*60*	*expect*	*33*
think/thought (n + v)	*61*	*know*	*56*	*believe*	*25*

Table 13. Mental process verbs in the Research Diary corpus.

– modality markers (of course minus modal verbs, which have been eliminated by the stoplist):

seem	*72*	*certain*	*21*	*probably*	*17*

Table 14. Lexemes marking modality in the Research Diary corpus.

– evaluative adjectives and adverbs:

interesting	*57*	*good*	*34*	*useful*	*15*
well	*48*	*important*	*18*		
right	*35*	*wrong*	*16*		

Table 15. Evaluative lexemes in the Research Diary corpus.

5 The distinction cannot easily be upheld, but close readings of the journals suggest that the expressions given were really used in one of these functions.

Wordlists just give a general view of the content of the diaries. They do, however, not allow a deeper understanding of the role that students assigned to themselves in their explorative work with corpora. This is also a relevant aspect, considering that autonomy is an important principle in the approach. We therefore looked at the uses of the first person singular pronoun *I*. With the help of the Collocation function in WordSmith, we established a list of the most common verbs which take *I* as their subject (we allowed a space of 3 words so as to include progressive, perfect and other complex forms). The list was manually lemmatised.

Once again, the verbs can be categorized, allowing insights into which processes are foregrounded. By far the largest and most varied group are verbs that simply describe the practical processes of working with a corpus and a concordancing programme:

try	75	*carry out (a search)*	2	*expand*	1
search	43	*collect*	2	*experiment*	1
start	41	*compare*	2	*finish*	1
work	40	*create*	2	*gather*	1
look at	31	*extend*	2	*include*	1
make	29	*fill*	2	*invest (time)*	1
use	22	*limit*	2	*list*	1
choose	21	*move*	2	*merge*	1
change	9	*produce*	2	*pick*	1
check	8	*skim*	2	*play*	1
add	6	*skip*	2	*process*	1
take a look	6	*accumulate*	1	*reduce*	1
begin	5	*activate*	1	*save*	1
run (a search)	5	*adjust*	1	*retrieve*	1
succeed	4	*close*	1	*re-try*	1
deal with	3	*compose*	1	*separate*	1
end	3	*decode*	1	*sort*	1
proceed	3	*divide*	1	*switch*	1
stop	3	*employ*	1	*take into consideration*	1

Table 16. Verbs of practical activities used with *I* in the research diaries.

A prominent subgroup describe (clearly) computer-related activities:

save	*15*	*install*	*4*	*click*	*1*
cop	*13*	*browse*	*2*	*scroll*	*1*
type	*12*	*enter*	*2*	*store*	*1*
download	*11*	*convert*	*2*	*unzip*	*1*
open	*9*	*google*	*2*		
upload	*7*	*press*	*2*		

Table 17. Verbs concerned with practical work with the computer used with *I* in the research diaries

Verbs directly referring to the process of interpretation are rare.

analyse	*7*	*conclude*	*1*	*present*	*1*
mean	*2*	*explain*	*1*	*verify*	*1*
argue	*1*	*interpret*	*1*		
attribute	*1*	*investigate*	*1*		

Table 18. Verbs of analysis used with *I* in the research diaries.

This, however, is not revealing in itself because verbs of description do not feature at all, unsurprisingly, we might say. After all, if we describe a phenomenon, we talk of the latter and not of ourselves.

Perhaps the relation between the two approaches is more noticeably reflected in the use of verbs denoting mental processes. These represent a very large group in the set. The most interesting comparison is between verbs of perception and verbs of cognition because these categories seem to be associated with description and observation on the one hand and with interpretation on the other.

Description/observation			
find	*134*	*come across*	*6*
notice	*16*	*encounter*	*5*
see	*14*	*hear*	*3*
discover	*9*		

Interpretation					
think	*46*	*believe*		*understand*	*2*
decide	*32*	*assume*	*2*	*wonder*	*2*
expect	*30*	*concentrate*	*2*	*associate*	*1*
know	*27*	*consider*	*2*	*figure out*	*1*
focus	*11*	*forget*	*2*	*imagine*	*1*
realize	*10*	*learn*	*2*	*presume*	*1*
suppose	*8*	*remember*	*2*	*suspect*	*1*

Table 19. Verbs of perception and verbs of cognition used with I in the research diaries.

The fact that *find* is by far the most frequently used verb with the first person singular pronoun indicates that students are often engaged in the description of (raw) data. However, a look at the figures for cognitive verbs – in addition to the large number of different lexemes – suggests that interpretation may have played a more prominent role than the content analysis of the research diaries revealed. Students at least did not just go about their task mechanically and thoughtlessly.

Another interesting detail in the set of mental verbs regards the two categories of volition and emotion. These could be interpreted as representing planning and systematic progress on the one hand, and feelings on the other.

Volition		*emotion*			
want	*49*	*like*	*12*	*appreciate*	*1*
intend	*3*	*hope*	*11*	*lose (my mind)*	*1*
plan	*3*	*feel*	*6*	*mind*	*1*
insist	*1*	*experience*	*3*		
persevere	*1*	*prefer*	*2*		

Table 20. Verbs of volition and emotion used with *I* in the research diaries.

The small gap in token frequencies suggests that the emotional factor (if not really the pleasure factor) does not lag that far behind the goal of proceeding systematically. This is again a positive aspect.

4.3 Questionnaire

The questionnaire was primarily intended to provide insights into whether the participants' views and perceptions in any way reflected the conclusions we have drawn from our analyses of the research diaries. We additionally wanted to find out about students' emotions, likes and dislikes.

4.3.1 Method

The questionnaire consisted of 42 statements with which students could agree/disagree (five levels: 1 = totally agree, 5 = totally disagree).

4.3.2 Results

Unfortunately, the results obtained were only of limited value. Firstly, only 9 completed forms were returned. Secondly, there were a number of misunderstandings, as revealed by inconsistencies in the data itself or by questions posed by the students afterwards.

The first group of questions were concerned with the intrinsic motivation of students and their appreciation of learning autonomy. Contrary to our general impression in teaching linguistics, students considered themselves highly interested in language and in its study, irrespective of course requirements or immediate usability. Although the contradiction may seem surprising at first, on second thought students' positive perception of their own interests suggests that intrinsic motivation is generally something positive for them and thus something they would like to associate themselves with. It also suggests they may be aware that teachers want them to be interested in things for their own sake. Claiming and possibly assuming that they are interested and motivated has, we however suppose, no bearing on how well they actually cope with an exploratory approach.

We also asked a few questions (or gave a few statements to assess) concerning autonomy, and here too we can see certain inconsistencies, even within the questionnaire itself. On the one hand, students appreciate the idea of working on their own according to their own interests and learning styles. On the other hand, they also want teachers to give clear guidelines and to state very explicitly what they expect of them.

A second group of questions concentrated on the benefits of the project in the participants' eyes. Generally speaking, the major positive effect the students saw was that they had learned that there were alternative ways to examine texts. This was partly relativised by the fact that they nonetheless did not think that they had gained knowledge about the potential of concordancing programmes for text analysis. Students were also relatively positive that their awareness of the great role that language plays in society, and how little elements can have large effects, had risen. The majority also thought that they had become more careful and more conscious readers and listeners.

Students also had to choose from a list of factors responsible for any positive effects of the project. The most influential aspect – and this was a positive finding for us – was, according to the participants, their own work with WordSmith and the corpus. Our input, no matter whether as handouts or in-class introductions, was considered less relevant.

We were also interested in what they liked and what they disliked about the project. With respect to the positive aspects, the topic of intelligent design got the best rating, while aspects to do with its exploratory nature (freedom, not targeting correctness, etc.) were not appreciated that much. The latter seems to corroborate the findings from the research diaries. The fact, however, that most students were eager to change from the Intelligent Design corpus to other text collections seems to contradict the claim that the topic was readily accepted as positive.

As far as concerns things they disliked, the first thing to strike the eye is that the positive aspects got higher ratings than the negative ones. This may suggest that in the students' eyes, the beneficial effects outweighed the shortcomings. But we have to take into account that they knew that they were expected to be more positive than negative. The only factor with a mean rating clearly below 3 (which marks the indifference line) was that they would have liked more immediate comparative discussions of findings and results in class. They did not think they needed more input from the teachers. This is interesting because it seemed the first choice for improving the effects of exploratory learning in the project.

4.4 Evaluation of seminar papers

As the final product of the seminar, their term papers should have highlighted how students had benefited from their work with corpora in the course of the project. A systematic assessment of the effects on the quality of the paper was, however, impossible, because of the low number of participants (13 handed in a paper) and the lack of a comparative basis (there was no control group). We will therefore restrict ourselves to a few subjective general comments.

4.4.1 Methodological awareness

The main benefit of the project was that it seems to have made students aware that text analysis can proceed along very different paths from those they are used to. While only some of the students actually employed corpus analysis (and none exclusively), even those resorting to more traditional in-depth analysis of individual texts often felt obliged to say why they had not considered the investigation of a corpus feasible or useful. The project has thus enhanced students' conscious knowledge of and sensitivity to the use of different methods of analysis, raising their methodological awareness.

4.4.2 Language awareness

We do at least also see a tendency to a tighter connection between the levels of form, meaning and socio-political significance. Through the emphasis on linguistic data in the corpus project, we still saw many analyses that were primarily descriptive, but the number consisting only of data-independent speculations markedly decreased.

5. Conclusions

Students' autonomous explorations of corpora may have had some positive effects with respect to methodological and linguistic awareness and perhaps – taking a biased and selective perspective – also with respect to intrinsic motivation and self-confidence. But overall, the outcome and effects do not fully correspond to our expectations. Why should this be?

There are three possible answers to this question:

- There are problems with the methods of evaluating the outcome.
- There are problem with the implementation of the approach.
- There are problems with the expectations.

5.1 Problems with the methods of evaluating the outcome

Due to the low return rate and the apparent ambiguity of some of the questions, the questionnaire itself is highly questionable so that findings have to be taken not with a pinch but with harmful amounts of salt. However we still believe that the qualitative analysis of the research diaries has provided a lot of relatively reliable results (despite all the problems connected with qualitative studies).

5.2 Problems with the implementation of the approach

With the benefit of hindsight and the analysis of the research diaries, we think that students' explorations would probably benefit from slightly more interventionism and feedback and slightly less autonomy. This is not however in agreement with what the students said in the questionnaires.

What we consider an absolute must is the introduction of discussion sessions of results after each week. Whether this should take place only among students or whether the teachers should also take part is another matter. We probably underestimated the relevance of the social and interactive factor of learning, which provides an extra boost in energy and motivation. This might help students get unstuck and not lapse into repetitive patterns too quickly. The social side could also be strengthened by students, for instance, forming working groups.

Probably, exploratory learning will also profit from more input, especially more practical work with WordSmith in class. Special – perhaps even explicit – emphasis should be laid on the difference between unique, singular phenomena and regular ordinary patterns, and the importance of the latter for Critical Discourse Analysis.

Although students are highly interested in Intelligent Design according to the questionnaire, we still think that the main corpus provided could be of more immediate appeal.

As many students chose to create their own small corpora in the course of the project, the expansion of input should also include a session on corpus design and text selection.

These aspects might have improved the project. They do, of course, not say anything about how exploratory learning might be implemented in the regular procedure of a course, at our Department or elsewhere.

5.3 Problems with the expectations

The more deeply we dived into the analysis of the project, the more we realized how little we know and how little we had thought about the didactics of linguistics. It is good to have these catchy pedagogical principles. But we naively assumed that they would somehow work on their own, which they obviously did not. There is still plenty of room for ideas and research in the area of the didactics of linguistics, it seems.

References

Bernardini S. (2000) Systematising serendipity: proposals for concordancing large corpora with language learners. In Burnard L. & T. McEnery (eds) Rethinking language pedagogy from a corpus perspective. Frankfurt a. M.: Peter Lang, 225–234.

Bernardini S. (2002) Exploring new directions for discovery learning. In Kettemann B. & G. Marko (eds) Teaching and learning by doing corpus analysis, Amsterdam: Rodopi, 165–182.

Conway J. (1997) Educational technology's effect on models of instruction. <http://copland.udel.edu/~jconway/EDST666.htm> [accessed 27 February 2007].

Johns T. & P. King (eds.) (1991) Classroom concordancing, Birmingham: University of Birmingham (English language research journal 4).

Johns T. (2002) Data-driven learning: the perpetual challenge. In Kettemann, G. & G. Marko (eds.), Teaching and learning by doing corpus analysis, Amsterdam: Rodopi, 107–117.

Mukherjee J. (2002) Korpuslinguistik und Englischunterricht. Eine Einführung, Frankfurt a. M.: Peter Lang.

Ormrod J. E. (1995) Educational psychology: principles and applications, Englewood Cliffs, NJ: Prentice-Hall.

Schönborn C. (2005) Finding design in nature, New York Times, 15 July 2005. <http://www.nytimes.com/2005/07/07/opinion/07schonborn.html?ex=1172638800&en=c99704260e1589be&ei=5070> [accessed 26 February 2007].

Scott, E. C. (2004) Evolution vs. creationism. An introduction, Berkeley & Los Angeles: University of California Press.

Scott, M. (1999) Wordsmith Tools 3.0, Oxford: Oxford University Press.

Shanks, N. (2004) God, the devil, and Darwin: A critique of Intelligent Design theory, Oxford: Oxford University Press.

WebCorp: <http://www.webcorp.org.uk/wcadvanced.html> [last accessed 6 May 2008].

WebCT: <http://xanthippe.edu.uni-graz.at/webct/entryPageIns.dowebct> [last accessed 6 May 2008].

Wikipedia (n. d.) "Constructivism (learning theories)". <http://en.wikipedia.org/wiki/Constructivism_(learning_theory)> [last accessed 26 February 2007].

The ID Corpus

Behe M. (1996) Darwin's blackbox. The biochemical challenge to evolution, New York: The Free Press.

Behe M. J., W. A. Dembski & S. C. Meyer (eds) (2000) Science and evidence for design in the universe (Proceedings of the Wethersfield Institute), Ft. Collins, CO: Ignatius Press.

Dembski W. A. (2004) The design revolution: Answering the toughest questions about intelligent design, Downers Grove, IL: InterVarsity Press.

Dembski W. A. (ed.) (2004) Uncommon dissent. Intellectuals who find Darwinism unconvincing, Wilminton, DE: ISI Books.

Johnson P. E. (1993) Darwin on trial (2nd edition), Downers Grove, IL: InterVarsity Press.

Pullen S. W. (2005) Intelligent design or evolution? Why the origin of life and the evolution of molecular knowledge imply design, Raleigh, NC: Intelligent Design Books.

Simmons G. & W. Dembski (2004) What Darwin didn't know, Eugene, OR: Harvest House Publishers.

Wells, J. (2002) Icons of evolution. Science or myth? Why much of what we teach about evolution is wrong, Washington, DC: Regnery Publishing.

GILL PHILIP

"...and I dropped my jaw with fear": The role of corpora in teaching phraseology

Abstract

This study addresses corpus-aided phraseological production in advanced learner writing. The writing task at the heart of the study is outlined in § 2. This is followed by an analysis of phraseological patterns produced by learners, who are grouped by their preferred look-up medium: corpora, monolingual dictionary, or Internet. The analysis suggests that corpora particularly aid archetypically good language learners, who add corpus use to their inventory of language learning strategies.

1. Introduction

This research reports an ongoing study into phraseological production in advanced learner writing. While most studies of learner production, whether corpus-based or not, investigate problems and their likely causes, this study compares successful and less successful uses of language. The *Phrasebuilder* task, a semi-structured writing activity designed to elicit multiple versions of a single base text (see § 2), makes this comparative approach possible, and is qualitatively different to the more commonly-used types of vocabulary elicitation, such as gap-fill, used in studies by Deignan et al. (1997) and Boers (2000) amongst others.

On-line corpora, paper and electronic dictionaries, Internet search engines and encyclopaedias were all familiar sources of language reference for the learners whose work is examined in the following sections[1]. All the students were given basic training in corpus use during the course, including how to carry out some of the more frequently-

1 The data presented in this study was gathered from five groups of learners following advanced (C1) general English courses at the University of Bologna, Italy.

used advanced search techniques such as those involving multiple nodes, POS tags and wildcards. Merely possessing these skills is no guarantee that corpora will be used efficiently, appropriately, or, indeed, at all. The task therefore was given a twofold purpose – to determine how proficient the students were at combining the keywords in running text, and to see which language resources they made use of in tackling the different phraseological challenges that the exercise presented. Some of the questions to be addressed in this contribution are:

- How can the effects of corpora on the language learning process be effectively assessed?
- Does corpus use aid students in a measurable way?
- Is there a marked qualitative difference between the work of students who make use of corpora in their studies and those who do not?

In other words, does corpus use necessarily lead to an improvement in students' language production, and if so, in what ways?

2. The *Phrasebuilder* exercise

The *Phrasebuilder* task is an exercise in guided creative writing. It consists of a fixed sequence of keywords and collocations, presented sequentially on flash cards or slides, forming the basic skeleton of a story which students must flesh out to produce their own short narratives. The keywords appearing on each consecutive slide collocate with each other, and they may also collocate with the keywords on the preceding or following slides. As with all language, however, they can also be used compositionally. The students' task is to write their own version of the story using all the words provided, sticking as closely as possible to the order in which the keywords are presented and avoiding changes to the word form provided (plurals should remain plural, tenses of verbs should not be modified). The keywords used in this study come from a version of the task devised by Goldsmith (2003): they are reproduced in their order of occurrence in the Appendix, alongside a model version of the story which incorporates them in the required sequence.

The *Phrasebuilder*'s guided approach to creative writing is similar to the one described by Martinez (in Lewis 1997). However, the specific exercise described in this study is more complex than Martinez's version, built up around a single delexical verbs and its collocates, despite the apparent constraints that fixed keywords in a fixed sequence might suggest. In the first place, students are provided with the raw materials for constructing a story which are general enough to allow them to use their imagination, yet structured in such a way as to provide a beginning, middle and end – to ensure that the story will be complete – and limited in scope so that the task can be completed in a single session (in this case, a 2 hour lesson). Secondly, the presence of a well-delimited set of keywords allows the teacher and/or researcher to identify areas of language where students are in need of additional instruction, whether grammatical or lexical.

Although not designed with corpus research in mind, the potential for such tasks in learner-corpus studies is immediately apparent. A small corpus can be compiled from the students' contributions, differing from other learner corpora in that the texts are all variations of a single, hypothetical original. This can be likened favourably to Bowker & Bennison's (2003) approach to translator training, in which the multiple texts examined are all translations of a single source text. Such a corpus makes it possible to analyse general tendencies in language production over a large sample, in a much more detailed and systematic way than can be hoped for with manual correction alone. The guaranteed presence of the keywords in all the texts[2] means that the researcher can easily identify areas of language to analyse, safe in the knowledge that concordances will be retrievable with sufficient numbers to ensure that findings are relevant. S/he is also in a position to observe how a restricted set of keywords are made to combine in text, whether as collocations proper or in a looser, more compositional way. It is this feature that will form the main focus of the present study.

2 Obviously, misspellings and typographical errors can have an affect on the location of keywords in the corpus.

The decision to turn the paper exercise into a digital one was based on several factors, corpus construction actually being quite low in the order of priorities. Several disadvantages became immediately apparent in the paper version, first among which was the difficulty of reformulating the texts in the light of new keywords as the story progressed. Space on paper is limited, and students soon tired of having to score out text and re-write chunks. There were also, unsurprisingly, repercussions on legibility. Timing also proved problematic. Students were presented the keywords on slides, and while some were quick to incorporate the new elements into their existing texts, others inevitably fell behind and missed parts of the sequence. It also became evident that students working at their desks with pencil and paper did not think of switching on their computers to make use of the reference sources available to them on the Internet. As a result, the students completing this task the first time it was run rarely used reference tools, which was hardly ideal as the task was intended as a language learning exercise, not an assessment.

Switching the exercise from paper to computer solved all three of these problems, with the added advantages of obtaining finished texts that were legible enough to correct and easily convertible into corpus material. Students worked one to a computer, with several windows open on the screen in front of them – one with the slides, so they would work at their own pace, one with a word-processor, and at least one other with monolingual or bilingual dictionaries, a search engine (usually Google), or a concordancer (typically WordBanks Online).[3] There were also paper copies of the main advanced learner dictionaries available in the room.[4]

3 <http://www.collins.co.uk/corpus/corpussearch.aspx>.

4 Macmillan English Dictionary for Advanced learners, Longman Dictionary of Contemporary English, Collins COBUILD Advanced Learners English Dictionary, Oxford Advanced Learners Dictionary.

3. Outline of the study

The findings discussed here are the result of the analysis of five groups' work, with data gathered over four academic semesters. A total of 41 students completed the exercise, and for the purposes of analysis they have been divided into four groups: *corpus users*, *Googlers*, *mixed-resource users*, and *dictionary users*. These groupings were made on a post-hoc basis, after observing which resources each individual tended to make most use of. As a means of evaluating the usefulness of corpora and the Internet in particular, the presence of a control group was indispensable. This group of ten students completed the task without the aid of any on-line resources, and accounted for ten of the *dictionary users*. Of the remaining 31 students, the *corpus users* numbered six, the *Googlers* three, *dictionary users* two, with the vast majority of students falling into the *mixed-resource users* group.

The *corpus users* were those who not only used the corpus, but, most importantly, were also happy to experiment with advanced searches, for example in order to find a suitable adverb to complete a verb phrase. Some even used the corpus as a source of ready-made examples which they could copy and paste into their text. The *Googlers* eschewed traditional forms of language reference, preferring to use fairly elementary single-word searches on the Internet as a means of locating possible expressions, by counting the number of hits, looking at the short extract accompanying the retrieved URLs, and occasionally going into the full text. The *dictionary users* not belonging to the control group appeared uncomfortable with corpora and the Internet, preferring to use only dictionaries, usually in paper or hand-held electronic form, which they habitually brought to class with them: those in the control group might of course have belonged elsewhere had they been given the option. The *mixed-resource users* used all resources to a greater or lesser extent, although it should be pointed out that within this group, there is a range running from students who selected particular sources to address different kinds of linguistic problems to ones who displayed no apparent sense of purpose in their choices, and/or made minimal use of reference tools. Were this experiment to be repeated, it might be useful to adopt a query record sheet such as that used by Frankenberg-Garcia (2005) to log the students' referencing behaviour.

A few unanticipated problems arose within the task itself. On some occasions, students changed the order of occurrence of the keywords, or indeed omitted one or more of them, despite being able to self-pace. As far as the individual compositions are concerned, this matters very little, but if viewed in the light of investigating students' ability to recognise potential collocations, omissions caused some disruption to the data set as a whole. In a similar vein, despite instructions to avoid alterations to the word forms, many students were tempted to use alternative inflected forms of the keywords provided, changing their meanings in the process. Different inflected forms collocate in distinct ways, and the apparently innocuous change from singular to plural noun can play havoc with phraseological meaning: *I lost my nerves* does not express the same meaning as *I lost my nerve*. A third problem, from the point of view of corpus analysis, is that keywords were at times misspelled, whether as a result of typographical mistakes at the keyboard (*sleeep* for *sleep*), persistent spelling errors (*toughts* for *thoughts*), or imprecise copying of less familiar words from the slides to the composition (*jew* for *jaw*). Inaccuracies such as these affected retrieval of the keywords from compositions using corpus query software.

The problems outlined above were infrequent, and hence only a minor cause of trouble On the whole, students had no difficulty in carrying out the task, and every one of them came up with an individual interpretation of the underlying story, in spite of the apparent constraints imposed by the keywords. The next section discusses the ways in which students dealt with four different types of phraseological meaning that the keywords were intended to elicit, demonstrating some of the differences in the quality of the writing produced by the *corpus users*, the *Googlers*, the *mixed-resource users*, and the *dictionary users*.

4. Phraseological production in the *Phrasebuilder* task

The Phrasebuilder task is designed to elicit phraseological language through the presentation of particular word forms in a predetermined sequence. Essentially, four types of phraseological language are involved, and each of these is discussed in the subsections that follow. The most simple is the formation of collocations, such as the decision to combine keyword nouns to make a compound or the addition of known collocates in order to incorporate the keywords into running text. This can be contrasted with non-formation of collocations, whereby the keywords are treated compositionally, occurring at some distance from one another in the text. The second type is the generation of phrases from a single keyword – typically one which has relatively low frequency and/or is presented in a precise inflected form which is expected to trigger the recognition (or location in reference works) of a limited range of expressions. The third type is the use of 'filler' phraseology, the lexical and grammatical choices made by students in order to link keywords which collocate strongly in the real world but fit rather more weakly in the text. Finally, the problems posed by figurative and idiomatic meaning are examined, by observing how well students are able to recognise when a keyword should not be used in its literal sense, to appreciate its intended meaning and to tackle its integration into their text.

4.1 Collocation versus free combination: wine + party

The keywords used to investigate students' awareness and use of collocation, as opposed to a compositional treatment of language, are *wine* and *party* (see Appendix for their place in the overall sequence). These words can form a compound or be used in a looser collocation which still conforms to the standard definition of collocation as being words which co-occur within five words of the node (Sinclair *et al.* 1970/2004: 5).

It may be surprising to learn that only one student produced the compound *wine party*, with all others settling for the looser type of collocation relating to the real-world occurrence (especially true for these Italian students) of *wine* being drunk at *parties*. This is an example of the influence of 'psychological collocation' (Partington 1998: 16–17) intruding on textual collocation, and this tendency is nicely illustrated in the data for these keywords. Apart from the lone occurrence of *wine party*, one other compound was present (*wine cellar*), and five occurrences of other collocations: *bottle of wine* (2) and *glass of wine* (1), as well as *red wine* (2). By far the most frequent collocate for *wine*, however, was *drink* (14), usually accompanied by the colligational feature of quantifiers (of which *too much* occurred in 9 of the 14), completing the picture of people drinking wine to excess at parties:

(1) *It was a strange* ***party****, the alchool was flowing like a river, I had drunk too much* ***wine*** *and I was very drunk.*

Given that *wine* and *party* are both high-frequency and easily contextualisable, there were no great differences in students' approach to their inclusion in texts, though *dictionary users* produced remarkably consistent results, shown in Fig. 1. The student who used *wine party* was an assiduous *dictionary user*, not from the control group, while all but one of the control group used a variant of the pattern *drink too much wine*, with *party* appearing in the cotext nearby.

Yesterday, we drank a lot of	**wine**	at the party. When I went to bed
to a party, where I drank too much	**wine**	. Not only the headache and
to sleep because I drank too much	**wine**	at the party, and so I had a
Last night I drank too much	**wine**	to a party and when I went to
onfusing...maybe I drank too much	**wine**	. Now I feel a terrible headache
in my house and drank too much	**wine**	. How could I lay down and sleep
to sleep. Maybe I drunk too much	**wine**	at the party.A terrible headache
went to a party. I drunk too much	**wine**	. Now, I feel a terrible headache
like a river, I had drunk too much	**wine**	and I was very drunk. That
and I think to have drunk too much	**wine**	, in fact when I came back home
I had really exaggerated with red	**wine**	! Considered that I mustn't have
my standard. Because I went to the	**wine**	party with my colleagues. It

Fig 1. KWIC concordance for *wine* – dictionary users only.

There were few apparent instances of free combination with this pair of keywords, though in a number of instances they were too far separated to qualify statistically as collocates. They were produced by all groups of students except the *dictionary users*, though the worst culprits were the *Googlers*. Examples (2) and (3) show typical examples of free combinations, while (4) illustrates a case where the keywords were moved around or indeed omitted (*party* should occur between *sleep* and *wine*, with *headache* at the end of this sequence).

(2) *This morning I went to a* ***wine*** *cellar, to buy 50 liters of Sangiovese for the* ***party*** *I and my girlfriend would give in the evening.*

(3) *I went to my kitchen desperately looking for a glass of* ***wine****, maybe there was one bottle left after the* ***party****!*

(4) *They say: "If you can't* ***sleep****, if you've got an* ***headache****...just drink some red* ***wine****, and you'll be better in a while!"*

That only one student used the compound *wine party* may serve as proof that students on the whole did not feel the need to look up *wine*, being quite convinced that they already knew its meaning(s). Had any of them checked in the corpus, they would not only have found confirmation that *wine* and *party* do collocate closely, but they would also have discovered that the pair actually tend to form a trio with *cheese*. It is easy to forget, both as teachers and as learners, that looking up common words can be a worthwhile exercise in vocabulary building and – as in this instance – in the unearthing of cultural information.

4.2 Building collocations: nerves

Nerves – note the plural form – is the keyword that was chosen in order to investigate how students tackled the generation of phrases from a single keyword. *Nerve* is not a very frequent word, but it is polysemous, with some of its meanings being restricted to the plural inflection alone. This detail proved crucially important, as did the mismatch between *nerve(s)* and its Italian equivalent, *nervi*, whose semantic range and phraseological patterns only partially overlap. But apart from the expected learner errors caused by calquing, some of the unexpected collocations that occurred cannot reasonably be ascribed to L1 interference (see (5) and (6) below). There appears to have been real confusion regarding the meaning of this keyword, yet the data suggests that few students actually turned to a dictionary to clarify the meaning or to look up possible phrases to use.

(5) *I shooked my **nerves**, trying to forget it was less than ten minutes I was awake.*
(6) *Noise and silly conversations were the cause of Jack's headache; his **nerves** were too tired to bear meaningless smiles and honey words.*
(7) *In addition to this, it started rainning. In fact, it really got me **nerve**.*
(8) *In my personal point of view rain is the third kind of weather that stand on my **nerves**, snow is the second and windy is the first.*

Examples (7) and (8) also appear not to have been produced with the help of a dictionary, but merely used in a half-remembered, or back-translated form. In these examples, the underlying meaning can be identified, but the word forms used are not the ones (*got on my nerves* in both instances) that typically communicate the intended meaning. As Hanks points out, "linguistic behaviour among users of a language is highly stereotypical, even in matters of fine detail" (2004: 246). Such fine detail includes limitations on which inflected forms can express particular meanings, as the examples above illustrate. One pedagogical question that inevitably arises is how and when such detail should be taught, given that language teaching tends not to devote as space much to the fine details of lexis as it does to those of grammar.

Of the four groups of students, none produced flawless texts, but the use of appropriate collocations with *nerves* was quite obviously the preserve of those who had looked the word up in one or other of the language reference tools available.[5] The *Googlers* produced expressions which verged on the incoherent, featuring the collocates *calm* and *break down* (see (9) and (10) below). Even allowing for the fact that *calm* + *nerves* is acceptable, its use in the text points to a lack of com-

5 It is worth remembering that students are unlikely to have looked up every single keyword in the task: by comparing the tendencies of each group, however, a general picture emerges, and from this it is possible to determine which choices were influenced by reference tools and which were not.

prehension, and a consequent inability to contextualise the phrase appropriately. The phrase may well have been found on the Internet, but the student failed to look further than the search results page to check its meaning in cotext.

(9) *. so the party finished and we had to calm ours* ***nerves*** *backing home a little bit drunk*

(10) *I had spent all the morning working hard – and the rain didn't make things easier –, my* ***nerves*** *broke down and I went into a heavy depression.*

The *dictionary users* were also guilty of making up collocations, including *irritate one's nerves* (11), and they also fell into the trap of thinking that the plural form could substitute the singular in collocations such as *lose one's nerve* (12). Overall, however, when the students in this group used acceptable collocations such as *get on one's nerves* (13), and *nerves + on edge* (14), they did so correctly, presumably due to the presence of examples in the dictionary entry.

(11) *More, a strong wind and an incessant rain irritated my* ***nerves****.*

(12) *…I lost my* ***nerves*** *and I had so much fear that my jaw was moving itself without my will.*

(13) *…a terrible storm was shaking my house, and the rain on the windows was getting on my* ***nerves****.*

(14) *I began to walk towards my home when it began to rain. My* ***nerves*** *were on edge.*

(15) *Outside the window an heavy rain was falling. It hurted my* ***nerves****.*

(16) *I shooked my* ***nerves****, trying to forget it was less than ten minutes I was awake.*

(17) *That night were getting on my* ***nerves****!*

(18) *…I could even perceive the light smell of the rain I began to be a bundle of* ***nerves****.*

(19) *I listen a strong wind, which is starting to get on my* ***nerves****; it's pouring with the rain...*

(20) *…I felt anxious, I made an effort to calm my* ***nerves****.*

The collocations produced by the *mixed-resource users* were much like the *dictionary users*' ones: a few invented collocations such as *hurt one's nerves* (15) and *shake one's nerves* (16), some standard collocations (typically *get on one's nerves*), and a couple of instances of more idiomatic phrases such as *bundle of nerves*. The general level of textual accuracy was lower than that of the *dictionary users* group: (17) and

(18) illustrate how the phrase itself can be faultless but yet not run on seamlessly from the preceding text. This error was not present in the *corpus users*' texts (19) and (20), whose use of collocation was phraseologically accurate, with the chunk being incorporated into the rest of the text with no apparent breaks. It may be the case that when corpora are used, the phrasal boundaries are less clearly cut than they appear in a dictionary entry, so a student using corpus data for reference will have a better model of how to mould the cotext around the chunk to make it fit properly. Clearly, this is the reason why dictionaries include example phrases, but a KWIC concordance makes repeated patterns more immediately recognisable, and so may have more influence on a student's choice of words.

4.3 Filler phraseology: heart + chest

While identifying correct or suspect collocates for a keyword is a fairly straightforward procedure, the analysis of filler phraseology is often relegated to second place in collocation studies, especially those dealing with learner data. A lot of filler phraseology is grammatical, and perhaps this is the reason why it tends to be ignored in favour of the more colourful lexical collocates. However filler phraseology, both grammatical and lexical, is an important part of language production. It is the glue with which lexical chunks are stuck together. This subsection investigates the lexical and grammatical choices made by students linking the keywords *heart* and *chest*.

In the real world, *hearts* are found in *chests*; or, to be more specific, the heart muscle is located within the chest cavity. It is not normally deemed necessary to make this sort of specification, but both of these keywords are polysemous, and it is really only by virtue of their proximity that we are inclined to interpret them both as parts of the body. One student did exploit the polysemy (25): for the others there was no question that the meaning was anatomical, especially since the language was intended to describe the emotions felt by the narrator in the light of the events up to this point in the text. Fear, trepidation and anticipation are all manifested by physical responses, typically including an increased heart rate. But how did the students express this familiar intercultural concept in a foreign language?

The four groups of students followed distinct patterns of usage in their filler phraseology, though the same general structures were adopted in order to express the idea of the heart beating fast within the chest. One interesting recurring feature in the students' filler phraseology was the presence of verbs such as *beat* and *bump* in the progressive aspect or gerund form (following *start* or *begin*), which emphasised the immediacy of the events. A further interesting aspect was the presence of adverbs, which were not used a great deal elsewhere in the texts.

his **heart** beating in his chest:
my **heart** is beating fast in my chest.
my **heart** was beating more fast
My **heart** started beating madly.
My **heart** started beating incredibly fast
My **heart** began to beat so rapidly that...
my **heart** started to beat very quickly
the **heart** in my chest and his beating was almost deafening
The **heart** begins bumping in my chest
my **heart** began to thump wildly in my chest.
My **heart** jumped out of my chest!

Fig. 2. Verbs collocating with *heart.*

The *Googlers* used simple, high-frequency verbs, did not use any adverbs and used compositional language throughout ((21) and (22)).. While the cartoon-style image of a heart literally jumping out of somebody's chest is clearly intended in both these examples, they both lack the conventional wording which would make this meaning immediate. Similar meanings are expressed more successfully in (23) and (24) (produced by a *dictionary user* and a *mixed-resources user* respectively).

(21) *That's the reason why, I suppose, when I suddenly heard someone knocking at the door, my* ***heart*** *tried to escape from my* ***chest****.*

(22) *I couldn't open the door and my* ***heart*** *was got off my* ***chest***

(23) *My* ***heart*** *started beating incredibly fast I thought it would have popped out of my* ***chest****.*

(24) *My **heart** began to beat so rapidly that I feared it was going to jump out my **chest**.*

(25) *My **heart** started beating madly. How could I save myself? The **chest**! I jumped inside.*

(26) *The **heart** begins bumping in my **chest** with the decise sound similar to foot-steps on a stairs.*

(27) *I suddenly heard something strange and my **heart** began to thump wildly in my **chest**.*

(28) *I suddenly heard a door slammed just over me. Even more violently slammed the **heart** in my **chest** and his beating was almost deafening.*

Of the remaining three groups, patterns in verb and adverb usage are discernable. The *dictionary users* opted almost invariably for the verb *beat* accompanied by a range of adverbs relating to speed, including *quickly* and *fast*, as well as adverbs of manner such as *madly* ((23) and (25)). *Mixed-resource users* drew upon a wider range of verbs, including *bump*, *run* and *pound*. While *beat* was invariably accompanied by adverbs (24), the more specific verbs tended not to be, though there are some interesting run-ons, such as that in (26). Finally, *corpus users* used a wide range of verbs, usually in combination with specific adverbs, as illustrated in (27) and (28).

4.4 Figurative language: my jaw…

Jaw is not a word in everyday usage: *jaws* do not arouse a great deal of interest and are not brought up in conversation very often. It was therefore unsurprising that many students felt perplexed by the presence of this keyword near the end of their task. While *heart* and *chest* were easy to fit into the story, *jaw* appeared not to be. Why should this part of the head be important?

A proficient user of English should recognize that *my jaw*... (and not *jaws* plural) leads into a restricted set of possible verb collocates, namely *drop* or *clench* and their synonyms. Even an advanced student may not have come across either of these expressions, and it should not be surprising that even at this level students do not realise that the keyword is intended to elicit one of these metaphors (probably the former, given the context). Yet problems are not wholly negative. The confusion that *my jaw* caused had the fortunate consequence of prompting students to look up possible uses, and as a result only eight students chose to interpret the word literally (29).

(29) *Too tired and angry to switch the light on I jumped in the bed hitting* ***my jaw*** *on the floor: it was the wrong direction.*

The *Googlers*, in line with their previous tendencies, either gave a literal interpretation or miscued on the necessary wording ((30) and (31)). Most *dictionary users* completed the phrase with *dropped*, although *clenched* also appeared once, alongside four literal, compositional interpretations ((32)–(34)).

(30) *I was surprised too when opened* ***my jaw*** *and I realized that it was the wrong house.*
(31) ***My jew*** *fell down to the floor.*
(32) ***My jaw*** *dropped, my heart started to beat very quickly and my chest was almost hurting!*
(33) *My mind was completely flooded by frightful thoughts,* ***my jaw*** *was clenched.*
(34) *Ok, now is the moment – I'm at the end of the bed! I feel a soft ache in* ***my jaw****. I can call my neigbour, he's doctor.*

The tendencies displayed by the *mixed-resource users* ((35)–(36)) were similar to the *dictionary users*' ones, using *dropped*, but there were several instances of the less common active form of the verb (36). This also occurred amongst the *corpus users*, who also produced some unexpectedly inventive interpretations of the keyword (37). This burst of inventiveness is strikingly uncharacteristic in the light of the corpus users' performance elsewhere in the task, as is the literal interpretation shown in (38). Why does this apparent lapse occur at this stage?

(35) *It took some seconds, but when I realized what had just happened* ***my jaw*** *dropped.*
(36) *My teeth were chattered and I dropped* ***my jaw*** *with fear.*
(37) ***My jaw*** *was clicking like a typewriter for the fear.*
(38) ***My jaw*** *hardened to an unsustainable degree, all my muscles were stiff and, because of the fright, I could hardly breath.*

At this point, it is enlightening to take a closer look at the corpus data. There were only 14 occurrences of *my+jaw* in the WordBanks Online data when these students completed their task, all of which are reproduced in Fig. 3. Although the conventional collocate *dropped* is present three times – twice to the right of the node (lines 3–4), and once to the left (line 12) – these frequencies are inadequate for any tendencies to be identified. This may well account for the presence of active forms of the verbs amongst the *mixed-resource group*.

A second glance at line 8 in the concordance explains the mystery of (37).

1	and my camera, not to mention	**my jaw**, free-fell to the floor. Japan's
2	in a hotel without dislocating	**my jaw** on my knees. I can sleep in tents
3	you propose to get it out [p]	**My jaw** dropped Oh God, I never thought
4	in open water. I glanced up and	**my jaw** dropped, for only thirty feet
5	and I felt horribly miserable.	**My jaw** ached from grinning all night
6	out at about 2.45am. Whether	**my jaw** muscles simply retired hurt, or
7	me but about the pain in	**my jaw**. Mind you, judging by the stares
8	Worse still, my teeth ached and	**my jaw** was clicking like a typewriter.
9	me on the head Another said:	'**my jaw** fell to the floor and fractured
10	from my stomach clear up to	**my jaw**. The peace symbols swirled
11	thigh, then landed squarely on	**my jaw**. I kept both hands on the wheel.
12	I asked, trying not to drop	**my jaw**. I admire Gail. She's one of the
13	[M02] No I dislocate	**my jaw** all the tie. I [ZGY] smashed
14	a ha ha. No. No. Please no more	**my jaw**'s aching all [tc text=pause]

Fig. 3. my+jaw (WordBanks Online: all concordances).

Is it right to criticise students for cherry-picking their way through corpora rather than restricting their interest to frequent, recurrent forms? Corpora provide native-speaker models, real examples of language in use that are there for the taking, and this student should probably be applauded for having embraced corpora so warmly. High-frequency patterns have to be learned in order to communicate effectively, but this does not necessarily mean that low-frequency forms have to be ignored completely. Should learners be denied the right to be creative and opportunistic for no better reason than the fact that they are non-native speakers? This previously hidden aspect of learner corpus use is incredibly interesting, and certainly worthy of more detailed investigation before any pedagogical conclusions can be drawn legitimately.

5. Corpora, users, and language learning

Relatively few students in this study chose to use the corpus as their main source of language reference. One immediate reason for this is that it was a newly-encountered tool: even those who had used corpora in previous courses had only ever encountered them in their university studies, while they had been using dictionaries since primary school. A further reason, unlikely as it may sound, is that there are still students reaching degree level who are barely computer-literate and who avoid using the computer whenever there is an alternative available. In order to gain the maximum benefit from what corpora have to offer, students need to have training in how to formulate search queries so as to obtain the data that is most relevant to their needs. Such training takes precious time away from other aspects of language learning, and as not all teachers are prepared to invest time in cultivating corpus skills, many advanced students fail to reap the full benefits offered by corpus data. Although the success of a query is dependent on the effectiveness of the search syntax used, learning the query language for any corpus seems worthwhile – not least because of its knock-on effect of improving use of search-engine syntax. An accomplished *corpus user* also becomes a more efficient *Googler*.

So corpora and corpus-based reference tools both aid students' vocabulary learning demonstrably, but this can only be true if they are indeed consulted. The data presented here, as well as other learner data discussed in Philip (2005, 2006) confirms the fears of many language teachers: advanced students limit their looking up to the bare minimum, usually only to check the meaning of new words. Some students see consultation as a sign of weakness, believing that only less-proficient students need to check meanings (form appears to come even lower down the priority list). Thus, out of embarrassment or fear of shame, they relegate dictionaries and corpora to tasks where they are explicitly required. Other students fall foul of the belief that once a word has been encountered, it has been 'learned', forgetting that such learned lexis is rarely revisited, hindering the learning of sub-senses, figurative extensions and phraseology. Students generally encounter words in their literal sense first, match them to a translation equivalent in their L1, and from then on, unless instructed otherwise, use the word in calqued forms of the L1 phraseology. The relative success of this strategy effectively masks the underlying problem, which is more serious than simply getting collocations wrong. Persistent calquing actually prevents students from acquiring a sense of the word's conceptual range in the L2, negatively affecting textual fluency and cohesiveness.

The data presented here demonstrate that corpora do indeed have a positive effect on language production, but the advantages are not restricted to hands-on use. Corpus-based advanced learner dictionaries condense and select information from the corpus and also provide examples and usage notes. The differences identified between *corpus users* and *dictionary users* are not easily quantified, but this study shows some of the qualitative differences present in students' written production when aided by dictionaries as opposed to corpora, or indeed by a combination of the two. At the same time it suggests that the Internet, while undeniably useful as a linguistic ready-reckoner, fosters neither accuracy nor variety in the acquisition and use of lexis and phraseology.

One of the most interesting points to emerge from this study was the observation that higher-quality texts are not produced by *corpus users* simply because they are using a corpus, but because the *corpus users* display traits associated with the archetypal 'good language learner' (Oxford 1990). These traits are shared to a lesser extent by the more discerning amongst the *mixed-resource users*, as well as the control-group *dictionary users* (though these students were explicitly asked to consult their dictionaries as often as possible). Adventurous *corpus users* are students who are motivated enough to make the effort to learn to use the query syntax. They then take care to identify precisely what forms of language they wish to locate, and are prepared to try various permutations of their queries before they settle on the data that best satisfies their needs. They appear to actively avoid translating directly from their L1, especially when the language is figurative, preferring to copy the native-speaker models present in the data. In other words, they are students who have simply added corpus use to an already productive repertoire of effective language learning strategies.

References

Boers F. (2000) Metaphor awareness and vocabulary retention. *Applied Linguistics* 21, 553–571.

Bowker L. & P. Bennison (2003) Student translation archive: design, development and application. In Zanettin, F., S. Bernardini & D. Stewart (eds) *Corpora in translator education*. Manchester: St Jerome.

Deignan A., D. Gabrys & A. Solska (1997) Teaching English metaphors using cross-linguistic awareness-raising activities. *ELT Journal* 51, 352–360.

Frankenberg-Garcia A. (2005) A peek into what today's language learners as researchers actually do. *International Journal of Lexicography* 18, 335–355.

Goldsmith P. (2003) Working wonders with words. Paper presented at 37th IATEFL conference, Brighton 22–26 April.

Hanks P. (2004) The syntagmatics of metaphor and idiom. *International Journal of Lexicography* 17, 245–274.

Lewis M. (1997) *Implementing the lexical approach: putting theory into practice*. Hove: Thomson Heinle LTP.

Oxford R. (1990). *Language learning strategies. What every teacher should know*. Boston: Heinle & Heinle.

Partington A. (1998) *Patterns and meanings. Using corpora for English language research and teaching*. Amsterdam & Philadelphia: John Benjamins.

Philip G. (2005) From concept to wording and back again: features of learners' production of figurative language. In Barnden J., S. Glasbey, M. Lee, A. Wallington & L. Zhang (eds) *Proceedings of the Third Interdisciplinary Workshop on Corpus-Based Approaches to Figurative Language*. Birmingham: Birmingham University Press, 46–53.

Philip G. (2006) Metaphor, the dictionary, and the advanced learner. In E. Corino, C. Marello & C. Onesti (eds.) *EURALEX Proceedings of the XII International Lexicography Congress*. Alessandria: Dell'Orso, 895–905.

Rundell, M. (ed.) (2002) *Macmillan English Dictionary for Advanced Learners*. Oxford: Macmillan.

Sinclair J., S. Jones & R. Daley (1970/2004) *English Collocation Studies: The OSTI Report*. 2nd Edition, R. Krishnamurthy (ed.), London & New York: Continuum.

Sinclair, J. M. (ed.) (2006) *Collins COBUILD Advanced Learners English Dictionary*. 5th edition. Glasgow: HarperCollins.

Summers, D. (ed.) (2003) *Longman Dictionary of Contemporary English*. Harlow: Pearson Education.

Wehmeier, S. (ed.) (2005) *Oxford Advanced Learner's Dictionary*. 7th edition. Oxford: OUP.

Appendix

Phrasebuilder: *keywords in sequential order*

I; bed; unable to sleep
went to
wine; party
headache; stomach; wind
rain; nerves
remember; film
turn; key; lock
suddenly heard; door
heart; chest
footsteps; stairs
thoughts; my mind
think; save myself
door; open
something; end of the bed
my jaw
neighbour; wrong house

Phrasebuilder: *model text*

Last night **I went** to **bed** but I was **unable to sleep**. I had got home late after my friend's **party**, and I'd definitely had too much **wine**. I had a terrible **headache** coming on, and my **stomach** was churning. Outside the **wind** was howling, and the **rain** battering on my window was getting on my **nerves**. For some strange reason, it made me **remember** a **film** I'd seen.

The sound of a **key turn**ing in the **lock** downstairs brought me back to earth. I **suddenly heard** my own front **door** slam shut. My **heart** started pounding in my **chest** as I realised that I had an intruder in the house! I heard **footsteps** steadily making their way up the **stairs**. All manner of **thoughts** went through my **mind**, as I tried desperately to **think** how I could **save myself**. But there was no time. I lay in terror as the **door open**ed slowly, and in the darkness of my bedroom I could make out **something** near the **end of the bed**.

My jaw dropped when the light was abruptly switched on and I came face to face with my **neighbour**, James, who had been at the party with me. He was in a worse state than I was, and had come back to the **wrong house**!

ALEX BOULTON

Bringing corpora to the masses: Free and easy tools for interdisciplinary language studies

Abstract

Despite huge promise, direct applications of corpus linguistics (CL) have yet to make substantial inroads to the language classroom. The main stumbling block is perhaps psychological: even when they are aware of the possibilities, teachers and learners alike may hesitate to change established practices and challenge traditional roles. It is difficult to alter such mindsets, but it should be possible to make corpus linguistics more user-friendly. In particular, we argue here that even using only free on-line tools with minimal training, learners are quick to see a variety of applications in language learning and other areas. This paper describes a CL option in an English MA course where students are allowed considerable freedom to discover the tools and possibilities for themselves, and pursue them to their own ends. An analysis of 30 resulting research papers highlights the diversity of approaches and topics which can be studied through CL, and discusses the wide range of skills learned in the process.

1. Introduction

Few fields of human inquiry have been left untouched by the advent of powerful computer tools for the processing of vast quantities of data. In language studies, this has given rise to complete new fields of study, including corpus linguistics (CL). CL in turn has made its influence felt in various areas connected with language teaching and learning, most especially in informing teaching and reference materials as well as considerations of content. However, and despite a plethora of research articles and projects, when it comes to direct applications in the classroom in the form of "data-driven learning" (Johns 1991a) or DDL, the trickle-down effect has yet to turn into the predicted torrent (Leech 1997: 2).

To explain this lack of uptake, we cannot ignore a number of obvious potential disadvantages to DDL, whether real or perceived. For example, the changes to current practices might be thought too big to be absorbed in a single step, and perceived as not "serious". DDL definitely constitutes a challenge to teacher and learner roles: the former might resent a loss of power and control, while the latter might not like having to take greater responsibility for their learning. Both might also lament the "fuzzy" nature of language inherent in corpus work, preferring the certainty and comfort (even if illusory) which accompanies a traditional rule-based approach. Some might argue they have insufficient facilities in terms of computers, software and space, or the money to acquire them. Even with extensive technological resources, teachers and learners can also feel threatened if they lack sufficient skills to use them. Some training would seem essential for DDL to be of use, but any "learning to learn" can be perceived as a waste of time, serving only to delay the language learning itself.

Many powerful arguments can of course be marshalled to overcome these objections. The widely reported advantages to DDL include promoting autonomy, language awareness and noticing skills in a learner-centred approach using authentic language by applying inductive, hands-on discovery learning. As all of these are central in current research on language teaching and learning, it might be argued that objections to DDL are largely a gut reaction. In a nutshell, learners and teachers simply aren't convinced.

If DDL is to break out of its current research confines and reach a wider audience, it should be seen to offer maximum return on minimum investment. For this to happen, a number of things are necessary:

- *The tools should be free*. Many working teachers are unaware of the considerable resources available for free on the internet; all that is needed to exploit them is a single computer with internet access and a printer. A fully-equipped computer laboratory and expensive software certainly allow greater possibilities, but they are by no means essential to DDL.
- *The software should be easy to use*. Specialists aside, few people are likely to exploit the full potential of the sophisticated software available; more important is that it should be user-friendly and ready to use with only a few minutes' exploration, even for those with limited ICT

skills. Freely-available software has increasingly intuitive interfaces, and is frequently accompanied by concrete examples, guided tours, tutorials, help facilities, etc.
- *The techniques should be flexible and transferable*. If CL is a methodology rather than a discipline (e.g. Scott & Tribble 2006: 4), then it might have applications in a variety of areas above and beyond linguistics and language learning (itself a derivative). The more widely it is used for a variety of purposes, the more likely it is to continue to be used.

This paper presents a course in corpus linguistics which attempts to put these criteria into practice. In particular, it discusses the tools that learners find free on the internet, and looks at the topics they choose to explore when allowed to use them to pursue their own interests.

2. An option in corpus linguistics

The course in question is part of an MA in English offered entirely at distance by the *Centre de Télé-enseignement Universitaire* (CTU) at Nancy Université in France, and the typical student profile is correspondingly quite specific (see also Boulton & Wilhelm 2006). Most of our learners are mature students with French as a mother tongue, but enrolments come from all over the world. They have relatively advanced language abilities as well as a specialist interest in English, and are comparatively autonomous and used to managing their work alone. Motivation is thus a key factor in such an isolated learning environment, as students try to reconcile their degree with work and family commitments in sometimes very difficult circumstances.

2.1 Course considerations

In accordance with the prevailing paradigm in France, language forms the common core of the MA supported by three major options in literature, cultural studies and linguistics, and a number of subsidiary specialisations (e.g. French as a foreign language). Of the three main options, linguistics is the least well-known, and statistically the least popular. It is important then to find a course which appeals to a wide range of interests, does not require too much prior knowledge, and relates to other studies. CL seems to fit this bill on a number of counts. On a practical level, it is unlikely students will have come across it before, thus placing them all on an equal footing despite their varied prior experience of linguistics in general. Apart from a computer and access to the internet, no extra costs are involved in the form of required reading or expensive tools, nor any specialist knowledge of ICT. The focus is on learning about CL by applying it to language areas students are interested in. This highly practical approach aims to downplay the common perception of linguistics as abstract theorising, and fosters a set of skills which are transferable to and from other areas of study, and indeed to non-academic life. Evaluation is confined to the final research paper submitted at the end of the semester. This system lends itself well to distance learning at MA level, as students can pursue their own interests and work at their own rhythm, with teacher back-up available as required. The paper is a 20-page report (not counting appendices etc.) on a research project they define and conduct themselves on an area of their choice. We have deliberately kept the guidelines for the research paper as flexible and open as possible so that learners can develop their own questions in regard to their own interests, which go well beyond language learning, the only restriction being that it should involve English and CL. Indeed, as Bernardini (2001: 228) points out, "it would be inherently contradictory to prescribe a methodology when the aim of the approach is to give learners the instruments to develop their own methodologies and make their own discoveries." The mark accordingly is less concerned with the product than with the process "defining the question, choosing the corpus, finding the appropriate tools, using their ingenuity to overcome the problems they will inevitably encounter, and reasoning their way through the whole procedure." A number of past research papers are made available on line as well as a list of all past titles and the most popular sites used. Guidance is also given on the appropriate structure, style and format of a research report in English, linguistics generally requiring rather different styles from research in literature or cultural studies.

Descriptions of a number of CL courses have been published elsewhere. Maia (1997), for example, imposed broad topics (e.g. sport or ecology) on her translation students but required a very specific product for evaluation, namely a bilingual glossary. Others (e.g. Dodd 1997; Jackson 1997; Bernardini 2000; Cheng et al. 2003; Chambers 2005) have used the research paper for evaluation purposes in undergraduate degrees; however, most of these are very explicitly language-oriented courses, often with the language topics for investigation provided by the teachers. Jackson (1997) is the exception in allowing his students considerable choice in their research, although the projects are confined to a CL analysis of literary style. All of these courses thus impose constraints of one type or another on what students can do, none allowing the freedom in the CTU course. In the light of Johns' (1991a: 2) oft-repeated comment that "research is too serious to be left to the researchers," we agree with Leech (1997: 10) that individual choice is essential in giving the student "thc realistic expectation of breaking new ground as a 'researcher', doing something which is a unique and individual contribution". CL would certainly seem to be a fruitful ground for this, as "the traditional divisions between, on the one hand, teaching and research, and, on the other, literary and linguistic analysis, are to an extent arbitrary" (Burgess & Kohn 1995: 63).

2.2 Introducing corpus linguistics

As students are often wary of linguistics, and CL can be terrifyingly technical on first encounter, it is essential to find a way to make the course as unthreatening as possible. Bowker and Pearson, in their "practical guide to using corpora" (2002: 108), attempt this by leaving their "introduction to basic corpus processing tools" (frequency lists, concordances, clusters, collocates, etc.) to chapter 7, half-way through the book. Another way is to provide easy, accessible, and familiar examples wherever possible, and leave much of the work to the learner to discover not just the language, but how to go about tackling it through CL. Learners need differing amounts of guidance, and back-up has to be available on demand, but in general students quickly see the point, and discover much of the rest for themselves in a relatively short time (cf. also Bernardini 2001).

The introductory section to the course thus aims to show how applications of CL can be quite concrete in a familiar environment, which also highlights the variety of applications of corpus methodologies. For example, students are generally familiar with amazon.com, but few have explored the "inside this book" and "search inside" functions, some of which offer insights into CL. Looking at a well-known book such as Dan Brown's *Da Vinci Code*, visitors to the site can read various extracts including the blurb and the first pages, and are introduced to "statistically improbable phrases" with a brief discussion of what that entails (*cilice belt, seeded womb, pope interred, corporal mortification, rosewood box*, etc.); these are hypertext-linked to the actual occurrences in the text. Other features provide an introduction to important concepts including frequency, search strings, concordances, collocations, co-text, and so on. The statistics provided here can be intriguing, and even the more fanciful ones serve to keep the introduction accessible: the book rates 9.1 on the Fog Index, indicating that 80% of books are harder to read; it has 11.1 words per sentence (82% of books have more); the reader gets 14,105 words to the dollar, and 11,425 words per ounce, meaning that each word costs €0.000056 at today's prices and weighs 0.0025 grams. The first 500-odd words of the novel can easily be copied into VocabProfiler[1] to show other features that texts can reveal, highlighting the importance of lexical frequency within the text. The statistics can also be compared to the language as a whole based on the most frequent words in bands of 1000. Other concepts introduced at this stage include types, tokens, lemmatisation and etymology.

1 URLs to the various sites mentioned can be found in Appendix A.

Standard search engines provide another familiar entry point. Although students know and use google.com for example, few have ever got around to exploring the advanced search features, which can make all the difference to the relevance of hits. The implications for corpus searches are made explicit, including the importance of domain-specific searches, reliability of websites, etc. The limitations of such tools are also explored, showing how they are information-oriented rather than language-oriented. This allows a lead-in to the web as corpus (see e.g. Kehoe & Renouf 2002), and especially the possibilities of the more linguistic WebCorp. There is an introduction to large public corpora "the British National Corpus (BNC) and the Bank of English (BoE) among others" as well as the common tools associated with them: concordances, collocates and frequency lists, as well as tagging, query language and tips for conducting successful searches. Other "non-linguistic" corpora are mentioned (e.g. Shakespeare, or Old English), as well as the possibilities for students to create and analyse their own corpora. For this, a number of free on-line tools are presented briefly (e.g. Web Frequency Indexer and the demo version of WordSmith Tools), and links are given to numerous other resources on line, including other tutorial pages.

Descriptions of such tools are kept to a minimum as the idea is that students should explore and find out for themselves; in a sense, learners become their own teacher-researchers. This would seem to be particularly appropriate in CL, which, "almost more than any other branch of linguistics, […] requires that students have 'hands on' experience of the subject […] Only through using corpora can one gain a first-hand sense of their potential" (Leech 1997: 7). This works precisely because CL, "by its very nature, has a highly practical and applied orientation" (Hatzidaki 1996: 263). We would agree in this with Kirk (2002: 156), who also found with experience that his "focus has shifted from *teaching* corpus linguistics to that of *learning* to do corpus linguistics". In a way such a discovery approach is really little more than an extension of the data-driven learning philosophy where learners explore language rather than being told about it; there seems little reason why a similar approach cannot be adopted with the tools and methodologies of CL as well as for language learning.

3. Student research papers

This section provides an overview of the most popular tools, methods and corpora used by our students, followed by an analysis of the research topics chosen. We look at 30 research papers submitted between 2002 and 2005 – not an entirely random selection, as it includes only those which were submitted electronically and got a mark of at least 60%. It also excludes papers which adopted a different approach from that described above: for example, some were more theoretical, while others discussed possible applications of CL in language teaching and learning, and so on. A list of the 30 papers can be found in Appendix B along with a brief summary of each.

3.1 Corpora and corpus tools

Surprisingly perhaps, only six papers used the internet itself as a corpus with various tools: WebCorp, Edict VLC, and To Google or Not to Google; Google and Yahoo were also used for searching the web as corpus in various languages. This is perhaps disappointing given that the internet is a "fabulous linguists' playground" (Kilgarriff & Grefenstette 2003: 333) and that there is enormous potential for using the web as corpus (see e.g. Kehoe & Renouf 2002; Bergh 2005). However, almost all of the corpora which were used were collected from the internet for obvious reasons of variety, availability and cost (Aston 2002). As Table 1 shows, there were two basic types: 18 papers used one or more large, ready-made reference corpora, while 27 involved at least one home-built corpus of their own.

		home-built corpora					
		0	*1*	*2*	*3*	*4*	*total*
reference corpora	*0*		3	6	1	2	12
	1	1	2	4		1	8
	2	2	4	3		1	10
	total	3	9	13	1	4	30

Table 1. Types of corpora used.

The majority of students made use of some kind of large reference corpus, most frequently the BNC (14 papers) or the BoE (12 papers).[2] Two used the Brown corpus, three used different specialist corpora (Old English, Switchboard, W3Corpora). In eleven of these cases, two or three of these large ready-made corpora were used for comparison purposes, or simply to collect more data. Only three students relied entirely on such reference corpora, the others compiling ones of their own. Among these, the majority analysed one corpus (9 papers) or two (13 papers); the remaining five used three or four. In eighteen cases both types of corpus were used, either with the reference corpus as a starting point before moving on to the home-built corpus (12 papers), or the other way round with the reference corpus serving to check the results of the purpose-made corpus (6 papers).

The most popular single source type was inevitably online newspapers for reasons clearly outlined in Rademann (1998). Not only are the texts easily available, but (depending on the newspaper) they have minimum standards of language and content, are up-to-date, cover a wide range of areas, and are arguably more representative than other registers in that they are written by multiple authors and read by millions (cf. Burnard 2002: 58). This does not mean the students are necessarily interested in the news as such, but as long as they are aware of the limitations of newspapers and do not overgeneralise their findings, newspapers would seem to be a fine source in general (Partington 2001a: 63).

2 See e.g. Aston (1996) and Bernardini (2000) for exploiting large corpora in language learning.

Twelve students based part or all of their corpora on British or American press found on line, although others were considerably more specialised.

It seems then that learners can see the attraction of both large existing corpora and small purpose-built ones (see Aston 1997a for a comparison). In the former case our students used only the dedicated software provided with the corpus (e.g. Sara with the BNC); in creating their own corpora, however, they made use of a variety of different tools available free on the internet.[3] One of the most popular was the Web Frequency Indexer (WFI), used by 15 students. 16 papers made use of WordSmith Tools (WST), although there were occasional alternatives. Tagging was rarely used, perhaps because of the limited availability of free on-line taggers such as CLAWS or the Brill tagger, which are often restricted to very small samples. Word frequency lists from the BNC proved popular, lemmatised or not, as did VocabProfiler and the Compleat Lexical Tutor in more recent papers. Other software included numerous online dictionaries, pgAdmin, Filemaker, the ubiquitous Microsoft Word and Excel, as well as occasional locally-available tools.

With the exception of general-purpose software (notably MS Word and Excel), what all the above tools have in common is that they are free and easily available on the internet. Although the free versions of some are limited, returning a reduced number of hits or allowing only short texts, they were frequently sufficient for most purposes. A number of students showed surprising ingenuity in finding ways around the limitations, especially with carefully formulated search commands, or cutting the text into small sentence or paragraph-length fragments containing the target language; a handful of others were sufficiently hooked to buy full licences for WordSmith Tools. Another point which bears mentioning is that not all of these tools were mentioned in the course: the students located them and found how to use them on their own.

3 A list of the most popular websites and software can be found in Appendix A.

3.2 Research topics

Although CL has permitted many quite revolutionary techniques, in some ways it is "nothing but a methodology" (McEnery & Wilson 2001: 1) – at least in the sense that its methods are not limited to linguistics alone. This can be seen in the description of a new journal entitled *Corpora: Corpus-based Language Learning, Language Processing and Linguistics*. One of its "three main features" is:

> Interdisciplinarity: the journal will actively seek to promote a cross fertilization of ideas and techniques across a range of areas… and disciplines… in the belief that these areas have something to offer to each other through their common focus on corpus data.[4]

Hatzidaki (1996: 262) argues convincingly for the introduction of CL as a taught course in undergraduate language degrees precisely because of its "strong interdisciplinary character… CL is applicable to a whole gamut of linguistic, and, arguably, non-linguistic disciplines." Partington (2001b) and Adolphs (2006) are among those who point out that the vast majority of social sciences use corpora in one way or another, from psychology to philosophy and beyond. Kettemann and Marko (2004) ask if the L in TaLC can stand for literature, and this can easily be extended to cultural studies, history, sociology, translation, etc., as well as the pursuit of personal interests. All of this suggests that CL may have applications in far wider areas than just "language" (Boulton 2006), a factor which it would seem churlish not to exploit, and even key in ensuring continued use of the methodologies beyond the course itself. Indeed, if corpora are to be effective, it seems extremely important to allow students to use them in domains that are of interest to them (Maia 1997), especially if texts are "only useful insofar as the learner is able to authenticate them, i.e. to create a relationship with the texts" (Braun 2005: 53; also Widdowson 1998). And what better way for students to authenticate a corpus than for them to choose the texts based on their own interests?

4 <http://www.eup.ed.ac.uk/journals/content.aspx?pageId=1&journalId=12801>, accessed May 2007.

Given the students' overriding interest in literature and cultural studies, their research projects frequently have a bias towards these and related areas.[5] The tools and procedures needed for the course are quite different from what the students are used to in these other fields, however; even where they have used a "corpus" in the past, the methods involved are likely to be substantially different. The idea is not to oppose the different approaches, but to treat them as complementary (Kettemann & Marko 2004: 187). However, the students quickly adapted to the quantitative measures needed, generally supplemented with a sensible qualitative eye. Of the 30 papers looked at here, arguably only 6 started with a purely linguistic question, typically a language point that is difficult to grasp or to translate into the L1. These included phrasal verbs, pairs or groups of close synonyms (e.g. *barely / hardly / scarcely*; *speak / talk*), and spelling differences (*civilise / civilize*; *enquire / inquire*). A number of others were interested in translations of key items, although only two had a parallel corpus as such. Many others were inspired by their own learning experiences, although again, few made this a major focus of the paper. About two thirds of the students started with a specific question (a bottom-up approach); the other third started with the corpus (a top-down approach).

A brief look at the titles of the research papers submitted shows the wide range of other interests pursued (Table 2). Top of the list were cultural issues revolving around politics, current affairs, and social issues such as feminism; other cultural topics related to their studies included history, and especially British and American cultural comparisons, confirming or rejecting stereotypes. Five papers were mainly concerned with literature, although many others had this as a minor element, especially in the form of stylistic comparison. Translation and language learning/teaching formed the core of four more, again relating to other courses offered in the degree. Outside interests can be found in music and popular culture, professional life, ICT, religion, and personal contacts with a particular part of the English-speaking world.

5 A list of the titles plus a brief description of each paper can be found in Appendix B.

Many papers managed to combine several of these interests quite explicitly. Such a broad range of topic areas supports Seidlhofer's (2000: 208) claim that CL can provide "an overarching theme" relevant to many if not all aspects of studies.

	topic area	*number of papers*
1.	politics / current affairs	9
2.	music / popular culture	8
3.	history	6
4.	literature	5
5.	GB / US differences	5
6.	work	4
7.	translation / teaching-learning	4
8.	ICT	3
9.	personal contacts	3
10.	religion	3

Table 2. Popular topic areas

4. What did they learn?

The course outlined here is, first and foremost, a course in *corpus* lin guistics for language students. As a result, students should end up with more than a passing knowledge of key concepts involved in CL, and be able to use them in the future. These include, in no particular order, an awareness of concordances, KWICs, frequency lists, keywords, distribution plots, collocates lists and tables, mutual information and *t*-scores, stoplists, picklists, batches, left and right sorting, and so on. Using corpora entails an understanding of the importance of balance and statistical evidence in relation to topic, text type, size, date, language variety and register, number of contributors, text length, representativity, and extrapolation from samples to populations. As with Chambers' (2005: 114) course, few if any of our students have an "ambition to become experts in CL, any more than they desire to become lexicographers when using the dictionary", but it is another potentially useful set of tools for them even without specialist in-depth knowledge (Hatzidaki 1996: 256).

In producing their research papers, students knew they would be assessed on the "processes rather than products, on methods rather than outcomes, on resourcefulness, awareness and reflectiveness rather than learnedness" (Bernardini 1997: 5). In other words, inconclusive or unexpected results do not automatically entail a low mark. As Maia (1997: 5) found in her course evaluation, "although the *product* of each of the assignments varied in quality, the knowledge gained from the *process* was considerable". There is inevitably a degree of serendipity involved (Bernardini 2000), but the students are thus sensitised to the cyclical nature of research, involving continuous feedback and rethinking rather than a strictly linear process. The discovery approach involves defining the question, choosing the corpus, locating appropriate tools and experimenting with their use, using their *nous* to deal with problems they will inevitably encounter, and reasoning their way through the whole process in a clear and rational way. All of this leaves the students better equipped to use CL techniques in the future.

It is also however a course in corpus *linguistics*, and students certainly learned a lot of linguistics in the process „ perhaps indeed more effectively as the practical approach can make many quite theoretical linguistic concepts that much more "real". Amongst other things we could mention:

- The concept of "word" (lemma, lexical item, etc.), function vs. lexical words, and the separation of lexis and syntax, and associated ideas (affixation, inflection/derivation, compounds, multi-word units, lexical phrases, chunks, collocations, discourse, cohesion/coherence), including the inherently "fuzzy" nature of language, which allows learners to be more confident with approximations.
- The importance of frequency, lexical density, type/token ratios etc.; semantics, polysemy, homonymy, part of speech, etymology, borrowings, cognates, polysemy, translation, etc.
- The importance of text type (genre/register, style, speech vs writing, etc.) and variation, especially between different varieties of English (geographic, socio-economic, diachronic, etc.); the concept of "error" and standard vs. non-standard varieties.

Clearly, a course such as this is not primarily concerned with language learning *per se*, but language was by default the mainstay of all projects. Where the specific research question had a language focus, one would hope that the point concerned would be better understood. More importantly as regards language learning, the processes involved are likely to increase noticing and sensitivity to various aspects of language, leading to more efficient learning in the future (Allan 2006). To use a hackneyed analogy, it would seem better in the long term to provide the hungry with a fishing rod rather than with a fish. As Kettemann and Marko (2004: 171) point out, "we do not want to make students aware of something, we want them to be able to become aware on their own". This kind of language awareness is what Mair (2002) calls the "hidden surplus value of corpora in continental English departments".

The first port of call for many students was a range of standard reference works, either on paper or on line. These include the dictionary, thesaurus, textbook, usage manual, grammar book, style guide, and so on. Notoriously, such materials are found to be inaccurate descriptions of what actually happens in many languages. Confronting such reference works with corpus evidence, learners might be expected to use them more efficiently or more sensitively in future; even when they are "accurate", they can rarely be complete, and a corpus approach can be seen to add to this (cf. Dodd 1997). A degree of scepticism and critical thinking is also needed in regard to teacher explanations and folk wisdom "not to mention the learner's own ideas" including an ability to think of alternative explanations for apparently simple phenomena (Kettemann & Marko 2004).

The entire process as outlined here involves a great deal of "authenticity" of text, purpose and activity (Stevens 1995), whether as the main focus or more indirectly, almost as a form of task-based learning. This includes following the course, understanding and using the tools in English, and encountering and manipulating tremendous quantities of English data in their chosen corpora. The lack of an explicit "language learning" aim is therefore not only not a problem, but can be seen as a positive advantage (Kennedy & Miceli 2001); Aston (1997b: 210) even claims that learners *should* "approach the corpus with non-linguistic goals". If, as Johns (1991b: 30) has claimed, "effective language learning is itself a form of linguistic research", one wonders if the converse might not also be true in many cases, i.e. that linguistic research can be an effective form of language learning (see also Boulton & Wilhelm 2006). Following Maia's 1997 article, "making corpora: a learning process", Mauranen (2004: 99) claims that "corpus skills constitute a learning task in themselves [...] Once acquired, they facilitate learning greatly and need not be constantly refreshed".

In such a course, students inevitably discover an awful lot about using ICT, in particular using the internet more efficiently: finding and evaluating sources of texts and tools, advanced functions of search engines and query language, recovering broken links, downloading and copying. Students often found the tools themselves, which means they should be better able to do so again in the future as resources come and go; they also had to find out how to use them by experimentation, as complete description is not possible „ or, as we have argued, desirable „ in the course itself. We could also mention OCR scanning, transcription, screen shots and image editing, among other things.

The students learned a lot about more advanced functions of software they thought they were already familiar with, in particular MS Word and Excel. This includes the manipulation of layout and formatting, tables and graphs, images and automatic tables of contents, page numbering, spell-checking in different varieties, keyboard shortcuts, find and replace functions, etc. As the final research paper was in English and in a style similar to professional academic articles, there was the obvious opportunity of providing a style guide similar to those frequently found in professional linguistics journals (cf. Jackson 1997). If these students do continue to do research, they should be better placed to produce an appropriate paper, with considerations of format, structure, style, the importance of evidence, the respective merits and roles of quantitative and qualitative approaches, interpretation and generalisation, background reading and referencing, and so on. Some students took the initiative to contact researchers, publishers and copyright holders in their chosen area; some explored local university and other resources; some acquired experience in doing fieldwork. Most should also be more sensitive to the dangers of preconceived ideas in the formulation of their research.

Finally, the whole problem-solving, hands-on approach using limited tools encourages all sorts of useful behaviour which may serve in future (see also Kettemann & Marko 2004: 185 ff.). The initial idea has to be formulated and framed in such a way that it becomes a valid topic for research; frequently the original research questions cannot be addressed with a simple command, requiring considerable lateral thinking to overcome the problems, especially given the limits placed on much of the free demonstration software. For example, creative thinking was required to formulate a number of separate but compatible search requests to obtain more than 50 hits with BoE or BNC, how to measure syntactic complexity, alignment of different texts, and so on. Students also needed to be aware of issues of repetition (e. g. with song lyrics), features of spoken *versus* written language, non-standard spellings, the presence of other languages or non-Roman scripts. Even if not confronted with these specific problems again, the fact that they have had to solve such problems in the past would seem to put students in better stead to solve new problems as and when they arise in the rest of their studies and beyond.

5. Conclusion: If…

Corpus linguistics is a hugely promising field with a wide variety of applications, but language courses as a whole; the uptake so far has been extremely limited. If CL is to play any role here beyond materials development and syllabus design, we have to make sure it is not perceived just as "trendy" research that is irrelevant to the working teacher and the "average" learner (cf. Braun 2005: 47, 48). For language learning as such, we need to show that CL can almost immediately produce results which are "illuminating and very helpful" (Sinclair 2004: 288).

Clearly, such an approach increases learner autonomy, but more than that "it is now possible for the learner to be autonomous in ways it was previously impossible" (Uzar 2003: 153). This applies whether the explicit focus is on language or something else, and the crossover for learners like ours is essential if they are to keep using CL in any form.

Several are applying it in their other studies, including the long Master's dissertation and subsequent doctoral thesis; others have provided informal feedback that they also use it outside the academic context. The crossover is by no means guaranteed: Chambers (2005) found her students in Ireland had great difficulty in making the connection. This might be in part because her students were focusing exclusively on language questions, while a wider range of non-linguistic questions and greater room for learner choice to follow their own interests may maximise the versatility of corpus methodologies.

> If corpus consultation… is to become a common activity for learners across the broad spectrum of language studies (general language learning, literary studies, languages for specific purposes, translation, etc.), it would seem necessary for developments to take place in a broader context… It is perhaps outside the classroom that the next important step in research in this area will take place. (Chambers 2007: 13)

Like Römer (2006: 105), our aim has been to "equip our students with a tool box, containing skills that are transferable from problem to problem across sub-disciplines". Multifunctional tools tend to be kept to hand and used repeatedly, while specialist tools tend to be confined to a dusty drawer and brought out on rare occasions, if they are not forgotten altogether. Although the tools generally used in CL may have been designed with specific purposes in mind, it is a tribute to their power, simplicity and versatility that they can find a range of other uses. Screwdrivers too can be used for opening tins of paint.

References

Adolphs S. (2006) *Introducing electronic text analysis: a practical guide for language and literary studies*. London: Routledge.

Allan R. (2006) Data-driven learning and vocabulary: investigating the use of concordances with advanced learners of English. Centre for Language and Communication Studies, Occasional Paper 66. Dublin: Trinity College Dublin.

Aston G. (1996) The British National Corpus as a language learner resource. In Botley S., J. Glass, A. McEnery & A. Wilson (eds) *TALC 1996. UCREL Technical Papers* 9, 178–191.

Aston G. (1997a) Small and large corpora in language learning. In Lewandowska-Tomaszczyk B. & J. Melia (eds) *Practical applications in language corpora.* Lodz: Lodz University Press, 51–62.

Aston G. (1997b) Involving learners in developing learning methods: exploiting text corpora in self-access. In Benson P. & P. Voller (eds) *Autonomy and independence in language learning.* London: Longman, 204–263.

Aston G. (2002) The learner as corpus designer. In Kettemann B. & G. Marko (eds) *Teaching and learning by doing corpus analysis.* Amsterdam: Rodopi, 9–25.

Bergh G. (2005) Min(d)ing English language data on the web: what can Google tell us? *ICAME Journal* 29, 25–46.

Bernardini S. (1997) A 'trainee' translator's perspective on corpora. In Aston G., L. Gavioli & F. Zanettin (eds) *Corpus use and learning to translate.* http://web.archive.org/web/20031231010215/http://www.sslmit.unibo.it/cultpaps/paps.htm [accessed May 2007]

Bernardini S. (2000) Systematising serendipity: proposals for concordancing large corpora with language learners. In Burnard L. & T. McEnery (eds) *Rethinking language pedagogy from a corpus perspective.* Frankfurt: Peter Lang, 225–234.

Bernardini S. (2001) 'Spoilt for choice': a learner explores general language corpora. In Aston G. (ed.) *Learning with corpora.* Houston: Athelstan, 220–249.

Boulton A. (2006) When linguistics isn't linguistics: interdisciplinary approaches to corpus linguistics. *Interdisciplinarité dans les études anglophones.* Nancy: Université de Nancy.

Boulton A. & S. Wilhelm (2006) Habeant corpus – they *should* have the body. Tools learners have the right to use. *Asp* 49, 155–170.

Bowker L. & J. Pearson (2002) *Working with specialized language: A practical guide to using corpora.* London: Routledge.

Braun S. (2005) From pedagogically relevant corpora to authentic language learning contents. *ReCALL* 17(1), 47–64.

Burgess J. & J. Kohn (1995) The use of parallel concordancing for literary and linguistic text analysis. In Gimeno A. (ed.) *EUROCALL '95. Technology enhanced language learning: Focus on integration*, 61–72.

Burnard L. (2002) Where did we go wrong? A retrospective look at the British National Corpus. In Kettemann B. & G. Marko (eds) *Teaching and learning by doing corpus analysis.* Amsterdam: Rodopi, 51–70.

Chambers A. (2005) Integrating corpus consultation in language studies. *Language Learning & Technology* 9(2), 111–125.

Chambers A. (2007) Popularising corpus consultation by language learners and teachers. In Hidalgo E., L. Quereda & J. Santana (eds) *Corpora in the foreign language classroom.* Amsterdam: Rodopi, 3–16.

Cheng W., M. Warren & X. Xun-Feng (2003) The language learner as language researcher: putting corpus linguistics on the timetable. *System* 31, 173–186.

Dodd B. (1997) Exploiting a corpus of written German for advanced language learning. In Wichmann A., S. Fligelstone, T. McEnery & G. Knowles (eds) *Teaching and language corpora*. Harlow: Addison Wesley Longman, 131–145.

Hatzidaki O. (1996) Corpus linguistics as an academic subject. In Botley S., J. Glass, A. McEnery & A. Wilson (eds) *TALC 1996. UCREL Technical Papers* 9, 254–265.

Jackson H. (1997) Corpus and concordance: finding out about style. In Wichmann A., S. Fligelstone, T. McEnery & G. Knowles (eds) *Teaching and language corpora*. Harlow: Addison Wesley Longman, 224–239.

Johns T. (1991a) Should you be persuaded: two examples of data-driven learning. In Johns T. & P. King (eds) *Classroom concordancing. English Language Research Journal* 4, 1–16.

Johns T. (1991b) From printout to handout: grammar and vocabulary teaching in the context of data-driven learning. Revised version in Johns T. & P. King (eds) *Classroom concordancing. English Language Research Journal* 4, 27–45.

Kehoe A. & A. Renouf (2002) WebCorp: Applying the web to linguistics and linguistics to the web. *WWW2002 Conference*, Hawaii. <http://www2002.org/CDROM/poster/67/> [accessed May 2007].

Kennedy C. & T. Miceli (2001) An evaluation of intermediate students' approaches to corpus investigation. *Language Learning & Technology* 5(3), 77–90.

Kettemann B. & G. Marko (2004) Can the L in TALC stand for literature? In Aston G., S. Bernardini & D. Stewart (eds) *Corpora and language learners*. Amsterdam: John Benjamins, 169–193.

Kilgarriff A. & G. Grefenstette (2003) Introduction to the special issue on web as corpus. *Computational Linguistics* 29, 333–347.

Kirk J. (2002) Teaching critical skills in corpus linguistics using the BNC. In Kettemann B. & G. Marko (eds) *Teaching and learning by doing corpus analysis.* Amsterdam: Rodopi, 155–164.

Leech G. (1997) Teaching and language corpora: a convergence. In Wichmann A., S. Fligelstone, T. McEnery & G. Knowles (eds) *Teaching and language corpora*. Harlow: Addison Wesley Longman, 1–23.

Maia B. (1997) Making corpora: a learning process. In In Aston G., L. Gavioli & F. Zanettin (eds) *Corpus use and learning to translate*. <http://web.archive.org/web/20031231010215/http://www.sslmit.unibo.it/cultpaps/paps.htm> [accessed May 2007]

Mair C. (2002) Empowering non-native speakers: the hidden surplus value of corpora in continental English departments. In Kettemann B. & G. Marko (eds) *Teaching and learning by doing corpus analysis*. Amsterdam: Rodopi, 119–130.

Mauranen A. (2004) Spoken corpus for an ordinary learner. In Sinclair J. (ed.). *How to use corpora in language teaching*. Amsterdam: John Benjamins, 89–105.

McEnery T. & A. Wilson (2001) *Corpus linguistics,* 2nd edition. Edinburgh: Edinburgh University Press.

Partington A. (2001a) Corpus-based description in teaching and learning. In Aston G. (ed.) *Learning with corpora*. Houston: Athelstan, 63–84.

Partington A. (2001b) Corpora and discourse strategies in action: from 'footing' to 'fooling'. In Lewandowska-Tomaszczyk B. (ed.) *PALC 2001: Practical applications in language corpora.* Frankfurt: Peter Lang, 263–279.

Rademann T. (1998) Using online electronic newspapers in modern English-language press corpora: benefits and pitfalls. *ICAME Journal* 22, 49–71.

Römer U. (2006) Where the computer meets language, literature, and pedagogy: corpus analysis in English studies. In Gerbig A. & A. Müller-Wood (eds) *How globalization affects the teaching of English: studying culture through texts.* Lampeter: E. Mellen Press, 81–109.

Scott M. & C. Tribble (2006) *Textual patterns: key words and corpus analysis in language education.* Amsterdam: John Benjamins.

Seidlhofer B. (2000) Operationalizing intertextuality: using learner corpora for learning. In Burnard L. & T. McEnery (eds) *Rethinking language pedagogy from a corpus perspective.* Frankfurt: Peter Lang, 207–223.

Sinclair J. (2004) New evidence, new priorities, new attitudes. In Sinclair J. (ed.) *How to use corpora in language teaching.* Amsterdam: John Benjamins, 271–299.

Stevens V. (1995) Concordancing with language learners: Why? When? What? *CAELL Journal* 6(2), 2–10.

Uzar R. (2003) A toolbox for translation quality assessment. In Lewandowska-Tomaszczyk B. (ed.) *Practical applications in language and computers: PALC 2003.* Frankfurt: Peter Lang, 153–162.

Widdowson H. (1998) Context, community, and authentic language. *TESOL Quarterly* 32, 705–716.

Appendix A. Popular websites

The URLs here were provided by the students themselves; all were operational at the time of the TaLC7 conference in 2006.

Large reference corpora:

- BNC (British National Corpus): <http://www.sara.natcorp.ox.ac.uk>.
- BoE (Bank of English): <http://www.titania.cobuild.Collins.co.uk>.
- Brown corpus: <http://www.ldc.upenn.edu/cgi-bin/ldc/textcorpus?doc=yes&corpus=BROWN#A>.
- Old English CorpusSearch: <http://www-users.york.ac.uk/ang22/YCOE/doc/corpussearch/CSRefToc.htm>.
- SwitchBoard: <http://www.ldc.upenn.edu/readme_files/switchbrd.readme.html>.
- W3 Corpora (Project Gutenberg): <http://clwww.essex.ac.uk/w3c/>.

The web as corpus (in addition Google, Yahoo and AltaVista in various languages):

- WebCorp: <http://ww.webcorp.org.uk>.
- To Google or not to Google: <http://cli.la.asu.edu/togoogleornot.htm>.
- Edict Virtual Language Centre: <http://www.edict.com.hk>.

Concordancers:

- WordSmith Tools: <http://www.lexically.net/downloads/download.htm>.
- MonoConc: <http://www.athel.com/mono.html>.
- Concord: <http://132.208.224.131/Concord.htm>.
- Larkin Concordance: <http://www.concordancesoftware.co.uk>.

Taggers and parsers:

- CLAWS demo tagger: <http://www.comp.lancs.ac.uk/ucrel/claws/trial.html>.
- Brill tagger: <http://www.ccl.umist.ac.uk/resources/ccl/BrillExec.zip>.
- Memory-Based Shallow Parser: <http://ilk.uvt.nl/cgi-bin/tstchunk/demo.pl>.
- Tilburg parse tagger: <http://pi0657.kub.nl/cgi-bin/tagdemo/tcl.cgi>.

Other tools:

- Web Frequency Indexer: <http://www.georgetown.edu/cball/webtools/web_freqs.html>.
- BNC frequency lists: <http://www.comp.lancs.ac.uk/ucrel/bncfreq>.
- VocabProfiler: <http://www.lextutor.ca/vp/eng>.
- BNC lemmatised frequency list: <http://www.itri.brighton.ac.uk/adam.Kilgarriff/bnceadme.html#lemmatised>.
- Compleat Lexical Tutor: <http://132.208.224.131>.
- The Internet Archive WayBack Machine: <http://www.archive.org/index.php>.

Appearing in papers not included in this selection:

- VLC Web Concordancer: <http://vlc.polyu.edu.hk/concordance/default.htm>.
- AntConc: <http://www.antlab.sci.waseda.ac.jp>.
- Variation in English Words and Phrases (VIEW): <http://view.byu.edu/>.
- Michigan Corpus of Academic Spoken English (MICASE): <http://micase.umdl.umich.edu/m/micase/>.
- Corpus of British Academic Spoken/Written English (BASE/BAWE): <http://www2.warwick.ac.uk/fac/soc/celte/>.
- EAGLES: <http://www.ilc.cnr.it/EAGLES96/home.html>.
- Corpora4Learning: <http://www.corpora4learning.net/>.
- ICT4LT: <http://www.ict4lt.org/en/index.htm>.
- TropesZoop: <http://www.acetic.fr/demo.htm>.
- KWiCFinder: <http://miniappolis.com/KWiCFinder>.

Appendix B. Research topics

Below are the full titles and a brief description of each of the 30 projects discussed in this paper, most recent first.

1. From screen-plays to fan fiction: A corpus-based study.

Interest in reading and writing science-fiction leads to a comparison of home-built corpora from the internet of *Star Trek* scripts and amateur "fan fiction" (45K words each). WST is used for various functions to check "techno-babble" overall, then focusing on the 10 most frequent items in each.

2. Basic English versus Standard English.

Experience teaching English in Germany provokes interest in the core lexicon of English (in terms of frequency, coverage, Germanic origin). Corpora of literary texts in SE and Ogden's BE (25K words each) are compiled from the internet using FileMaker; this allows analysis of the definition of "word" claimed for the 850-item vocabulary of BE. Comparative statistical analysis is conducted using Larkin and VocabProfiler.

3. Analysing Sting and the Police lyrics.

to analyse maturity of Sting's lyric writing. Focus is on the most frequent nouns using MonoConc (also WST), plus a qualitative interpretation for semantic fields, KWICs and collocates etc.; the results are checked against BNC written/spoken frequency lists.

4. The religious vocabulary in U2's lyrics.

A musical interest in the group instigates background research into their religious inclinations. Lyrics are compiled from the internet in two periods (8K and 12K words), and analysed for religious/spiritual lexical words and collocates using WFI and WST.

5. *Fancy*, *like* and *love*: Expressing liking and feeling.

Words don't always have one-to-one translations, and emotions are a particularly difficult area. After looking in dictionaries and comparing translations, these verbs were checked in BoE and BNC, as well as W3Corpora. To Google or Not to Google was used for the target items plus *someone* or *something*.

6. Building a lexical map of Nick Cave's lyrics: From The Boys Next Door to The Bad Seeds.

The lyrics were found on the web and compiled into two unbalanced corpora from different periods (5K and 30K words), and compared against BNC spoken corpus (keyword frequencies, collocates etc.). WFI and WST were used but a qualitative comparison was necessary too for syntax and meaning, collocation and idiom, concentrating on emotive lexical words.

7. Should we *enquire* or *inquire* about something?

Different varieties of English lead to confusion, and dictionaries and etymology are of little help. Usage is compared in relevant subcorpora of BNC and BoE, then in home-built corpora from GB and US newspapers and literature on line (total 25K words). Analysis of key words in each corpus is conducted with WFI and WST: frequencies, collocates and KWICs are used to compare meanings.

8. The different meanings and uses of the word *concern* and its derivative forms in Tony Blair's and George Bush's speeches.

This paper unites interest in politics and the intuition that *concern* is a "false friend": dictionaries etc. are found unconvincing regarding meaning and use. Two corpora of semi-scripted interviews are compiled from GB and US leaders (120K words each) and tagged with CLAWS. MonoConc and WFI were used to compare different senses and uses in the corpus against frequencies in Brown and BNC, the web as corpus using Virtual Language Centre, KWICs and frequencies etc.

9. The simplified novel, a case study: The Fall of the House of Usher.

The interest here is in literature and reading in a foreign language, as well as vocabulary acquisition. Corpora are compiled from an original text (7K words) and an OCR-scanned simplified reader (2K words). VocabProfiler is used to compare vocabulary (Anglo-Saxon vs. Greek/Roman/French origins), as well as CLAWS and WST for syntax, text structure, omissions and additions; the tagging also helps to check against the simplification guide. The results are compared against 5 other similar novels from the internet.

10. *Civilise* or *civilize*? A comparative study of the verbs ending in *-ise* and those ending in *-ize* and their respective nominalizations.

A common problem where dictionaries, usage manuals, etymology and style guides are not much help. On the claim that it may be a US/GB distinction, examples are checked against Brown and BNC, including BNC frequency lists. Two balanced corpora (12K words each) are then compiled from online newspapers from GB (*Guardian, Independent, Telegraph, Mirror*) and the US (*USA Today, Washington Post, New York Times, LA Times*) over two weeks. Other software includes SwitchBoard, VocabProfiler and WST.

11. Stylistic features of verbatim reports of speeches in European Parliament debates: The passage from the tapes to the final transcripts.

Working at the European Parliament with access to in-house and published documents generates an interest in politics and speech/writing differences. The corpora are from unscripted EP speeches by native speakers, comparing transcribed and subsequently edited texts (6K words each). The focus is on spoken features, redundancy, syntactic complexity, connectors, etc. using WFI and WST.

12. Near synonyms for *woman* in Old English: A corpus analysis.

Interests lie in literature, language evolution, the “real” meaning of words, and gender studies. Synonyms from OE dictionaries are checked against online parsed OE corpora (1.5M words of prose, 75K words of verse); relevant segments are analysed with WFI.

13. A corpus-based approach to the speeches made by Gerry Adams since the Good Friday Agreement.

Contacts in Ireland and subsequent interests in politics and history inspire a corpus analysis of Adams’ speeches before (45K words) and after (62K words) the GFA, as well as Paisley’s speeches (16K words), all from the internet. The corpora are tagged with CLAWS, frequencies checked with WFI, and compared to each other and to BNC subcorpora and frequency lists; the focus is on aspects of scripted speeches with written/spoken styles. All corpora are checked for religious words and loaded language (WFI, WST) and against WebCorp on British newspapers.

14. Some French words and expressions in English.

Motivated by the crackdown on Anglicisms in France, this looks at the causes of borrowing and the shared history of French and English: Frequency, prestige, accommodation, semantic shifts, etc. Definitions and etymology of French borrowings and Anglo-Saxon synonyms are compared in monolingual and bilingual dictionaries, then in KWICs and frequencies in different subcorpora of the BoE. There is also a comparison between US and GB English from editorials of newspapers (total 36K words) using WFI.

15. E-words.

From a combination of previous experience in linguistics (including lexicology) and the IT focus of the course, ICT words are noted in general contexts. New coinages are compared against BoE and BNC frequency lists, and subsequently against an international newspaper corpus (35K words) as well as the web as corpus (Yahoo in different languages). Relevant contexts are downloaded and pasted into WFI.

16. *Make* or *do*? That is the question.

A long-standing dissatisfaction with traditional explanations of generalisations or idiosyncrasies is reason to check synonyms and translations for common points in BNC and BoE. A corpus is built from the internet *Guardian* Friday review and analysed with WST, looking also at translations back into French. Semantic, collocational and structural patterns are compared.

17. *Land*, *country*, *nation* and *state*: Scotland in focus.

In interest in politics combines with time spent in Scotland and an awareness of Scottish autonomy. Dictionaries and etymology are found unconvincing for the target words, so two corpora are compiled from the *Guardian* and SNP websites (27K words), the key words checked for frequency, collocates and KWICs with relation to Scotland using WFI, and compared against BoE.

18. Latin and French derivatives in the Guardian Unlimited and the Sun Online.

French borrowings are frequently claimed to be more formal in English. After historical research, corpora were built using pgAdmin to compare the prestigious *Guardian* and the popular *Sun* newspapers (12K words each); the corpora were further subdivided into news (more formal) and sport (more popular). Typically French affixes were the key focus.

19. A corpus comparison of the verbs *speak* and *talk*.

These verbs posed problems in translation which dictionaries did not answer satisfactorily. BoE was used to provide KWICs of the verbs + preposition, as well as collocates, and translations back to French were compared.

20. A study of two phrases: *To go on strike* and *to be on strike*.

Current affairs prompts an interest in phrasal uses of *strike*, which are compared first with French and German equivalents. The key words are analysed in BoE and then a newspaper corpus of *Guardian* articles covering the event, and the relevant text is checked for various uses, PoS, idioms, argument structure etc.

21. French words in English cuisine.

An enthusiasm for cooking and English recipes prompts interest in borrowings and history. BNC and BoE KWICs allow analysis of accommodation in morphology and structural use as well as semantic coverage against French. A corpus of recipes is compiled from MSN, downloading borrowings for analysis with WFI.

22. *Freedom* and *liberty* in George W. Bush's speeches.

Reactions to 9/11 highlight one Germanic/French doublet in English with a lack of comparable difference in French. This leads to work on etymology, but dictionary differences remain unclear. A corpus is built from the official White House site (27K words) and fed into WST; KWICs, WFI and structure provide insight to differences in meaning and use.

23. Corpus study of non-standard past irregular verbs in Appalachian and Piedmont English.

Living in the US, this student's family is critical of the non-standard local variety (especially *do*). The corpus is largely from a university audiobank supplemented with 3 local informants: interviews, own transcriptions of relevant past forms and focus on the 7 commonest verbs. There is a comparison of (non)standard usage and variation of form and meaning by register and speaker using tools from the same university.

24. *Clone, cloned, cloning*: New terms in modern language.

A retired doctor looking at "new" words since Dolly was cloned in 1997, especially as a buzzword outside medicine. WFI and WST were used to compare 4 registers (20K words each) of fiction, newspaper, science and "ethical" texts; collocates by PoS.

25. Technical and non-technical uses of forestry terms.

Working at the Office National des Forêts and reading professional documents, this student compiled two corpora of journal abstracts in fundamental (42K words) and applied (84K words) forestry science over a 4-year period. Lexical word frequencies are compared using WST, as well as technical and sub-technical language (especially compounds), and KWICs for semantic coverage and reference.

26. Is the verb *to maintain* solely reflective of the maintenance department activity or is it part of the group of synonyms *to repair* and *to fix*?

Working at LuxAir with access to trade documents, this paper presents a home-built corpus from professional documents comprising 6 manuals (230K words). The corpus is parsed with the Tilburg parse tagger, and WST is used to check frequencies, KWICs and collocates against BNC and BoE.

27. Investigating use of the adverbs *barely*, *hardly* and *scarcely*.

Meaning and usage (syntax) are confusing for these words, and dictionaries and manuals unconvincing. To find out more, frequencies and collocates are gathered from BNC and BoE, as well as KWICs for word order; also WST for a minicorpus.

28. The initiatory book: A case study of *The Little Prince*.

An interest in literature and "initiatory" books as well as translation prompts the comparison of two corpora of the novel in French and English (17K words) from the internet. Ten "interesting" words of *f*>5 were compared against BoE (frequencies and KWICs); a quantitative and qualitative analysis of translation is provided, especially pronominal replacement; WFI is also used.

29. British and American spelling – *meter* or *metre*? That is the question.

Different spellings can be intriguing but confusing. After researching historical, cultural and pronunciation differences (homophones etc.) between the two varieties, some of the commonest differences are picked out. These are checked in BoE and BNC subcorpora for frequency and collocates. Two home-built corpora comprise GB and US papers using WFI.

30. *In* in phrasal verbs.

Phrasal verbs often pose problems for French speakers. After checking definitions, the commonest ones are checked in BNC and BoE KWICs and frequencies, and compared against a home-built corpus of fashion magazines (23K words) using WST; other references include Switchboard, ICE and W3Corpora.

ANGELA CHAMBERS

Language learning as discourse analysis: playing games in a corpus of French journalistic discourse

Abstract

Although the use of authentic texts is now the norm in language teaching, invented, decontextualised examples are still very much in evidence in the teaching of grammar. This chapter shows how corpus data can provide a rich variety of examples of actual use to complement and reinforce individual instances found in a given text. After briefly situating the study in the research context of corpora and language learning, and describing and justifying the corpus which is used, verbal forms of the lemma JOUER *in a corpus of journalistic discourse are analysed. As we shall see, the corpus is a rich source of examples of expressions involving* JOUER *in literal and metaphorical contexts. The study is set in the context of intermediate and advanced learners of French, in the later stages of secondary education or in higher education.*

1. Introduction

Within the communicative approach to language learning and teaching, the integration of the explicit teaching of grammar and of lexico-grammatical patterns continues to give rise to debate among researchers. Carter & McCarthy (1994: 1–2) propose a discourse-based view of language for language teaching and learning, in contrast to an approach based on "a static, decontextualized view of language as a particular set of forms". Course books, they note, tend to emphasise single sentences or minimal units, reflecting "dominant paradigms for the description of, for example, grammar, vocabulary and the sound system of English, which have tended to concentrate on decontextualized units of language" (1994:xi). This approach is also evident in course books for French and other languages, although within the communicative approach the explicit teaching of grammar now tends to be inserted in chapters which are based on genuine examples of spoken or written texts. Indeed, this development was accompanied in the 1990s by a number of publications on discourse analysis specifically intended for language teachers (Cook 1989; McCarthy 1991; Nunan 1993; Carter & McCarthy 1994; Celce-Murcia & Olshtain 2000). All this, however, does not exclude the addition of decontextualised, invented examples, and it is easy to understand the recourse to them by authors and teachers. If a reference to playing football, for example, is encountered in a French text, the author of the coursebook, adopting a weak communicative approach and including some explicit teaching of grammar, may decide to include invented examples of JOUER + À used to denote playing sports, and to add examples of JOUER + DE for playing musical instruments. As the space available for such examples is limited in the coursebook, the teacher may add a worksheet with additional invented examples. Thus, even within a communicative approach based on genuine texts, the emphasis on invented, decontextualised minimal units can easily remain dominant.

The aim of this chapter is to show that corpus data can provide a rich variety of examples of actual use without undermining the emphasis on genuine texts studied in context which is central to the communicative approach. After briefly situating the study in the research context of corpora and language learning, and describing and justifying the corpus which is used, verbal forms of the lemma JOUER in a corpus of journalistic discourse are analysed. The aim is to show how these can be used in an approach to language learning which combines an explicit focus on grammatical structures at times, and at other times the focus on discourse recommended by Carter & McCarthy and others. As we shall see, the corpus is a rich source of examples of expressions involving JOUER in literal and metaphorical contexts. The study is set in the context of intermediate and advanced learners of French, in the later stages of secondary education or in higher education.

2. Small corpora and language learning and teaching

From the mid-1980s and particularly in the 1990s, research on the pedagogy of corpora and language learning and teaching focussed not only on what language is taught, but also on how it is taught, including what type of resources are most suitable for learners to consult. Empirical studies of learners' actual use of corpus data (Stevens 1991; Cobb 1997; Kennedy & Miceli 2001; O'Sullivan & Chambers 2006) tend to be based not on the vast corpora created for the purpose of research (Bernardini 2000 and Cheng et al. 2003 are notable exceptions), but on small corpora created specifically for use by learners. A number of developments (Burnard 2004; Chambers & Rostand 2005) involve using corpora of approximately one million words,[1] which Dodd (1997: 131) describes as "enough to make a valuable teaching aid and [...] realistically within the reach of most teaching institutions". These corpora tend to be of two types, on the one hand corpora of texts from one genre which the learners hope to master (Aston 2002; Flowerdew 2002), and on the other corpora of a more general nature, based on familiar texts such as newspaper articles, course material and fiction. Johns (1997: 103–104), for example, used "a 3-million word corpus chosen to give a rough reflection of an overseas student's life in Birmingham, both on and off the campus", including lectures, scientific journals, newspapers, 'domestic' texts on childcare and household management, and "one or two 'interloper' texts [...] for example Frederick Forsyth's *The Day of the Jackal* to give an occasional glimpse of sex-and-violence". As we shall see, the familiar nature of resources such as these must be taken into account in any consideration of the issue of context in the use of corpus data with learners.

There has been much controversy concerning the presence or absence of context in concordance data. Widdowson's (2000: 7) well-known description of corpus data as decontextualised language exists alongside publications which confidently use the term 'context' in rela-

1 *BNC Baby* (Burnard 2004) consists of four subcorpora of approximately one million words each.

tion to learner consultation of corpora (Cobb 1997: 302–303; Johns 1997; Roe 2000; Stevens 1991: 48). While Widdowson's comments may refer to the vast corpora combining many text types and genres, the other researchers all explicitly refer to small corpora of texts belonging to one genre or to familiar texts. The intention is that the learner will have sufficient familiarity with the text types in the corpus for it to be possible for them to select the information they need, despite the fact that they are not studying each individual text in detail. This is particularly relevant in the present case, where it is proposed that the data will provide multiple examples of naturally occurring discourse to reinforce an occurrence in a genuine complete text being studied, replacing the recourse to invented examples.

3. JOUER in a corpus of journalistic discourse

The corpus used in this study (Chambers & Rostand 2005) consists of 1723 articles from *Le Monde*, *L'Humanité* and *La Dépêche du Midi* in 2002 and 2003, covering the rubrics editorial, cultural, sports, national news, international news, and finance, for a total of approximately one million words. The hypothesis is that this will form a useful resource for teachers and learners at intermediate and advanced levels, providing them with examples of actual language use to complement their study of complete texts in a communicative context. To create the resource the teacher must undertake a journey of exploration in the corpus, beginning with consultation of the 592 occurrences of JOUER to find simple examples of JOUER + DE and JOUER + À, and additionally uncovering a very substantial number of non-literal uses of the verb.[2] In addition to direct references to playing games, musical instruments and theatrical roles, the corpus includes a large number of metaphorical expressions, such as SE JOUER, and references to cards and roles. In a study of the importance of discourse analysis in language teaching, Olstain et al. (2001: 717) emphasise the need for language teaching to

2 The concordancer used here is *Wordsmith Tools* Version 4.0 (Scott 2003).

focus on various discourse features. In the context of listening they underline the importance of providing learners with the opportunity to recognise "lexicogrammatical signals, such as discourse markers, lexical phrases, and word order". It is easy to see the relevance of this for the other three skills, and to add that learners, particularly at advanced level, should also be encouraged to be aware of lexicogrammatical features of texts such as non-literal uses of the simple expressions which they learned as beginners.

For the author of a course book or a teacher wishing to find examples of JOUER with the prepositions À and DE referring literally to playing sports and musical instruments, the corpus is a useful source of data, with genuine examples from registers familiar to the learners. All the occurrences are listed below.

« Jean RoyFressinge ***jouait*** *au golf à Fontainebleau.*
j'ai tout de suite saisi que Marco avait ***joué*** *au football sérieusement,*
Elles voulaient tout simplement ***jouer*** *au foot. »*
« Moi, mon père ne voulait pas que je ***joue*** *au foot, raconte Miriam, 16 ans.*
Sans oublier qu'aux Minguettes, quand tu ***joues*** *au foot, l'environnement fait que*
« Des filles qui ***jouent*** *super bien au foot et qui ne peuvent pas venir au club, il y en a plein*
« Il m'a appris à jouer. Je ne savais pas ***jouer*** *au tennis avant lui.*
on n'a pas encore trouvé les moyens de ***jouer*** *au golf sur 2 000 mètres carrés.*
« S'il arrive un jour à ***jouer*** *au basket, j'arrête d'entraîner. »*
le dimanche suivant, on ***jouera*** *aux échecs au jardin du Luxembourg*
à l'heure où les valeurs vedettes ne cessent de ***jouer*** *au Yo-Yo, Renault est le*
Il prend plaisir à raconter des histoires, à ***jouer*** *au jeu du chat et de la souris, précise François Scherer, psychologue.*
orchestrée par la musique haletante de John Williams, et que les bolides ***jouent*** *à cache-tampon avec les gratte-ciel en de vertigineuses plongées*
Empocher le magot des assurances. Aux Paralympiques, les athlètes sont loin de ***jouer*** *à ce genre de jeu, pourtant leur classification par handicap peut donner*
Quant à l'intéressé, il ***joue*** *toujours aux jeux vidéos et se passionne pour les voitures de course.*
Sapporo (Japon), envoyé spécial. A Sapporo pays de base ball on ne ***joue*** *pas au soccer sous la pluie.*
Pendant le dernier Lancôme, beaucoup de gens qui ne ***jouent*** *pas au golf venaient me demander des autographes.*
Il doit continuer à apprendre le jeu, car nous, Américains, y ***jouons*** *depuis notre enfance.*

« Comme on le nomme le rat trompette, il ***joue*** *de cet instrument ».*
Hasna ***joue*** *de la guitare électrique, du oud, de la derbouka, du bendir et même du banjo*
AU « GUINNESS BOOK RECORDS » ? ***Jouer*** *du violoncelle en même temps que du didjeridoo et laisser sa main pianoter*
Cette troupe de cinq musiciens ***jouera*** *des instruments anciens comme la bombarde ou la cornemuse.*
Alors qu'il veut apprendre le saxophone, ses proches lui répondent que personne n'en ***joue*** *dans la famille et qu'il ne fera pas exception.*
Si Alice est censée être au piano, Agathe Alexis fait simplement mine d'en ***jouer*** *en agitant ses doigts.*

These genuine examples, in particular the reference to the *Guinness Book of Records*, remind one of Dodd's (1997: 133) comment that "no text book would come up with such a range of examples". The inclusion of examples of *y* JOUER and *en* JOUER also provides greater variety than is found in a number of coursebooks. It is important to note that this exploration of a corpus of written texts is not intended to replace consultation of spoken corpora. Significantly, in the French corpus of teen talk within the European SACODEYL project[3], "je fais du football" is more common than "je joue au football".

Given that the rubrics included in the corpus include sport and culture, it is perhaps surprising to find so few direct references to playing games and musical instruments. Indeed these form only a very small proportion of the occurrences, 24 out of 592, 18 for À and six for DE. While this might not provide the teacher introducing this structure to 11 or 12 year olds with a large number of simple examples, it could provide suitable, interesting, and perhaps therefore memorable reinforcement for more advanced learners who may still not use these expressions correctly. In addition to providing adequate resources for revision, the corpus can also provide the teacher and learner with serendipitous discoveries, to borrow Johns' (1988:21) phrase. The 592 occurrences include two occurrences of JOUER *le tennis*, and one of JOUER *à deux pianos*, which initially surprise the nonnative speaker of French.

3 SACODEYL (System-Aided Compilation and Open Distribution of European Youth Language). <http://www.um.es/sacodeyl/>.

> *Si Serena* ***joue*** *le meilleur tennis de sa vie sans faire de faute [quoting French player Amélie Mauresmo]*
> *Si j'arrivais à* ***jouer*** *le tennis que j'ai joué aujourd'hui, je savais que je pouvais réussir un très bon match, [quoting Peruvian player Luis Horna]*
> ***Jouer*** *à deux pianos demande des heures, voire des années, de pratique*

These expressions, while grammatically correct, provide examples to the nonnative speaker which are not readily available in language-learning materials.

Among the examples of JOUER with the prepositions *à* and *de*, it is interesting to note that we encounter four metaphorical uses, including a reference to playing yoyo in the context of the stock market, and to players taking advantage (or not, as the case may be) of insurance claims. This is far from being the only metaphorical reference to playing in the context of sport. The reference to playing chess, although not metaphorical, is particularly interesting in the context of culture and language learning. The source of this occurrence is an article by Maurice Ulrich, "Ces jours qui ont changé la France", published in *L'Humanité* on 4 May 2002, charting the development of the reaction of the Left in France to Le Pen's success in the first round of the presidential elections. The article begins with a reference to the cultural practice of playing chess in the Jardin du Luxembourg, builds up a dramatic account of the horrified reactions and protest marches which followed the news of the election results, and ends with a fervent hope, highly unusual for *L'Humanité*, that Chirac will win. "La météo annonce que dimanche il fera beau, et le dimanche suivant, on jouera aux échecs au jardin du Luxembourg, au milieu des rires des enfants, entre les arbres aux fleurs mauves. Peut-être." The references to playing chess in the Jardin du Luxembourg refer to that cultural practice in Paris in a symbolic sense, alluding to the fact that things will hopefully have returned to normal. The corpus data thus provide a variety of examples of the use of these simple structures which could easily replace the invented examples found in course books and supplementary materials, adding a genuine quality and providing interesting discoveries. For adult learners in particular, they add a 'real' quality (Chambers 2005: 120), and in this case also a cultural dimension, to what can otherwise be perceived as the chore of learning grammar.

In addition to a substantial number of literal references to sport, and a smaller number to music and theatre, the 592 occurrences of JOUER include metaphorical uses, a detailed quantification and analysis of which is beyond the scope of this paper, and also unlikely to represent an interesting task for a teacher or learner other than in the context of a dissertation on metaphors involving playing. A number of possibilities exist for the teacher wishing to use the corpus data to provide a greater variety of examples which learners can use to explore the literal and metaphorical uses of items they encounter in a text. For a study of the use of JOUER in general, 120 occurrences could be randomly selected and presented to the learners unsorted for them to discover the patterns of use of À, DE, Y, and EN, together with literal and metaphorical expressions. This reveals 60 literal uses (including the symbolic reference to playing chess in the Jardin du Luxembourg) and 60 metaphorical ones. The very high proportion of metaphors underlines the need to make learners, particularly at advanced level, aware of their importance (see also Low 1988; Cameron and Low 1999). Alternatively, the teacher can extract the results from one category, as in the examples given above for games and instruments.

The unsorted concordance works particularly well in the case of the 52 occurrences of the pronominal form SE JOUER, which is much more common in its metaphorical than in its literal sense, with only 11 references to sport and 5 to theatre (28 examples from the concordance are included as an appendix). It is not difficult for learners, at postgraduate level in the class in which I have used this concordance, but very probably also at undergraduate level, to identify the patterns which emerge in the nouns and noun phrases used as the subject of SE JOUER. In addition to the 16 literal references to sporting and theatrical performances, and 3 occurrences of SE JOUER DE, meaning "to make light of", the learner quickly discovers that the majority of the occurrences have the sense of "to be at stake" or "to hang in the balance". The corpus-based *Oxford-Hachette French Dictionary* suggests expressions with *avenir, sort, paix*, and *drame*. The concordance includes examples of all these with the exception of *paix*. In addition, *tout* occurs six times as the subject of the verb, and *beaucoup* once, alongside *l'avenir* (3), *le sort* (3), *le destin* (1), *la destinée* (1) *la catastrophe* (1), *la partie industrielle planétaire* (1) *le destin de la planète* (1), *ce combat manichéen* (1) and other expressions suggesting that major issues are at stake. When the scene is more limited than the entire planet, dramatic events are nonetheless depicted, "les traces de sang sur les murs disent le drame qui s'est joué ici", a reference, as consultation of the context reveals, to a terrorist incident in Morocco. The references to sport on the one hand, and to major events on the world stage or the lives of individuals caught up in them on the other, cannot always be clearly separated in this concordance. In two of the six occurrences with *tout* as subject, the reference is to sport:

Les compétiteurs sachant que tout ***se joue*** *sur les 28° d'inclinaison de la pente*
En se faisant étriller par la Russie (1–4). Tout ***se jouera*** *donc lors des dernières rencontres, le mois prochain,*

Thus, extending the definition given even in a corpus-based dictionary, the learner studying these examples discovers that major importance is a subjective category, which can refer to a major world event involving the lives of large numbers of people, or to the results of a sports event. In addition, playing on the usual connotations of major events, one journalist refers to "le petit drame qui s'est joué à l'arrivée". In conclusion, even in a world where corpus-based dictionaries are making a major contribution to the availability of resources based on actual language use, there is still room for individual discoveries by learners based on access to concordance data.

The corpus contains a variety of metaphorical expressions involving JOUER which could form the basis of a research project by a learner or, in the more limited context of a language class, of a study of an individual expression in a text backed up by multiple corpus-based examples. This combination of the study of metaphor in one or more complete texts, together with a corpus-based analysis of patterns across texts, is becoming increasingly common in discourse analysis (see, for example, Koller 2004). Among the most frequently occurring expressions in the *CRJF* are:

- JOUER + *rôle* (42);
- JOUER followed by *le/la/les* to indicate pretence (17)
- JOUER + *carte* (11)

In analysing the occurrences of JOUER + *rôle* it is easy for a learner to begin by finding the literal meanings, which number only 3, 2 theatrical and 1 sporting. A study of the other 39 reveals that, while this metaphor occurs frequently, it is largely used as a conventional metaphor,[4] where the reader is barely aware of the existence of the metaphor.

> *Sur le réseau Internet, qui* ***joue un rôle*** *majeur dans la coordination et dans le combat idéologique*
> *a pour objectif d'aider les élèves et les enseignants à découvrir* ***le rôle*** *joué par les satellites dans l'observation des océans*
> *"L'ONU doit* ***jouer un rôle*** *essentiel" dans "l'après-Saddam", ont prétendu Bush et Blair.*

In an expression such as "Accusé de jouer un rôle actif", for example, playing an active role is synonymous with being active, with no added connotations. For the native speaker or the researcher looking for interesting discoveries, it may seem boring to observe that JOUER + *rôle* is a common collocation, but it is nonetheless of interest to learners, as it is seldom if ever included in language-learning materials. Course materials, particularly at beginners level, but also at intermediate and advanced levels, tend to focus almost exclusively on non-metaphorical language use, in contrast to the views of researchers such as Lakoff & Johnson (1980) that metaphor is pervasive in everyday language. Indeed Cameron & Low (1999: 85), when identifying a research gap in relation to metaphor in second language development by children, add:

> *Also in need of investigation are the use of metaphor in foreign language teaching materials aimed at young learners, and the development of metaphor when an L2 is learnt in formal educational settings.*

Cameron & Low also point out that, despite research on the importance of metaphor in language learning, there is little evidence of this research being applied in the classroom.

4 Low (1988: 127) prefers the term 'conventional' to 'dead'. "Conventional metaphor can for the most part be identified positively as successful, which is to say widely adopted and integrated into the language, rather than negatively as 'dead'."

While references to playing a role have passed into everyday language use in French, more obvious metaphors in journalistic discourse also provide an interesting resource for advanced language learners. In the 11 occurrences of JOUER + *carte* the reader is immediately aware that the journalist is using the metaphorical form to create a specific effect. The methodologies employed by discourse analysts can provide a useful starting point here. Koller (2004: 56) distinguishes between the primary discourse of participants and the secondary discourse of journalists. Here journalists use the reference to playing a card to convey their view of the deliberate and often artificial nature of the activity.

Hue a incarné cette évolution de manière trop superficielle et narcissique en ***jouant la carte*** *médiatique à outrance.*
Le secrétaire général de la CGT devra lui aussi ***jouer la carte*** *de l'apaisement en direction de ses troupes.*
Le PS, lui, réinvestira ses présidents sortants et se dit prêt à ***jouer la carte*** *de l'union avec ses partenaires de gauche.*
arrêter le chef d'un gouvernement... » Son homologue australien, John Howard, ***joue la carte*** *de l'innocence.*
Le journal australien de Melbourne, The Age, n'hésite pas, lui, à ***jouer la carte*** *de l'ironie : « Le dicton dit que l'on n'est jamais assez prudent*
Moscou ***joue une carte*** *ouvertement américaine dans l'espoir de restaurer avec la bienvei*
Bari, Dominique Washington et Londres veulent ***jouer la carte*** *d'une nouvelle résolution au Conseil de sécurité pour arracher l'*
Après avoir ***joué une carte*** *ouvertement unilatéraliste, Washington se tourne vers ses alliés*

Similarly in the case of the 17 occurrences of JOUER followed by *le/la/les* to indicate pretence, the expressions are intended to persuade the reader to view the content from a critical distance.

Les militaires US, qui savent si bien ***jouer les candides****, invoquent la nécessité de « maintenir le moral des troupes »*
Rude tâche que celle de Premier ministre qui doit ***jouer les pères de la nation****, avoir le don d'ubiquité et mener le char de l'Etat*
De leur côté, les adversaires de l'ex-dictateur l'accusaient de ***jouer les « malades imaginaires ».***
Le gouvernement veut aller vite. Le MEDEF ***joue les épouvantails****, histoire de maintenir à distance le maximum de salariés.*

François Copé, qui l'a invité à "donner des conseils positifs" plutôt que de ***"jouer les oiseaux de mauvais augure"****.*
le président de l'Union cycliste internationale (UCI), mais il ne déteste pas ***jouer les shérifs****. Soutenu par le comité exécutif réuni la semaine dernière*

It is interesting to note that these metaphorical expressions either add an ironic note to what would otherwise be a sentence with little or no ironic dimension, as in the first example, or add to an already ironic phrase, as in the second. This brief analysis of some of the occurrences of JOUER thus leads the teacher or learner quickly from straightforward examples of the use of the verb with prepositions, to the varied contexts in which the pronominal form may be used, to examples of conventional metaphors such as JOUER + *rôle*, and finally to the use of other metaphors with JOUER to convey irony in the author's approach. A worksheet prepared by the teacher can thus enable weaker learners in a class to revise basic aspects of language use, while enabling more advanced learners to discover other uses of the verb in naturally occurring discourse.

4. Conclusion

It is important to note that this study does not imply that the traditional grammar class should be resuscitated in lexico-grammatical form, with concordance-based examples replacing the earlier invented examples. The analysis of JOUER is rather intended to illustrate that concordance data can enhance a text-based class in a much richer way than invented examples or recourse to a dictionary or grammar, enabling what Cobb (1997: 303) terms 'multicontextual learning'. In a study of the importance of metaphor in language learning, Low (1988:139) also recommends multi-text as opposed to single-text activities. Low, who is not in any way referring to corpus consultation and analysis, illustrates his recommendation with a simple exercise: making a written complaint to a shop; phoning them to follow up the complaint; reporting the shop to the police; writing to a friend about it, etc. While this is clearly very different from the discovery of multiple occurrences of an expression in different contexts in a concordance, there is nonetheless some similarity in approach. Learners encountering SE JOUER in a text about a major world event can can discover that it can be used literally for sport and artistic performances, that it can refer to an event of less major significance, or be used ironically with an expression such as *le petit drame*. In other words the corpus data can complement the communicative class based on one or a small number of texts, by at times providing access to a richer, multicontextual environment.

References

Aston G. (2002) The learner as corpus designer. In Kettemann, B. & G. Marko (eds) *Teaching and learning by doing corpus analysis*. Amsterdam; New York: Rodopi, 9–25.

Bernardini S. (2000) Systematising serendipity: proposals for concordancing large corpora with language learners. In Burnard L. & T. McEnery (eds) *Rethinking language pedagogy from a corpus perspective*. Frankfurt am Main: Peter Lang, 225–234.

Burnard L. (ed.) (2004) *BNC Baby* [CD-Rom]. Oxford: Research and Technology Service, Oxford University. Available at <http://www.natcorp.ox.ac.uk/babyinfo.html>.

Cameron L. & G. Low (1999) Metaphor. *Language Teaching* 32, 77–96.

Carter R. & M. McCarthy (1994) *Language as discourse: perspectives for language teaching*. London; New York: Longman.

Celce-Murcia M., & E. Olshtain (2000) *Discourse and context in language teaching: a guide for language teachers.* Cambridge: Cambridge University Press.

Chambers A. (2005) Integrating corpus consultation in language studies. *Language Learning & Technology*, 9, 111–125.

Chambers A. & S. Rostand (2005) (eds) *Le Corpus Chambers-Rostand de français journalistique / The Chambers-Rostand corpus of journalistic French.* Oxford, University of Oxford: Oxford Text Archive. <http://www.ota.ahds.ac.uk/ texts/ 2491.html>.

Cheng W., M. Warren & X. Xun-feng (2003) The language learner as language researcher: Putting corpus linguistics on the timetable. *System* 31, 173–186.

Cobb T. (1997) Is there any measurable learning from hands on concordancing? *System* 25, 301–315.

Cook G. (1989) *Discourse*. Oxford: Oxford University Press.

Dodd B. (1997) Exploiting a corpus of written German for advanced language learning. In Wichmann A., S. Fligelstone, T. McEnery & G. Knowles (eds) *Teaching and language corpora*. London/New York: Longman, 131–145.

Flowerdew L. (2002) Corpus-based analyses in EAP. In Flowerdew J. (ed.) *Academic discourse.* London: Pearson Education.

Johns T. (1988) Whence and whither classroom concordancing. In Bongaerts T., P. De Haan, S. Lobbe, & H. Wekker (eds) *Computer applications in language learning.* Dordrecht: Foris, 9–27.

Johns T. (1997) Contexts: The background, development, and trialling of a concordance-based CALL program. In Wichmann A., S. Fligelstone, T. McEnery & G. Knowles (eds) *Teaching and language corpora.* London; New York: Longman, 100–115.

Kennedy C. & T. Miceli (2001) An evaluation of intermediate students' approaches to corpus investigation. *Language Learning and Technology* 5(3), 77–90.

Koller V. (2004) *Metaphor and gender in business media discourse.* Basingstoke, Hampshire; New York: Palgrave MacMillan.

Lakoff G. & M. Johnson (1980) *Metaphors we live by.* Chicago: University of Chicago Press.

Low G. (1988) On teaching metaphor. *Applied Linguistics*, 9(2), 125–147.

McCarthy M. (1991) *Discourse analysis for language teachers.* Cambridge: Cambridge University Press.

Nunan D. (1993) *Introducing discourse analysis.* London: Penguin.

Olshtain E. & M. Celce-Murcia (2001) Discourse analysis and language teaching. In Schiffrin, D., D. Tannen & H. E. Hamilton (eds) *The handbook of discourse analysis.* Malden, Mass.; Oxford: Blackwell, 707–724.

O'Sullivan Í. & A. Chambers (2006) Learners' writing skills in French: Corpus consultation and learner evaluation. Journal of Second Language Writing, 15(1), 49–68.

Roe P. (2000) The ASTCOVEA German Grammar in ConText Project. In Dodd, B. (ed.) *Working with German corpora.* Birmingham: University of Birmingham Press, 199–216.

Scott M. (2003) *Wordsmith Tools* Version 4.0. Oxford: Oxford University Press.

Stevens V. (1991) Concordance-based vocabulary exercises: A viable alternative to gap-fillers. In Johns, T. & P. King (eds) *Classroom concordancing: English Language Research Journal 4.* Centre for English Language Studies: University of Birmingham, 47–63.

The Oxford-Hachette French Dictionary. (2001) Oxford: Oxford University Press.

Widdowson H. G. (2000). On the limitations of linguistics applied. *Applied Linguistics,* 21 (1), 3–25.

Appendix A
Extract from concordance of SE JOUER

« Notre avenir **se jouera** demain matin, au tribunal de commerce de Béthunes. Les dix derniers jo

Personne surtout n'avait suggéré avec autant de force comment en fait beaucoup **se joue** autour des mots et de la langue. La maladie s'était en effet pour la pre

lui auraient permis de prendre la mesure de la catastrophe qui était en train de **se jouer**. Cette démission est donc loin d'exonérer à peu de frais le ministre

Pour l'hôpital public français, une dernière chance est en train de **se jouer**

Pas un mot non plus sur de nouvelles sources de financement. Tout devra donc **se jouer** pour lui autour du trio infernal : baisse des pensions ; augmentation d

M. Chevènement a lancé: L'avenir de l'euro **se jouera** sur sa capacité ou non à aider l'Europe à conjurer la récession

La vie semble reprendre ses droits à Alger... El Lithem **se joue** au TNA le 20 janvier à 15 heures,

qu'au printemps auront lieu des élections régionales capitales au moment où **se joue** le deuxième acte de la décentralisation, une réforme-phare pour Jean-Pie

coupe d'Europe de rugby à XV entre le Castres- Olympique et le Munster (Irlande) **se jouera** à Béziers. Une décision espérée qui fait le bonheur de tous les rug

Nico Mattan nous a donné quelques indications. Le premier test grandeur nature **se joue** sur les routes françaises, direction le sud.

Ce film est également un psychodrame quasi clinique où **se jouerait** l'imaginaire québécois à travers la chasse, la forêt ou la convivial

Je sais par mon métier que tout peut **se jouer** dans une enquête sur un témoignage.

Aujourd'hui on sait un peu plus qu'hier que dans l'aventure polaire **se joue** aussi une part non négligeable du destin de la planète.

ligue des champions, nous sommes plus à l'aise à l'extérieur. La qualification **se jouera** sans doute la semaine prochaine, à Amsterdam, où l'Ajax sera obligé d'

Le silence est de mise dans l'attente du dénouement d'une lutte qui **se joue** département contre département,

Les séquelles en sont toujours présentes Enfin ce qui **se joue** en Serbie ressemble beaucoup à ce qui se passe

d'une grande compagnie européenne résume la partie industrielle planétaire qui **se joue** en coulisses pendant,

et interpréter encore un film et que ce combat manichéen est aussi celui qui **se joue** entre le noir d'une salle de cinéma et la lumière de l'écran. N'y aurait

aux comptes et hauts fonctionnaires, dont Jean-Claude Trichet, pour qui **se joue** la présidence de la Banque centrale européenne (BCE). Les neuf hommes

et atypique Jean-Louis Borloo sont tombés d'accord: « Le sort de la République **se joue** dans les quartiers.

Il s'inspire du halqa, cette forme ancienne où le théâtre **se joue** dans la rue, au marché le plus souvent.
Dans le box des accusés, celui-ci est tendu. Il sait que son sort **se joue** peut-être dans cette audience.
dérouleront le mois prochain à Salt Lake City. Les compétiteurs savent que tout **se joue** sur les 28° d'inclinaison de la pente. Les places en finale sont chères
laisse a laissé passer sa chance en se faisant étriller par la Russie (1–4). Tout **se jouera** donc lors des dernières rencontres, le mois prochain, entre la Russie
est devenue politique, au point que l'on peut supposer que tout, en réalité, va **se jouer**, maintenant, entre l'Elysée et la Maison Blanche.
course terminée, les ennuis ont commencé. L'acteur principal du petit drame qui **s'est joué** à l'arrivée, au télésiège du
avec Clemenceau et de Gaulle, parmi ces grands irréguliers dont la destinée **s'est jouée** sur un moment crucial où leur singularité l'a emporté sur tous les c
les chaises renversées, les traces de sang sur les murs disent le drame qui **s'est joué** ici, où trois kamikaze ont opéré. « J'ai entendu deux explosions. Ens

MAGGIE CHARLES

Corpus evidence for teaching adverbial connectors of Contrast: *however, yet, rather, instead* and *in contrast*

Abstract

This chapter uses two corpora of theses in Politics and Materials Science to examine the frequencies, grammatical patterns and rhetorical functions associated with the contrastive adverbs however, yet, rather, instead and in contrast. The data show that however is by far the most frequent adverb in both corpora (over five times as many occurrences). The grammatical patterns in which these adverbs occur vary considerably. Initial position is the most common for all the adverbs, although however and instead also show appreciable medial occurrence, and negation is highly frequent before instead and rather. Extended concordance lines are examined to shed light on the interpersonal aspect of contrastive connection. The adverbs are shown to perform several distinct rhetorical functions, including justifying the writer's own work, constructing a gap in disciplinary knowledge and making a criticism of the research of others. It is argued that an effective pedagogical strategy for improving connector usage is to raise students' awareness of the rhetorical purposes for which writers establish logical relations. The study of specific rhetorical functions provides a clear rationale for the use of a given adverb, thereby assisting students to develop a deeper understanding of appropriate adverb use.

1. Introduction

Ever since the seminal work by Halliday and Hasan on cohesion (1976), text connection has been seen as an important pedagogical issue. One of the ways in which cohesion is achieved is through adverbial connectors such as *however, therefore* or *in addition*, which establish logical relations within the text. A considerable amount of research has indicated that the use of these adverbs poses problems for writers who are non-native speakers of English (NNS) (e.g. Zamel 1983; Crewe 1990;

Liu & Braine 2005). Furthermore, comparisons of spoken and written genres show that adverbial connectors are highly characteristic of academic writing (Altenberg 1986; Biber 1988). In this area, a particular focus of work has been on studies that compare the written English of native-speakers (NS) and of NNS from various language backgrounds including, for example, French (Granger & Tyson 1996), Swedish (Altenberg & Tapper 1998) and Chinese (Bolton et al. 2002). Although the results of these studies are somewhat conflicting, they all reflect a concern with the frequency of the connectors examined and a concomitant stress on over- or underuse in relation to native-speaker occurrence.

While it is clear that both over- and under-use of adverb connectors can cause problems in the writing of NNS students, this paper proposes a shift in emphasis from frequency to function. Several researchers have drawn attention to the fact that connective signals carry out not only textual, but also interpersonal functions. Thus Sinclair (1993: 7) argues that connectors are 'part of the interactive apparatus of the language', while Hoey (1983: 55) notes that 'all signals, whether in signalling sentences, clauses or phrases, are evaluative'. The interpersonal element is also implicit in Biber et al.'s (1999: 875) definition of linking adverbs as those that 'state the speaker/writer's perception of the relationship between two units of discourse.' Stating the 'perception' of a relationship necessarily implies that the writer incorporates into the structure of the text their own view of the way the content is connected. Adverbial connectors, then, serve to organise the text, but in so doing they also indicate the writer's attitude towards the information given.

This paper explores the somewhat neglected area of interpersonal meaning in adverbial connection, focusing particularly on adverbs that construct a contrast. I argue that if NNS writers are to use such adverbs appropriately, it is important to raise their awareness of the interpersonal functions the adverbs perform. It is necessary for learners to understand not only how the adverbs structure the text, but equally importantly, the rhetorical purposes for which writers establish the logical relations. I return to discuss these questions in detail below. First, however, I provide information on the corpus, method and quantitative findings of the study.

2. Corpora, method and findings

This study draws on two corpora, consisting respectively of eight MPhil theses in politics/international relations, amounting to approximately 190,000 words, and of eight doctoral theses in materials science, totalling about 300,000 words. Further details can be found in Charles (2006a). Using WordSmith Tools software (Scott 1999), word lists were compiled for each corpus and possible adverbial connectors of contrast were identified. Contrastive adverbs were taken to be those that "mark incompatibility between information in different discourse units" (Biber et al. 1999: 878). Concordances were then generated for each of these words and the lines were examined in order to eliminate non-adverbial uses and non-contrastive meanings from the totals. All adverbs (or senses of adverbs) that occurred 10 or more times per 100,000 words in at least one corpus were included. This led to the identification of five contrastive adverbs: *however, yet, instead, rather* and *in contrast*. The data is shown in Fig. 1.

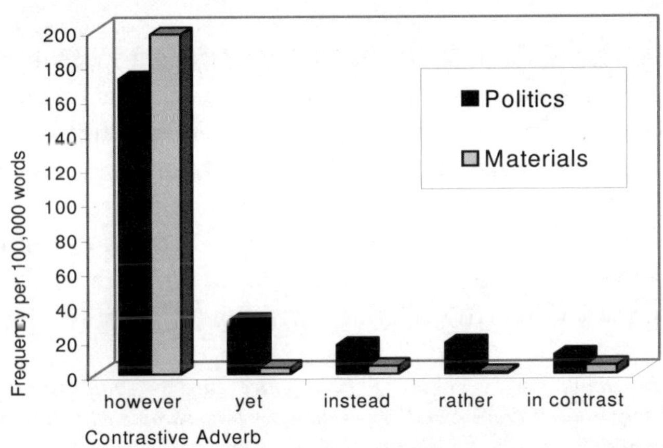

Fig. 1. Frequency of adverbial connectors of contrast per 100,000 words.

In the Politics corpus there are 472 instances of contrastive adverbs, giving a normed figure for the whole group of 248.4 per 100,000 words, while in the Materials Science corpus there are 635 occurrences, that is

211.7 per 100,000 words. Thus the Politics corpus records a slightly higher use of this group of adverbs overall. In conformity with the findings of other writers (Altenberg & Tapper 1998; Biber et al. 1999), both corpora show the predominance of the adverb *however* in constructing a contrastive relation. Frequency figures for this adverb are broadly similar in the two corpora, with Materials slightly higher than Politics at at 197.3 vs 171.6 per 100,000 words. However, there are considerable variations in the use of the other individual adverbs. In Materials there are no frequencies above 5 per 100,000 words, while in Politics *yet* (31.1) is roughly twice as frequent as *rather* (17.9) and *instead* (16.8), and about three times as frequent as *in contrast* (11.1). Thus the Politics Corpus makes greater use of a range of different contrastive adverbs.

3. Contrastive adverbs as interpersonal and textual markers

As noted above, a contrastive adverb establishes a logical relation of incompatibility between two units of discourse, thus acting as a textual marker. However, it is the writer who determines that the material forms two contrasting parts. Another researcher might not notice the phenomenon or might not perceive it to be a significant contrast. Thus the adverb also functions as an interpersonal marker. This is illustrated in the example below, where the writer uses the adverb to draw the reader's attention to the contrast he perceives between an effect in two samples:

(1) *This is a small effect very close to field centre since the radial component of the field here is numerically small.* ***In contrast****, a long sample will have surface area in the highly divergent parts of the field further from the centre.* (Materials)

Moreover, the construction of a contrast presupposes the existence of at least two opposing elements. This leads to a two-part interaction between writer and reader. First, the writer states or implies that the reader has a certain expectation which is based on shared knowledge.

In the second part, marked by the adverb, the writer presents the reality, which conflicts with the reader's expectation:

(2) *The problem of the exclusion of gender-related persecution as a basis for granting refugee status originates in international law.* ***However***, *the problem manifests itself at the national level of refugee determination systems* [...] (Politics)

Because *the problem originates in international law*, the reader's expectation is that it should *manifest itself* at that level. However, by using the contrastive adverb, the writer sets up a distinction between the problem's origin and its manifestation. In this way *however* performs a textual function. At the same time the writer also uses the adverb to signal that the reader's expectation is defeated. Thus the adverb carries out an interpersonal function as well.

In this example it is only when we read *However, the problem manifests itself* in the second sentence that we retrospectively interpret *the problem ... originates* in the first sentence as the first term of a contrast. In fact the two sentences could be understood quite readily without the adverb and its omission would not lead to a noticeable lack of cohesion, since the subject of the two sentences remains the same. However, under these circumstances we would read the text differently. It is the use of *however* that marks the relationship as one of contrast and is crucial to our understanding of these sentences in terms of a mismatch between expectation and reality. In this way, the use of an adverb normally associated with the textual function constructs an interaction between writer and reader, and in so doing carries out an interpersonal function.

4. Patterns of contrastive adverb use

Before moving on to investigate the specific rhetorical purposes achieved through the construction of contrast, I will deal with some of the grammatical patterns that occur. Considerable variation is seen in the patterns associated with individual contrastive adverbs. In this paper I will deal with just two: position in the clause and occurrence with negation.

4.1 Position of contrastive adverbs

It is a characteristic of adverbial connectors that they can occur in several positions in the clause (Biber et al. 1999; Conrad 1999). Three positions are distinguished, all of which occur in this corpus:

- clause initial, which for most examples in this corpus is also sentence initial;
- medial, for example, between subject and verb, after the operator;
- between the main verb and another obligatory element; clause final.

Adverbs which link phrases are not included in the data on clause position.

Fig. 2 presents the summed data of the two sub-corpora for each adverb position, expressed as a percentage of the occurrences of that adverb. In discussing these percentages, it should be borne in mind that the frequency of each adverb varies significantly, as noted above.

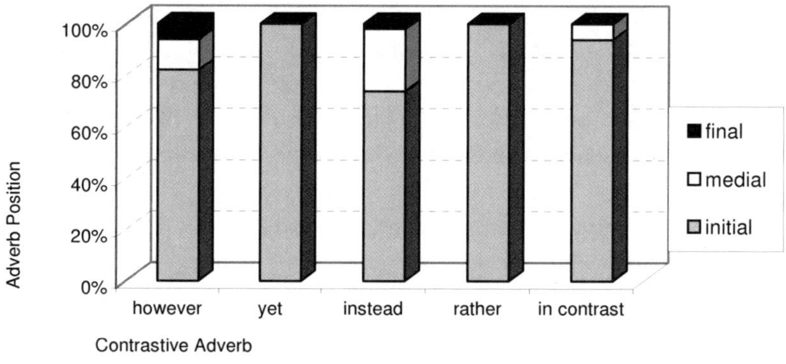

Fig. 2. Position of adverbial connectors of contrast.

From Fig. 2 it can be seen that all five adverbs tend to occur in initial position, although the actual percentages vary from 74% for *instead* through 82% for *however*, 94% for *in contrast,* to 100% for *yet* and *rather*. Medial position is the next most frequent with figures of 6% for *in contrast* and 12% for *however*, while *instead* records the highest frequency at 24%. Final position has the lowest use, with occurrences only of *however* (6%) and *instead* (2%). These findings are consistent with the overall figures for the position of linking adverbs in academic writing reported by Biber et al. (1999). As they point out, linking adverbs establish connections between two units of discourse and so it is reasonable for the connector to be placed at the point where this connection is made: in initial position before the second unit of discourse. Thus initial position may be considered the unmarked choice (Conrad 1999). Even in the medial instances, there is a tendency for the adverb to occur relatively close to the beginning of the clause, for example immediately after the subject. In such cases, the connector again provides an early signal of the logical relation:

(3) *Silicon,* ***however****, cleaves much less readily and produces a (111) plane.* (Materials)

A further explanation for preferring initial position, and one that is more specific to academic writing, may lie in the fact that academic texts are primarily concerned with the construction and development of arguments. Thus writers may choose initial position in order to enable the reader to process complex ideas more efficiently:

(4) *Clearly, in order for hypothesis 2 to be confirmed, we do not need the relationship to work with a continuous variable, but rather an ordinal one.* ***However****, since continuousness requires more than ordinality, if the test works for continuousness then it will also work for ordinality.* (Politics)

However, conflicting evidence on adverb position is presented by Tribble (1989) in an early comparative study of research articles and essays written by NNS students. He found that in the research articles only 25% of instances of *however* were sentence initial, whereas the figure for the essays was 81%. A similar preference for sentence initial *however* was also found in essays written in English by native-speakers of French and Chinese, though not of Dutch (Granger & Tyson 1996). However here, the difference between NNS and NS writers was much less extreme. Although initial position may be preferred by NNS writers because it is easier to handle, this does not provide an adequate explanation for the higher figures found for initial position in either the

Biber data or the present corpora. There are two other possible reasons for these discrepancies. First, Tribble's research article corpus was restricted to a single discipline, history, while Biber et al.'s corpus covers a wide range of disciplines. Much work has convincingly demonstrated the importance of disciplinary differences (see e. g. Hyland 2000); thus it may be that the pattern observed by Tribble is characteristic of history writing, rather than of academic writing more generally.

The difference between the present corpus and that of Tribble in the frequency of initial position may be due not only to the disciplines, but also to the genres examined: theses as opposed to research articles. In contrast to the writers of research articles, thesis writers have a dual role (Shaw 1991; Charles 2006b). They must operate simultaneously as candidates who have to convince examiners that they are competent and knowledgeable and as professionals who are making a new contribution to the field. It is possible, then, that the need to demonstrate the reliability and soundness of the arguments to examiners leads to a greater use of initial position as the clearest way of marking the logical relations. Further, the greater length of thesis texts in comparison with research articles may lead to more extended and complex discussions of the research; this again could lead to a greater use of initial position in order to achieve enhanced clarity of argument. Thus there are a number of factors that may influence the choice of adverb position, and further research on carefully controlled corpora of expert and non-expert academic genres are needed in order to understand this phenomenon better.

In medial position the figure for *instead* stands out as somewhat anomalous at 24%. Examination of the concordance lines shows evidence of a pattern which is characteristic of this adverb: it occurs in non-finite clauses between a participial verb form and a noun phrase. This position allows the participle to be more easily linked back to the main subject and also serves to place contrastive emphasis specifically upon the noun phrase. Thus in the following example the contrast set up is between *this pattern* and *a wide range of behaviour*:

(5) *The other middle powers did not fall into this pattern, displaying* ***instead*** *a wide range of behaviour.* (Politics)

4.2 Negation and contrastive adverbs

Two of these adverbs, *rather* and *instead*, are typically used to link a negative to an affirmative clause. A negative evaluates against the expected positive, creating a contrast between expectation and reality (Labov 1977). Textually, the use of the adverb reinforces this effect by introducing the reality statement with an added marker of contrast, while interpersonally, the adverb marks the writer's rejection of the reader's expected view and the substitution of their own:

(6) *Consequently, the UN Security Council was* <u>*not*</u> *directly involved in the political settlement process.* ***Rather***, *it fulfilled two duties.* (Politics)

By negating the first sentence, the writer both implies that the reader expected *the UN Security Council* to be *directly involved* and at the same time rejects this view. She then uses *rather* to substitute her own assertion, which reflects the reality of the situation. In this way, the writer's view is presented as the correct one and the use of the adverb serves to emphasise this by clearly marking the contrast between the expectation imputed to the reader and the reality given by the writer.

Instead operates in a similar way. In the following example the first main clause again negates the reader's positive expectation, while the adverb signals that the subsequent information reflects reality:

(7) *...the amorphous layers identified in section 4.2 of Chapter II of such material and attributed to those treatments were* <u>*not*</u> *seen in these cases.* ***Instead***, *etched graphene layers and exfoliated surfaces were detected.* (Materials)

However is also found in conjunction with negation, but there is a tendency in both corpora for the negatives to occur in the *however* clause itself:

(8) *Hence, large areas of particles could be scanned, the problems of the physical damage described in Chapter V were minimised, and any morphological changes towards the skeletal forms could be observed.* ***However,*** *during the trial,* <u>*no skeletal features were observed*</u>, *either forming or having formed.* (Materials)

In the first sentence the researcher shows the care taken to minimise problems and as a result the reader expects *skeletal forms* to be seen. Despite this, the use of the adverb *however* in the second sentence signals the defeat of this expectation.

5. Rhetorical functions performed by contrastive adverbs

I now move on to consider the purposes that writers carry out through the adverbial construction and marking of contrast. These rhetorical functions rest primarily on the establishment of some kind of problem in the research and thus can be seen within the context of the Situation-Problem-Result-Evaluation text structure described by Hoey (1983, 2001). The problems may concern the subject matter itself or conflicting views and procedures within the discipline. Problems may be past or ongoing and may be constructed in the writer's own work or that of other researchers. First I deal with rhetorical functions which primarily concern problems with the writer's own work; then I discuss those that relate to the work of other researchers in the discipline.

6. Dealing with problems in the writer's own work

6.1 Justifying the writer's own work

As we have seen, contrastive adverbs operate to set up and then defeat the reader's expectations, thereby revealing the writer's view to be the one that is consistent with reality. One way in which writers use this contrast is to set up a two-part pattern: first, criticisms are anticipated by acknowledging problems in the research, and then a justification is provided for the writer's procedures or methods. This interaction is an example of the 'two-part counterclaim' pattern noted by Barton (1995). The first sentence details the objections to the research procedure that the reader might make, putting them forward as conceded propositions.

In the adverbial clause, the writer then moves to counter the possible criticisms, by asserting the validity of the methods for the present research purposes. This function is carried out through the use of a negated sentence in the first part of the pattern, followed by the adverb *however* to signal the second part:

(9) *The models discussed in chapter two are rather primitive – there is no treatment of electron-hole correlation, no valence band coupling, and vital information about band line-up and surface states cannot be obtained.* ***However***, *in the context of this investigation, the limits of the model are quite adequate...* (Materials)

(10) *There is nothing essential in these categories, and they may not appear tenable to other scholars.* ***However***, *the assumption that socialization affects various registers of state practice differently is useful in analyzing...* (Politics)

A further form of justification is provided in the Materials Corpus, when the writer indicates that a practical limitation affects an experimental procedure. The first part, which is again negated, indicates the action that the reader might expect, but that the writer did not perform; the adverbial clause, signalled this time by *rather* or *instead,* gives the procedure that the writer did carry out:

(11) *Due to limited availability of space in the fume cupboards, it was not possible to proceed with the reactive gas work on semiconductors.* ***Instead,*** *it was decided to attempt a synthesis of small metal particles.* (Materials)

(12) *Since microscopy is a time-consuming and involved process compared to optical characterisation, not all colloids were examined in this way.* ***Rather,*** *the correlation observed between optical spectra and HRTEM micrographs was used to build up information...* (Materials)

By anticipating and dealing with problems and limitations in this way, writers demonstrate their awareness of the likely reactions of other researchers or examiners. They gain credibility by showing that they can assess their own work by the standards of their discipline and they display confidence in their own judgements by backing their own research decisions.

6.2 Demonstrating professional competence

The contrast between the setting up and defeat of the reader's expectations can also serve to show the writer's professional competence. In the following examples, the writer first indicates a possible interpretation of the research data, then problematises and counters it by substituting their own more reliable view. The two-part sequence is an example of Winter's (1994) Hypothetical-Real clause relation. In the first sentence of the examples the hypotheticality is indicated through the use of *seem* (first example), and *appears* (second example). The second sentence, connected by contrastive *however*, brings in the writer's view, which is signalled as reality:

(13) *This* [the awakening of the Herderian nation] *would seem to parallel the Marxist awakening of the proletariat from a class-in-itself to a class-for-itself.* ***However***, *this masks a difference in the epistemological capabilities of the awakening elites.* (Politics)

(14) *... there appears to be little difference between the uncycled and cycled samples in both cases. On closer inspection,* ***however***, *small differences are observed.* (Materials)

These examples show particularly clearly the stance of professional competence constructed by the writer: others might not notice the differences between Herder's and Marx's views or between *the uncycled and cycled samples*, but these writers do. By structuring the text in this way, writers succeed in showing themselves as both knowledgeable and astute, in that they see the possibility of drawing an erroneous conclusion, but avoid the pitfall themselves.

7. Dealing with problems in the work of others

When referring to the work of other researchers, the problem signalled by the contrastive adverb may exist among other researchers in the field or between the writer and other researchers. It may have been solved already, or it may still remain an open question.

7.1 Criticising the work of other researchers

One of the most important uses of contrastive adverbs, particularly *however, yet* and *rather*, is to introduce a direct criticism of the work of others:

(15) *Waltz presents competition and socialization as two alternative processes through which the international system indirectly causes unit behaviour;* ***however****, socialization and competition might not be quite as distinct as Waltz sometimes claims.* (Politics)

(16) *Ling and Anderson (1992) comment that non-random particle distributions are to be expected in view of the enhanced reduction in the interfacial energy of the system.* ***However*** *since non-random particle distributions lead to smaller pinned grain sizes it can be argued that they have precisely the opposite effect.* (Materials)

The writers begin by stating a piece of shared disciplinary knowledge concerning the work of other researchers. Then, with the use of the adverb, the writers signal the unexpected information that they do not accept the view of these researchers. They show the others' view to be problematic in that it conflicts with reality as the thesis writers see it and they turn from providing the general view, to making their own, new and contrasting point. A similar effect is achieved by the use of the adverb *rather*, following a negated clause. Here the writer puts forward their own critical view by appearing to correct a misconception:

(17) *... the problem is not to justify revolutionary dictatorship as Talmon's analysis implies.* ***Rather*** *it is to achieve an identity of the subjective will of the individual and objective standards...* (Politics)

7.2 Mitigating a criticism

Under some circumstances a direct criticism may appear too harsh, or even risky for a writer who is a candidate member of the field. One way of mitigating the effect of the criticism is for the writer to incorporate a positive evaluation of others' work or a concession to others' views, before putting forward their own, critical judgement. Again, this function is performed using the adverbs *however* and *yet*:

(18) *He* [Spijkerboer] *makes the valid point that such an approach presents women as active objectors rather than passive victims.* ***However,*** *there are several problems with this analysis.* (Politics)

(19) *For example, Françoise Hampson began her article, Law and War, with an interesting question:* [quotation omitted][22]. ***Yet,*** *she furnished no answer, except an analysis of the end result.* (Politics)

In the example below, however, the concession is more apparent than real:

(20) *... J L Talmon thinks that the similarities between Hegel and Mazzini are 'too obvious to be emphasised'.*[5] *Talmon is right that the similarities are not very hard to spot.* ***However,*** *the relationship between Hegel and Mazzini should not be dismissed as obvious because it is anything but that.* (Politics)

This form of the two-part pattern, then, serves to make a criticism less face-threatening. By first acknowledging the positive aspects of others' work, and only then bringing forward the negative points, writers show themselves to be measured and reasonable in evaluating the work of others and thus make it more likely that their criticisms will be accepted.

7.3 Constructing a gap

One type of problem constructed through the use of *however* indicates that there is a gap in the field (Swales 1990). Here the writer establishes that certain research has not been done, or that certain information is not known and thereby creates a research space which they can fill with their own work. In this case, the unfilled gap amounts to a problem for the discipline until it is resolved by the writer:

(21) *Evidence from isotope-fractionation experiments shows that primary nucleation occurs from the coalescence of individual carbon atoms[18], and the high temperatures in the plasma near the electrodes would certainly support this[19].* ***However***, *the question that remains to be answered is how the carbon atoms form the 'bucky-ball' from this highly disordered state.* (Materials)

There is no criticism of earlier work in this example, as evidenced by the use of *shows* and *certainly* in the first sentence. Rather, there is a recognition that research is not yet complete and therefore the writer's work can make a contribution. In empirical research such as that included in the Materials corpus, the prevailing form of knowledge-building is cumulative, with one person's work building on that of another (Becher & Trowler 2000) and lack of knowledge is often presented as a problem (Hunston 1993). In this way, potential conflict between the writer and other researchers is downplayed, since drawing attention to a lack of knowledge is not as threatening as making a direct criticism.

7.4 Discussing the development of the field

As part of a review of the literature, writers may discuss the development of the field, which they may present as a sequence of problems identified by other members of the discipline. In such cases, the adverb *instead* signals that an earlier inadequate research procedure or theory has been replaced by one that is more satisfactory:

(22) *Secondary-ion mass spectrometry (SIMS), spreading resistance (SRP) and capacitance-voltage (CV) profiling are commonly used to analyse the chemical and electrically activated dopant profiles of semiconductors, but are essentially one-dimensional techniques. In response to this limitation, interest has turned* ***instead*** *to microscopy techniques which have potential for high resolution profiling in two-dimensions (Vandervorst and Clarysse, 1992).* (Materials)

(23) *Only in the early-1980s did some international relations scholars begin to criticise realist and neorealist ideas as too narrow. They realised that not all interactions between states could be explained solely on the basis of power and calculations of self-interest.* ***Instead,*** *they proposed that rules and procedures could acquire importance, thus enhancing the likelihood of co-operation and interdependence in international relations.* (Politics)

In both these examples the writer states or implies their criticism of the earlier work. In the first example the noun *limitation* is used with reference to the *techniques*, while the use of the verb *realise* in the second sentence of the second example indicates that the writer accepts other scholars' evaluation of the work as *too narrow*. In this way, the writers ally themselves with the more up-to-date and satisfactory approach that has replaced the earlier work.

However the problem posed by conflicting views may also remain unresolved, as signalled by the adverb *yet*:

(24) *The carbon black is often imagined to be a nucleation centre for the spherulitic growth of the crystalline regions of the polymer*[229]*, and* ***yet*** *it is also predicted to be excluded from these regions*[227]. (Materials)

This examination of the functions of contrastive adverbs shows the wealth of rhetorical purposes that are fulfilled and highlights the many and complex ways in which individual connectors overlap with and are distinct from each other in terms of use. As the most frequent connector, *however* has the widest range of functions, including justifying aspects of the writer's research, constructing a gap in knowledge and criticising the work of others. *Yet* shares some of these functions, but is particularly associated with making criticisms of others' research. Both *rather* and *instead* provide a practical solution to a problem in the writer's own work, but vary in their uses to comment on others' work, with *rather* allowing the construction of a stronger criticism. Finally, *in contrast* is rarely used to perform rhetorical functions such as these and its interpersonal aspect seems much less noticeable.

8. Conclusions and pedagogical implications

This paper has examined five adverbs which are frequently used to carry out contrastive connections: *however, yet, rather, instead* and *in contrast*. It has revealed their grammatical patterning with regard to clause position and negation and some of the rhetorical functions they are used to perform. The data show that the grammatical patterns in which these adverbs occur vary considerably. Initial position is the most common for all the adverbs, although *however* and *instead* also show appreciable medial occurrence, while negation is particularly frequent before *instead* and *rather*. Perhaps more importantly, this study has highlighted the interpersonal aspect of contrastive connection. It has shown that, although all these adverbs belong to the same semantic area of contrast, there are several distinct purposes for which the contrasts are constructed. Among the most essential of these are justifying the writer's own work, constructing a gap in disciplinary knowledge and making a criticism of the research of others. Moreover the data show that each adverb tends to be associated with certain specific functions.

Clearly, this study has limitations in terms of the size of the corpora and the genre examined. It is not claimed that these are the only functions performed by contrastive adverbs, nor that the functions identified are carried out by these adverbs alone. Further research using larger corpora and with data on a number of disciplines and genres would be necessary in order to establish a more comprehensive picture of the interpersonal aspects of adverbial connection.

Despite these limitations, however, the findings suggest a number of recommendations for pedagogy. First, the provision of semantically grouped lists of connectors is of limited use (see also Crewe 1990; Granger & Tyson 1996; Bolton et al. 2002). The data on both grammatical patterning and rhetorical functions offers evidence to support the view that such lists are likely to be misleading in that they encourage learners to see the adverbs as interchangeable. In this regard I concur with Zamel (1983) that learners need to study the patterns of specific adverbs individually. It is also important that students are provided with sufficient context to enable them to perceive the logical relationship between the contrasted elements, a point also noted by several earlier researchers (Zamel 1983; Crewe 1990; Granger & Tyson 1996). Indeed it is often necessary to provide a whole paragraph in order for the function and purpose of the adverb to be fully understood.

However the emphasis here on the interpersonal functions of contrastive adverbs offers new insight into the teaching of adverbial connection. I would argue that tasks such as sentence combining, gap-filling and reformulation advocated in the literature (Zamel 1983; Crewe 1990; Tseng & Liou 2006) tend to place too much emphasis on the contrast and not on enough on what exactly is being contrasted and why. Thus, rather than concentrating on adverbial connection itself, I suggest a focus on teaching the rhetorical functions performed by the adverbs. In this approach, the whole two-part contrast is learnt as one single function and the connector can more easily be seen as an integral part of this larger textual pattern. Using awareness-raising tasks based on expanded concordance lines, students can be taught, for example, how to construct a gap in knowledge, a function which will give rise to the use of *however*. In so doing, they learn that a given connector operates as a signal of a specific function and the use of this connector is seen to be an effective means of achieving an important rhetorical purpose. This provides a rationale for the use of the adverb and helps students begin to develop both a sense of when an adverbial signal is required and a knowledge of which adverb is appropriate.

As noted at the beginning of this paper, adverbial text connection has long been considered an issue of pedagogical importance. In opening up the area of interpersonal functions to detailed investigation and description, this paper has added a further dimension to the study of adverbial connection which, it is hoped, can be effective in addressing students' concern with achieving grammatical and rhetorical competence.

References

Altenberg B. (1986) Contrastive linking in spoken and written English. In Tottie G. & I. Backlund (eds) *English in speech and writing*. Stockholm: Almquist & Wiksell, 13–34.

Altenberg B. & M. Tapper (1998) The use of adverbial connectors in advanced Swedish learners' written English. In Granger S. (ed.) *Learner English on computer.* London: Addison Wesley Longman, 80–93.

Barton E. L. (1995) Contrastive and non-contrastive connectives. *Written communication* 12, 219–239.

Becher T. & P. Trowler (2001) *Academic tribes and territories* (2nd ed). Buckingham: Society for Research into Higher Education and Open University Press.

Biber D. (1988) *Variation across speech and writing.* Cambridge: Cambridge University Press.

Biber D., S. Johansson, G. Leech, S. Conrad & E. Finegan (1999) *Longman grammar of spoken and written English.* Harlow: Pearson Education.

Bolton K., G. Nelson & J. Hung (2002) A corpus-based study of connectors in student writing. Research from the International Corpus of English in Hong Kong (ICE-HK). *International Journal of Corpus Linguistics* 7, 165–182.

Charles M. (2006a) The construction of stance in reporting clauses: a cross-disciplinary study of theses. *Applied Linguistics* 27, 492–518.

Charles M. (2006b) Revealing and obscuring the writer's identity: evidence from a corpus of theses. In Kiely R., P. Rea-Dickins & G. Clibbon (eds) *Language, Culture and Identity in Applied Linguistics.* London: BAAL and Equinox, 147–161.

Conrad S.M. (1999) The importance of corpus-based research for language teachers. *System* 27, 1–18.

Crewe W.J. (1990) The illogic of logical connectives. *ELT Journal* 44, 316–325.

Granger S. & S. Tyson (1996) Connector usage in the English essay writing of native and non-native EFL speakers of English. *World Englishes* 15, 17–27.

Halliday M.A.K. & R. Hasan (1976) *Cohesion in English.* London: Longman.

Hoey M. (1983) *On the surface of discourse.* London: George Allen & Unwin.

Hoey M. (2001) *Textual interaction.* London: Routledge.

Hunston S. (1993) Professional conflict: disagreement in academic discourse. In Baker M., G. Francis & E. Tognini-Bognelli (eds) *Text and technology: In honour of John Sinclair.* Amsterdam: Benjamins, 115–134.

Hyland K. (2000) *Disciplinary discourses: social interactions in academic writing.* Harlow: Longman.

Labov W. (1977) *Language in the inner city.* Oxford: Blackwell.

Liu M. & G. Braine (2005) Cohesive features in argumentative writing produced by Chinese undergraduates. *System* 33, 623–636.

Scott M. (1999). *WordSmith Tools 3.0.* Oxford: Oxford University Press.

Shaw P. (1991) Science research students' composing processes. *English for Specific Purposes* 10, 189–206.

Sinclair J.M. (1993) Written discourse structure. In Sinclair J.M., M. Hoey & G. Fox (eds) *Techniques of description: spoken and written discourse.* London: Routledge, 6–31.

Swales J.M. (1990) *Genre analysis.* Cambridge: Cambridge University Press.

Tribble C. (1989) The use of text structuring vocabulary in native and non-native speaker writing. *MUESLI News* June 1989, 17–20.

Tseng Y.-C. & H.-C. Liou (2006) The effects of online conjunction materials on college EFL students' writing. *System* 34, 270–283.

Winter E. (1994) Clause relations as information structure. In Coulthard M. (ed.) *Advances in written text analysis.* London: Routledge, 46–68.

Zamel V. (1983) Teaching those missing links in writing. *ELT Journal* 37, 22–29.

JOSTA VAN RIJ-HEYLIGERS

Breaking the chains of rhetorics in academia: Corpus-based research as tool for transformation in discourse?

Abstract

Today English functions as the lingua franca of communication in business and technology. Globalisation has further strengthened its position in higher education, with increasing numbers of students who have English as an additional language (EAL) flocking to universities in English-speaking countries. Also, regionalisation, such as the Bologna process, has led many European universities to provide instruction in English at the postgraduate level to enable the portability of degrees across borders. Similarly, universities in the Asia-Pacific region are offering more and more courses in English in order to be internationally competitive.

Clearly, English has acquired a position of 'worldliness' that gives the language power and its speakers status (cultural capital). Nowadays, however, speakers of English represent a diversity of cultures. In this context, the teaching of English for academic purposes (EAP) based on notions of Standard English fails to acknowledge that students' writing occurs in a space of "socio-culturally situated production and consumption of texts" (Doecke, Kostogriz & Charles 2004: 32). This space is imbued with tension between the prescribed genre of the dominant discourse community and students' 'own' voices. Corpus linguistics generally represents the standardisation of language as it aims to describe language as is spoken and written by native speakers. However, when rooted in critical discourse analysis, corpus-based methods can also bring to light the socio-political discourse of specific corpora through, for example, investigations of semantic prosody and transitivity. Moreover, when corpus linguistics incorporates a comparative methodology, it raises awareness of the "rich heteroglossic potentiality" (Doecke et al. 2004: 34) evident in the corpora of different disciplines, speakers of English, and time periods. Hence these approaches allow EAP practitioners and their students to explore academic discourse as variable and open to negotiation. This paper argues that corpus linguistics can make a significant contribution to the field of EAP when it injects a critical genre dimension into its analysis of academic texts. It presents the author's research in progress, incorporating aspects of corpus linguistics and genre/critical discourse analysis into the study of academic writing and teaching of EAP to research students from diverse backgrounds and disciplines.

> If English is imposing the world on our students, we as TESOL professionals can enable them, through English, to impose their voices on the world.
>
> (Warschauer 2000: 530)

1. Introduction

English is now an established lingua franca for business, education, and research and technology. Of 925,000 scientific articles published in major journals in 1997, for example, 95% were published in English (Bollag 2000). However, the spread of English to all corners of the world does not necessarily mean that first language speakers will set the standard of English in the future. The number of first speakers of English will shrink from 8% in 1950 to to 5% in 2050 (Wallraff 2000), the number of Chinese, Spanish, Hindi and Arabic speakers will increase (Graddol 1997), and second language speakers of English will soon outnumber first language speakers of English. Already there are more speakers of English as an additional language (EAL) than native English speakers (Crystal 1997), and half of the scientific articles mentioned above originated from authors in countries outside the English-speaking core. As these newcomers are not just passively learning but actively shaping the language, it follows that 'standard' English may soon be a concept of the past.

Notions of standard English still prevail, however, and they have an impact on how English is taught and learned. Yet as the language gains a position of 'world' power (e.g. Pennycook 1994), perceptions towards norms of English are changing. Gupta, for instance, observes that with the fortification of Europe as a single political identity, English with standard Anglo-American as model increasingly functions as a "link language between Europeans" and "a vehicle for cultural self-expression" (1999: 60). In former British colonies like India, Malaysia, Singapore and Hong Kong, however, the English language has developed into local varieties among bi- or multilingual communities. In these environments speakers use English as an additional language "to impact and change the world [...] to express their identity and make their voice heard" (Warschauer 2000: 530). Since English is now appropriated by an increasing majority of ESL speakers, the language is no longer the sole possession of its 'ancestral' speakers; rather it has become a 'world possession'. Accordingly, countries that take a restricted model of English as norm "will have to adapt to a more open perspective which recognises the diversity of English in the world" (Gupta 1999: 60). This open view pertains not only to European countries, but also to 'inner circle' speakers of English, and in the case of English for academic purposes (EAP), their academic communities.

As the EAL student population in many 'inner circle' universities now represents a variety of backgrounds, it has led to reassessments of what is taught (content), how it is taught (pedagogy) and why it is taught (purpose). In the case of academic writing, Ann Johns (2005) observes that 'traditional' approaches to language learning like Structuralist, focusing on discourse patterns and grammar; Expressivist, emphasising students' creativity and individual voice; and Process, formalizing a top down approach to the writing process, are no longer sufficient on their own. They tend to overlook the social context in which text production, authorship and targeted audience are situated, and ignore the fact that in modern societies "knowledges are increasingly constituted in multisemiotic ways" and that the information society of today is diverse and reflexive, "constantly reshaping our social practices on the basis of knowledge about those practices" (Fairclough n.d.: 3). This diversity and reflexivity produce conflict and tension between monoglossic, centripetal discourses, which "tend to centralise or standardise language", and heteroglossic, centrifugal discourses that tend to "decentralise and diversify language" (Doecke et al. 2004: 33).

Clearly, the 'worldliness' of English requires negotiation and critical reflection of its use across settings, and exposing EAL students to a variety of 'Englishes' so they can observe the different styles of written English and make the language their own (Booij 2001). To the EAP practitioner, corpora-based research offers a wealth of possibilities. On the one hand, quantitative methods of corpus linguistics, such as measures of word frequency, concordance and collocation, can draw attention to aspects of language that have not been visible before (Hunston 2002). On the other hand, critical discourse analysis, which considers the use and production of language beyond the level of syntax and lexicon, can raise awareness of the socio-political discourse context of a specific corpus. For example, investigations of semantic prosody, the tendency of certain words to co-occur with either negative or positive expressions, may unveil the hidden messages of a corpus and hence indicate its implicit norms, beliefs and assumptions. Similarly, studies of the transitive system can reveal ideological opinions and positions (e.g. centrality of human agency, responsibility or lack of control; see Huston, ibid). Finally, the use of comparative linguistics can highlight variations and changes in academic discourse across disciplines, speakers of English, both native and non-native, and time (in the case of diachronic corpora).

All these possibilities present the EAP practitioner with tools to raise awareness of the fact that academic discourse is not neutral nor is it fixed. In other words, corpora-based research may support students in developing their own voice. This paper advances the need of multiliteracy in EAP and the contribution corpus-based research can make to this field. The author further discusses and explores the relevance of corpus linguistics and genre/critical discourse analysis to her own discipline (education) and work (teaching EAP) through her research in these areas.

2. EAP Pedagogy for Multiliteracy

With the growing 'wordliness' of English, theories of discourse (a process orientation) rather than language (a product orientation) have emerged that see texts as socially constructed, 'ideologically saturated' (Bakhtin 1981) and as 'living documents' with which authors, audience and discourse communities interact (Johns 2005). From this viewpoint, texts are analysed through the study of discourse moves, stance and voice. Moves refer to the rhetorical patterns available to the writer to serve his or her purpose within a particular genre (e.g. the "Create A Research Space" (CARS) model proposed by Swales & Feak 1994). Teaching students these moves helps them to "identify the relationships between a text's structure, the [discourse] community, and the writer's purposes", hence making their interrelations more apparent (Johns 2005: 105). The writer's stance takes place within socially constructed frameworks derived from a community of experts and its discourse(s). Positions are expressed through, for example, the author's choice of words, opinions, degree of certainty (hedging) and politeness, and meta-textual features that organize the text. Voice is related to stance but is not seen as belonging to an individual: rather it is co-owned, involving a process of negotiation and conflict between what one wants to say and a disciplinary voice that either allows or restricts it (Johns 2005). Compared to an expert writer, the student novice has relatively less freedom in the discourse community. Yet, as new members they may still "challenge existing genres or bring with them expertise of other genres, helping to fuse, appropriate or transform existing ones" (Trayner 2004: 3).

The diversity of today's voices positions writers in their community historically and culturally. Within one discipline positivist, progressive, postmodern, postcolonial, feminist, critical or a combination of these voices can be observed. Although this multitude of voices is often more a characteristic of the soft disciplines than the hard sciences (Paltridge, n.d.), in order to become participating members every novice writer needs to know and consider what voices his or her discourse community enlists. Understanding that different discourses represent different perspectives and interests within a disciplinary domain helps students "to question and look beyond [existing discourses] so [as to] advance knowledge" (Fairclough n.d.: 3). Similarly to Johns, Doecke et al. (2004: 34) refer to this process as authorial discourse dialogised in heteroglossic utterances, where the act of writing no longer represents an individual voice, but rather permits a multiplicity of social voices.

In this heteroglossic environment, EAP instructors have to review positions that present a discipline as a specific academic culture, sets of norms, bodies of knowledge and modes of inquiry (Becher 1989). Academic disciplines or *territories* can no longer be seen as monolithic and unitary; rather they are made up of "individuals with diverse experiences, expertise, commitments and influence" (Hyland 2000: 9). This diversity is reinforced by the changing nature of disciplines towards interdisciplinarity, and by globalisation that brings experts and novices from different cultural and linguistic communities in closer contact with each other. As Fairclough (n.d.: 3) observes, teaching literacy as a set of skills to be taught so as to reproduce unitary knowledge is no longer tenable as knowledges "are in the business of evaluating and changing discourses". Instead, as Brian Paltridge (n.d.) argues, teaching and learning EAP in today's university environment requires an academic literac*ies* approach in the plural sense. The New London Group proposes the concept of multiliteracies as an alternative to literacy pedagogies that confine themselves to "formalized, monolingual, monocultural, and rule-governed forms of language" (New London Group 1996: 60). A central concern of this group is that cultural and linguistic diversity should pose no barrier to educational success. They similarly stress that our present *lifeworlds* – consisting of private, public and work spaces – have "become more divergent and their boundaries more blurred" (New London Group 1996: 68), and state that students should learn a multiplicity of discourses by way of a pedagogy that is anchored in *situated practice*, *overt instruction*, *critical framing* and *transformed practice*.

As literacy practices are embedded in social practices and beliefs and articulated in discourses and genres, *situated practice* highlights the importance of learners being engaged in meaningful contexts that allow for peer cooperation, negotiation of complex language items and evaluation of information learned (Warschauer 2000), leading to increased mastery. *Overt instruction*, which traditionally is associated with the banking or drilling of knowledge, here refers to the Vygotskian notion of scaffolding that helps to minimise the complexity of learning, and to sequence and accentuate the important aspects of valued discourse(s) in a community. However, the goal is "conscious awareness and control over what is being learned" (New London Group 1996: 83). Critical framing aids this process as it entails going beyond overt instruction of the valued but more narrowly defined discourse, by "critically interpret[ing] information and communication in a given social context" (Warschauer 2000: 528). The role of the teacher is to help learners to stand back and "make strange again what they have learned and mastered" (New London Group 1996: 84). By this distancing and critiquing, learners can (re)create a discourse that serves their purpose and transfer it to new social and cultural contexts. The transformed practice that results entails that the learner can juxtapose and integrate the different discourses, identities or interests (e. g. self and other or audience) that may historically have been at conflict, and in the process transform meaning of the discourse to make it his or her own (New London Group 1996).

As Luke & Freebody put forward, effective literacy incorporates a repertoire of practices that permits learners to break the code of discursive practices and conventions by recognising their basic features; participate in understanding and constructing meaningful texts; use texts purposefully through negotiation; and critically analyse and transform texts by "acting on knowledge that texts are not ideologically natural or neutral" (Luke & Freebody 1999: 5). For this to occur, the learner needs to develop coding, semantic, pragmatic and critical competence.

3. Corpus linguistics: an 'instrument' for multiliteracies in EAP?

With teaching and learning EAP taking place in diverse university communities, how can the use of corpora support students' need for multiliteracies and competencies? There has been growing interest in introducing corpus-linguistic methods in the EAP classroom, perhaps as they "support exploratory learning and are well-suited to encourage autonomous learning and teaching" (Braun 2005: 47). In addition, they are not incompatible with a pedagogy of academic literacies as proposed by Paltridge and the New London Group discussed above. Corpus-based studies provide rich, up-to-date and diversified information about actual patterns of language use (Braun 2005), and the data can be derived from different genres and settings. However, the field needs improvement. Existing corpora tend to represent the discourse of first language users (one of the exceptions is the International Corpus of Learner English: Granger et al. 2002). But as Graddol (1997) and Crystal (1997) indicate, many EAL students will use English mostly with non-native English speakers. Hence, students may not be overly concerned or motivated to comply with first language speakers' norms (as seen in not applying the 's'-rule to simple present verb forms in third person singular among many European and Asian speakers of English). In fact, as Hunston (2002) has pointed out, adherence to these norms may well represent a form of linguistic imperialism. Nevertheless, when it comes to writing for EAP, access to powerhouses that publish research articles may be hindered when the student writer does not take on the discourse conventions of his or her research community. In this case, the problem faced by the EAP teacher and learner is that few specialised corpora exist or are publicly available (and as higher education is increasingly linked to market forces, free information may become even more difficult to obtain).

Another limitation is that corpora were originally intended for research in linguistics, so their design and principles are not always of much use to the EAP instructor and learner. Braun (2005), for example, highlights corpus limitations pertaining to size, content and type of annotation. Mega-sized corpora are suitable data for the linguist but not necessarily for the language teacher/learner. Their large size makes data difficult to manipulate as too many results can lead to messiness, ambiguity and even misinformation. As Krieger (2003: 3) observes, use of corpora in the classroom is challenging as corpus results "[appear] to be so chaotic", making it impracticable to let students perform their own analyses; hence, it lacks the didactic element of *overt instructions* as proposed by the New London Group (1996). Moreover, findings of these general corpora may not be relevant to learning EAP. Data filtering is a possibility to make the results meaningful, but this filtering also takes away student control of what is being learned.

In addition, corpus content is generally transformed into statistical data and 'vertical readings' (lists of word frequencies and concordances). This allows researchers to cope with the large volume of data generated but at the same time decontextualises the obtained information from the wider co-text (Braun 2005). As Widdowson (2003) has pointed out, corpora represent bodies of texts isolated from their communicative setting; and as such they provide us with a "description [or traces] of text, not discourse" (Widdowson 2000: 9). And as the teaching and learning of EAP is concerned with language use rooted in real discursive practices, abstraction of text removes the authenticity of these practices. Moreover, many of the annotation schemes in use are often too detailed for language learning needs and application. Nevertheless, messiness is an aspect of authentic language and some types of annotation are helpful in raising students' awareness of language use (Braun 2005).

Despite these limitations, the use of corpora can be of benefit to the language teacher and learner. Indirectly, it has already born fruit in the dictionaries and teaching materials corpus-based research has generated. But since corpus linguistics has its shortcomings as a didactic and transformative tool, the challenge for the EAP instructor is how to make direct, relevant use of corpus data in the classroom and align it with a pedagogy of academic literacies so as to avoid a prescribed, monolingual/cultural, and rule-governed approach to learning EAP that may stifle students' voice as negotiation with and change in their discourse community.

4. Corpus linguistics as data driven learning

The recent interest of using corpora in the EAP context has focussed on data-driven learning (DDL). DDL is student-centred and based on discovery learning; students (as language detectives) ask their own questions as related to the task at hand, assess the (multiple) facts of language use from authentic texts, notice the patterns and make generalisations (Hunston 2002; Krieger 2003). Accordingly, a DDL approach to corpus linguistics is inductive and consciousness-raising. What students become aware of influences, and at times determines, the outcome of their learning. It also enables them to discover aspects of language use the teacher has failed to notice. As such, the DDL method gives students control over what is being learned. Corpus data, such as concordances, offer students no explanation (Gavioli 2001). Rather, they encourage students to investigate the various meanings of common words, useful phrases and collocations, the structure and nature of different discourses, and features more typical of certain text(s) than others (Willis 1998). Through these explorations students can build up the discourse knowledge required for participation in their academic community. Negotiation is possible as teachers (partly) relinquish their control and role as experts, help learners ask questions about the texts and the contexts in which they occur, and hence facilitate rather than bank knowledge(s). On the other hand, encouraging the learner as researcher to be immersed in rich and complex data can lead to students consuming too much time following wrong leads, or even diminish their control and awareness of what is worth knowing and doing. Consciousness-raising cannot automatically be assumed.

A related topic is that the use of corpus data in this inductive manner provides students with samples, not examples, for making generalisations (Gavioli 2001). Samples may not be accurate as they depend on the appropriacy of the corpus and the learner's ability to analyse and generalise them. As Gavioli (2001: 113) observes, *examples […] suggest certain generalizations quite explicitly and unambiguously; samples […] merely provide occurrences of varying tractability from which possible generalizations have to be worked out*. Examples in textbooks or from teachers represent particular instances of language in use. Those that do not neatly fit the general pattern are often excluded so as not to make information too messy for, in particular, the beginning learner. Samples can become sources of examples, but for this transformation to take place, samples first need to be analysed and selected. As students may well fail to understand and misuse samples (when treated as examples), they need training to arrive at generalisations from corpus data (Gavioli 2001). Gavioli thus proposes that students should be gradually introduced to corpus analysis, starting with a small corpus compiled from short texts of similar genres that are of interest to the class (requirements consistent with the New London Group's pedagogy of *situated practice* and *overt instructions*). The data of such a corpus become manageable whilst still containing sufficient instances of repeated language use. Students can start comparing concordance lines, moving from observing one recurrent feature to identifying and adding others. In the process, they become increasingly aware of "formal and functional similarities and differences" (Gavioli 2001: 117), so as to group like patterns and make generalisations, becoming "rapidly [...] more sophisticated in their observations" (Gavioli 2001: 120). However, it is not guaranteed that students will progress from this focussed process to critically interpreting data-driven information and changing practices.

5. Corpus linguistics and critical discourse analysis for EAP

To an EAP instructor the relevance of corpus data to students is of key importance. As Hunston (2002: 198) has observed, 'what to teach' is often more important than 'how to teach'. Hence, situated practice is of the foremost concern. What do students need to know about writing an essay, report or thesis in their discipline(s)? What are the text features they need to know to become members of their discourse communities? These questions are starting points for acquiring knowledge about language. But within a pedagogy of multiliteracies, student writers also need to know about the social and cultural contexts surrounding (their) texts. As stated earlier, the work of genre analysts (e.g. Swales 1990; Swales & Feak 1994) helps to examine the discourse moves in a certain genre. Genre-based studies also provide the background to make students aware that genres change over time (e.g. Bazerman's work, see Swales 1990), are situated in practice and their participation in that practice; include both form and content specific to purpose, context and point of time; represent duality of structure as members simultaneously constitute and reproduce social structures when drawing on genre rules; and represent "a discourse community's norms, epistemology, ideology, and social ontology" (Breure 2001: 2).

Whilst genre represents these norms and values, a critical discourse approach (CDA) to analysing texts helps learners explore the ways expert systems shape discourse and position the multiplicity of voices. As Janks (2005: 97) has pointed out, "all texts are positioned and positioning". CDA focuses on raising awareness that "language and discourse are not transparent or neutral means for describing or analysing the social and biological world"; monoglossic forces operate which "effectively construct, regulate and control knowledge [and] … practices as scholarship and research" (Luke n. d.: 2). As they work along side heteroglossic forces, these systems have the potential to open up new discourses. Nonetheless, "they remain affiliated … with particular conventionalised discourses … [and] thus both constrain and enable meanings and social relations between speakers and listeners, writers and readers" (Luke n. d.: 6). Each genre, albeit fuzzy and often subjective, dynamic, flexible and contested (Swales 1990), has a macro structure, a series of patterns, recognizable segments, movements and chunks that "shape and reshape what will count as knowledge … and textual practices" (Luke n. d.: 7). Hence, a moves analysis informed by CDA (infusing a contextual power element into the analysis) becomes a promising platform for meaningful and situated corpus-based investigations.

One of the significant contributions of corpus linguistic methods to genre/CDA analysis is that they make it possible to quantify the qualified (Hardt-Mautner 1995). Repeated paradigmatic relations cannot be observed from an individual text, or the holistic approach (Stubbs 2001) which characterises CDA (Hardt-Mautner 1995). A corpus-based approach helps to confirm as well as disconfirm what is observed by genre and CDA analysts or intuitively understood by expert members. For example, concordance and frequency methods to investigate choice of lexicon, agency (active or passive), pronominalisation (*we-they*), and action (tense and modality) at the sentence level can make transparent the recurrent patterns of authorial discourse (for a comprehensive list of analysable linguistic features, see Janks 2005). Starfield (2003), for instance, used concordance analysis in her EAP class to examine the structure of academic writing and use of language that establishes writers' credibility (e. g. reporting on other people's work). Her activities helped students discover the myriad of patterns typical of the genre. This wealth of information facilitated their access to and control of the discourse conventions, with the result that these students experienced marked improvements in their academic writing over time. Starfield's research suggests that once clarified, conventions previously opaque help students to establish an authoritative voice and contribute to (shaping) their discourse community. Once they are understood discursive norms can be appropriated, negotiated and manipulated, with students taking on active roles in "transforming the world" (Freire 1972: 75).

A discourse-based approach to exploiting corpora may thus well start from reading a small corpus of academic articles in individual disciplines (Hunston 2002). The observations obtained can then be tested by analysis of a larger corpus, which may either support or refute the initial findings.

6. Putting theory into practice

My limited knowledge of corpus linguistics places me in an ideal position to put theory to the test as a learner and researcher. In this position, combining a genre/CDA approach with corpus linguistics to advance discourse knowledge and (negotiated) voice can be assessed in terms of its relevance and practicality to novice students and teachers of corpus linguistics.

I started investigation from my work and interest (*situated practic*e) in EAP for research purposes using Swales & Feak's (1994) genre analysis of introductions to research papers. Although research involves multiple genres (needing multiliteracies), Swales & Feak simplify the process of writing introductions by proposing a rhetorical pattern with three main moves: establishing a research territory, indicating a gap or question in current knowledge, and occupying the research niche established. This pattern functions as a workable heuristic or as a framework facilitating overt instruction. It also increases the chance of 'making connections'. As Gledhill (1996) points out, connecting the presence of a word with its significance is difficult without knowing which section or part of text the word occurs in. Awareness of the move structure gives a novice corpus researcher the hooks to 'fish' into a pool of raw corpus data.

Heuristics as simplifications have their limitations. As Swales (1990) notes, the two first moves are hard to separate and the three moves 'recycle' in longer introductions. Nevertheless, all three moves were persistently observed. Performing a rough analysis on a 100 research papers from a range of disciplines Swales found that in move 2 negative or quasi-negative quantifiers, such as *no*, *little*, *none*, or *few*, were most frequently used to signal that a niche is being established, closely followed by lexical negation (e.g. *fail, failure, limited*). Swales & Feak (1994) point out that of interest to EAL students is the use of the quantifiers *little* and *few* (with the evaluative meaning of *not enough*) in comparison to *a* little and *a* few (with the neutral meaning of *some*). In indicating a gap in the research area of investigation, students' use of *little* and *few* without the indefinite article would indicate genre knowledge and hence competence.

The basis of my first corpus search was to observe these quasi-negative quantifiers in combinations likely to indicate a gap in the field. Since *little* collocates with the uncountable noun *research* and *few* with the plural noun *studies*, my first search was to perform a concordance search on MICASE for *little* + *research* and *few* + *studies*. However, no such collocations were found, which is no surprise as a corpus of spoken academic English understandably contains little reference to gaps in the research field. It proved, however, that these collocations belong to a specific written academic register, and showed that my lack of knowledge concerning the availability of specific corpora for written academic discourse hampered my investigation.

My next step was to investigate the British National Corpus using SARA, as this contains many written academic texts. An online search provided 79 occurrences of *little research* and 54 of *few studies*. Examination of these showed that:

- Both *little research* and *few studies* were mostly used as negative quantifiers for signalling gaps. However, *little research* was the preferred collocate (more than 80% of *little* occurred without an article compared to 60% for *few*).
- *Little research* was used with few verb types and predominantly with passive constructions.
- *Few studies* co-occurred with many different verb types, and passive constructions were much less frequent..
- *Little research* was also more often qualified by the adverb *very*.

The investigation thus provided support for the observations made by genre analysts but also added some richer information about their usage in text.

SARA, however, was not the most effective web tool for searches on the BNC sampler, given the difficulty of separating out academic writing in the corpus. I was advised to use view.byu.edu, where different genres in the full BNC could be examined separately. Concordance searches were performed on the academic writing subcorpus. These largely confirmed my previous findings:

- Passive feel of *little research*: *done, carried out, conducted, undertaken.*
- In active voice, *little research* collocates with *examines, focuses, looks, exists, takes place.*
- *Few studies* more often occurs as agent, and in many more verb combinations: *few studies challenge, seek, give, describe, examine, assess, evaluate, try, attempt, consider, purport, penetrate, take into account.*

View.byu.edu returned 52 hits for *little research* in academic writing, yet 61 for *few studies*. This apparent inconsistency with the SARA data was for the reason that the VIEW interface also retrieved occurrences of *a little research/a few studies*, which SARA excluded. Detailed examination confirmed *little research* as the preferred way of indicating a limitation or gap. Of the 52 hits only one was preceded by *a*, while of the 61 hits for *few studies*, 12 were preceded by *a*.

This search also highlighted other language features (colligations) occurring to the right of these expressions:

- *Little research* was most often followed (either immediately or after its verb collocate) by the prepositions *on* (17 hits), *into* (5), and *in* (4).
- *Few studies* was most often followed by the prepositions *of* (12), and *on* (4).
- *Little research* was also followed by *to* + infinitive (5) or *–ing* participle (2) phrases, whereas *few studies* was followed by *that* (5) or *which* (2) clauses.

Another feature of the view.byu.edu interface is that frequencies can be compared to those in other BNC subcorpora. For example, whilst *little research* occurred 52 times in the academic writing subcorpus, it only occurred 3 times in the news corpus, a difference of 94.4%, and twice in the spoken corpus, a difference of 96.2%. Similar differences were obtained for *few studies*: 61 hits in the academic writing corpus (of which 49 without an article), 3 hits in the news corpus (difference of 95.3%), and 1 sample in the spoken corpus (difference of 98.4%). Clearly, the expressions investigated are specific to the written academic genre.

While providing support for Swales & Feak's (1994) findings concerning *little* and *few*, the BNC academic writing subcorpus cannot be assumed to be representative of research paper introductions. As mentioned earlier, while a larger corpus can provide support for observations obtained from genre analysis, it is also likely to obscure variation in genre or register, and may thus fail to indicate important contextual data (Krieger 2003). As Swales' work is mainly based on science and applied linguistics research reports, it may not say much about other discourses. Hence, my next step was to compile a small corpus based on journal articles from the 'sociology of education' discourse community, as that is my area of expertise. The work proved time-consuming and I ended up with 31 articles in .txt format. As their introductions would only make up a 4000–5000 word corpus, I decided to explore them manually, performing a genre analysis (see Appendix) and locating whether and where *little research* and *few studies* occurred.

The first finding of interest was that 17 of the 31 journal articles did not refer to gaps, limitations or critiques of the existing literature and research in the field. They did not use move 2 (limitation of the field) of Swales & Feak's move-analysis. Instead, they provided background (move 1), sometimes formulated a problem (a move 2, but not in reference to prior research or theory in the field) and then outlined or gave the purpose of their paper (move 3). None used *little research* or *few studies*. The 14 articles that did provide a move 2 used a range of expressions. *Focussed on* was the only phrase occurring twice (but with different qualifiers: *largely*, *a narrow range*). My corpus was clearly too small to observe repeated lexical patterns. However, it did suggest a range of semantic synonyms, indicating the rich, creative way in which language can be used (see Appendix), and studying these could encourage learners to develop 'personal' voice within their discourse community. Of course, the choices observed in a micro-corpus can be investigated in a larger corpus to provide further evidence of their use, exemplifying the genre-analysis and corpus-based research cycle.

In addition, I observed the use of *little* and *few* in my own doctoral thesis (120,000 words) using the find option. *Little research* was used once in the opening chapter combined with the passive verb form *was instigated*. I mostly used *little* as a negative qualifier (35 occurrences versus 5 with a neutral meaning) with nouns like experience, time and value. *Few* I used mainly in its neutral form (16 occurrences preceded by *a*, 4 preceded by *the*; 9 without article to indicate negative evaluation). This analysis largely confirmed the patterns found in the academic writing subcorpus of the BNC.

7. Conclusion

All in all, my fishing in a pool of corpora indicates that corpus-based research raises the learner's awareness of collocates and surrounding text – of how certain language features are used. It also stimulates what Aston (1998) refers to as "serendipitous exploration". The learner as language detective is likely to explore and discover more, as my own explorations show. Clearly, the learner is in control of the investigations; thus corpora are tools to further autonomy and to make students less dependent on the instructor and textbooks (Aston 1998). However, researching a large corpus has its limits. Considerable time may be required, and it requires high motivation on the part of the learner. It also requires skills in the use of corpora. As Aston warns, "it takes time and practice to learn how to formulate queries which will effectively find what one is looking for" (1998). In that respect, I am still a novice. Also, only a limited set of patterns can be investigated at any one time and hence working on a corpus may be a slow means of learning the many aspects of research writing. Working in pairs or groups may help to "make enough sense of the data", and "maintain interest and motivation" (Aston 1998). It also helps in building more knowledge that is then shared (van Rij-Heyligers 2004). Finally, in comparison to whole-text analyses, findings in large corpora are generally taken out of context. Although the BNC allows the researcher to see the sentence in which hits occur and the source of material, this information does not necessarily provide the heuristic framework that genre analysis of a small corpus can offer, showing where words are situated in the text, and hence the strategies (such as moves) used. Genre analysis also illustrates the multiple ways students can express themselves within their field(s). Applying a critical discourse analysis approach to corpora and genre-analysis makes the learner aware that these texts are to be taken as social actions serving social conventions, such as how a research community indicates a gap in knowledge or uses passive and active constructions to indicate (lack of) agency. To transform practice through consciousness-raising and negotiation, students need to know the norms in order to flout them. A corpus-based approach informed by genre analysis and critical discourse analysis has the potential to indeed "break the chain of rhetorics" by raising awareness of the multiplicity of language.

References

Aston G. (1998). *Learning English with the British National Corpus.* Paper presented at the 6th Jornada de Corpus, UPF, Barcelona, May 1998. Retrieved 2 May 2008, from <http://www.sslmit.unibo.it/~guy/barc.htm>

Bakhtin M. (1981) *The dialogic imagination.* Austin: University of Texas Press.

Becher T. (1989) *Academic tribes and territories: intellectual enquiry and the cultures of disciplines.* London: Taylor & Francis.

Booij G.E. (2001) English as the lingua franca of Europe: a Dutch perspective. *Lingua e Stile,* 36(2), 347–357.

Bollag B. (2000) The new Latin: English dominates in academe. *The Chronicle of Higher Education: International,* 47(2), A73.

Braun S. (2005) From pedagogically relevant corpora to authentic language learning contents. *ReCALL,* 17(1), 47–64.

Breure L. (2001) *Development of the genre concept.* Retrieved 26 May 2005, from: <http:/cs.uu.nl/people/leen/GenreDevelopment.htm>.

Crystal D. (1997) *English as a global language*. Cambridge: Cambridge University Press.

Doecke B., A. Kostogriz & C. Charles (2004). Heteroglossia: a space for developing critical language awareness? *English teaching: practice and critique*, 3(3), 29–42.

Fairclough N. (n. d.) *Global capitalism and critical awareness of language.* Draft paper retrieved 25 May 2006, from: <http://www.schools.ash.org.au/litweb/norman1.html>.

Freire, P. (1972) *Cultural action for freedom.* Harmondsworth: Penguin.

Gavioli L. (2001) The learner as researcher: introducing corpus concordancing in the classroom. In Aston G. (ed.), *Learning with corpora*, Houston: Athelstan, 108–137.

Gledhill C. (1996) *Scientific innovation and the phraseology of rhetoric: posture, reformulation and collocation in cancer research articles.* Unpublished PhD thesis, University of Aston in Birmingham.

Graddol D. (1997) *The future of English?* London: British Council.

Granger S., E. Dagneaux & F. Meunier (eds) (2002) *The International Corpus of Learner English. Handbook and CD-ROM*. Louvain-la-Neuve: Presses Universitaires de Louvain.

Gupta A. F. (1999) Standard Englishes, contact varieties and Singapore Englishes. In Gnutzmann C. (ed.), *Teaching and learning English as a global language: native and non-native perspectives*, Tübingen: Stauffenburg Verlag, 59–72.

Hardt-Mautner G. (1995) *'Only connect': critical discourse analysis and corpus linguistics.* Wien: Institut fur Englische Sprache, Wirtschaftuniversitat Wien.

Hunston S. (2002) *Corpora in applied linguistics.* Cambridge: Cambridge University Press.

Hyland K. (2000) *Disciplinary discourses: social interactions in academic writing.* Harlow: Longman.

Janks H. (2005) Language and the design of texts. *English Teaching: Practice and Critique*, 4(3), 97–110.

Johns A. M. (2005) English for academic purposes: issues in undergraduate writing and reading. In Bruthiaux P., D. Atkinson, W. G. Eggington, W. Grabe & V. Ramanathan (eds), *Directions in applied linguistics: essays in honor of Robert K. Kapla*n. Clevedon: Multilingual Matters 133, 101–116.

Krieger D. (2003) Corpus linguistics: what it is and how it can be applied to teaching. *The Internet TESL Journal,* 9(3), 1–6. Retrieved 26 April 2006, from: <http://iteslj.org/Articles/Krieger-Corpus.html>.

Luke A. (n. d.) *Theory and practice in critical discourse analysis*. Retrieved 26 May 2006, from: <http://www.gseis.ucla.edu/faculty/kellner/ed270/Luke/SAHA6.html>.

Luke A. & P. Freebody (1999) *Further notes on the four resources model.* Retrieved 25 April 2006, from: <http://www.readingonline.org/research/lukefreebody.html>.

New London Group (1996) A pedagogy of multiliteracies: designing social futures. *Harvard Educational Review*, 66(1), 60–92.

Paltridge B. (n. d.) Academic literacies and changing university communities. Retrieved 26 April 2006, from: <http://www.arts.usyd.edu.au/committees/ArtsTLCtee/Projects/CIWE/paltridge.htm>.

Pennycook A. (1994). *The cultural politics of English as an international language.* London and New York: Longman.

Starfield S. (2003) Why does this feel empowering? Thesis writing, concordancing, and the 'corporatising' university. In B. Norton & Toohey K. (eds), Critical Pedagogies and language learning. Cambridge: Cambridge University Press, 138–157.

Stubbs M. (2001) Texts, corpora, and problems of interpretation: a response to Widdowson. *Applied Linguistics*, 22, 149–172.

Swales J.M. (1990) *Genre analysis: English in academic and research settings.* Cambridge: Cambridge University Press.

Swales J.M. & C.B. Feak (1994) Academic writing for graduate students: a course for nonnative speakers of English. Ann Arbor: The University of Michigan Press.

Trayner B. (2004) *Critical genre and discourse analysis.* Retrieved 26 May 2005, from: <http://btrayner.info/Genre/criticalgenrediscourse.html>.

van Rij-Heyligers J.A. (2007) To weep perilously or W.EAP critically: the case for a corpus-based critical EAP. In Hidalgo, E., J. Quereda & J. Santana (eds), *Corpora in the foreign language classroom.* Amsterdam: Rodopi, 105–118.

Wallraff B. (2000, November) What global language? *The Atlantic online.* Retrieved 2 February 2002, from: <http://www.theatlentic.com/issues/2000/11/wallraff.htm>.

Warschauer M. (2000) The changing global economy and the future of English teaching. *TESOL Quarterly,* 34, 511–535.

Widdowson H.G. (2000) On the limitations of linguistics applied. *Applied Linguistics*, 21(1), 3–25.

Widdowson H.G. (2003) *Defining issues in English language teaching.* Oxford: Oxford University Press.

Willis, J. (1998) Concordances in the classroom without a computer. In B. Tomlinson (ed.), *Materials development in language teaching.* Cambridge: Cambridge University Press, 44–66.

Appendix: Phraseology for 'gap' expressions in Sociology of Education introductions

The following phrases occurred in the Introduction section of 14 out of 31 articles

Contrastive adverbial linking words

- However, the assumption that … is challenged by (NP) …
- … (NP) is not simply (NP) … Rather, it has more complicated aspects that extend to (NP) …

Contrastive adverbial linking words, but making concessions

- *While* the study of … has provided invaluable insights, (NP) … have received less attention.
- *Though* research on …, other … research does not always reach out to (NP) …
- … (personal NP) have offered frameworks for (ing-participle phrase) … *Yet* relatively little use has been made of any of this work.
- … discourses offer wider and more sophisticated definitions of the problem, *although* still very much within (NP) …

Swales & Feak (1994) state that these structures are also common in Discussion sections, signalling the limitations of one's own research.

Phrases indicating insufficient theory or research

- With few exceptions, … studies have been based on (NP) …
- … most previous studies have focused on a narrow range of (NP) …
- … literature on … has largely focused on (NP) …, at the expense of (NP)
- … literature … rarely reflects on (NP) …
- … body of research and analysis has been carried out almost exclusively on (NP) …
- Work on … is thin in comparison with (NP) …
- … (NP) are under-studied and under-theorized.
- Only one unpublished paper dealt with (NP) …

Phrases indicating problems with validity or reliability

- … report conception fails to adequately take account of (NP) …
- …the mutual neglect of (NP) …
- … much of what passes for (NP) does not engage with the core aspects of (NP) …
- … only a concern with (NP) is a recurrent feature of work in (NP) …

- … (NP) promote rather minimal understandings of (NP) …
- It is yet to be established how (NP) …
- We cannot say whether the patterns described (NP) can be generalized to (NP) …
- Most specifically, the role of … is largely unexamined
- . … distinctive features may affect how (NP) …
- … (NP) lack the statistical evidence to accurately measure (NP) …

Miscellaneous

- The … report is suspicious of departure from (NP) …
- The model extends beyond (NP) … The model of… also sits as a counter to (NP) …

SYLVANA KRAUSSE

Semantic preference and semantic prosody in the specialist language class

Abstract

The paper offers a view on semantic preference and semantic prosody from the perspective of the domain-specific language of environmental engineering and illustrates with the help of corpus-based examples how these notions manifest themselves in text. This is done with a strong emphasis on their potential for use in the ESP class.

1. Introduction

The teaching of ESP has come a long way from the days of pure terminology to today's task-based or content-based approaches. As well as focussing on the language, these methods take into consideration the specific situations in which the language will be used by the learner. Without questioning these premises, I will argue that ESP teaching still needs to adjust its emphasis. It is widely recognised that meaning is not constituted in just single words but may be spread over several words, forming units of meaning (cf. Sinclair 1996a; Tognini-Bonelli 2002). It is also clear that lexis and grammar cannot be considered separate systems but cooperate in the creation of meaning. These ideas have unfortunately not yet entered materials design in ESP, in particular those which are of central interest in this paper – semantic preference and semantic prosody.

Together with collocation (recurrent lexical combinations) and colligation (recurrent combinations of lexical and grammatical features), semantic preference and semantic prosody make up Sinclair's extended unit of meaning (1996a). These four categories of relations, which together constitute units of meaning, need to be acquired by learners in order to achieve fluency and proficiency in the language. Only if "available as a single choice on the paradigmatic axis" (Tognini-Bonelli 2002: 91), and properly used within the restrictions set by these relationships, can a unit of meaning be used as a chunk in formulating and understanding speech, overcoming the stringing together of single words.

Semantic preference and particularly semantic prosody have been the object of lively discussion in corpus linguistics. This paper provides a view from the perspective of domain-specific language. It looks at cases of semantic preference and semantic prosody in a 2-million word corpus of environmental engineering texts, and discusses how these concepts can be applied in the teaching and learning of ESP.

The corpus comprises 2 million running words which are presented in 6 subcorpora. These subcorpora on the one hand represent the main topics the students of environmental engineering have to deal with at our university: Mining Reclamation, Soil Reclamation and Waste Disposal and Recycling. On the other hand, the subcorpora reflect various text types, like the subcorpus of web-based journals, that of technology fact sheets and that consisting of an introductory textbook. Within the text-type based subcorpora, efforts were made to ensure that at the same time the texts reflect the above-mentioned topics.

All in all, the subcorpora comprise one section of mining reclamation material (approx. 200,000 running words), one of soil remediation material (approx. 300,000 running words), approx. 200,000 words of technology fact sheets, 120,000 words from an introductory environmental engineering textbook, 400,000 words on waste treatment and recycling and approx. half a million words from web-based journals.

2. Semantic preference and semantic prosody in specialist language

There is little dispute about the concept of semantic preference. Most authors concur with Stubbs, who defines it as "the relation, not between individual words, but between a lemma or a word-form and a set of semantically related words" (2001: 65). Textbooks of technical English usually illustrate a few sets of this kind, such as verbs and nouns

indicating trends (*increase, decrease, rise, drop, fall,*), presenting these with the adjectives and adverbs which typically qualify them (*slight(ly), slow(ly), steadi(ly), gradual(ly), significant(ly), dramatic(ally)*). While ESP teachers may be able to think of other examples, there are not many such sets to be found in most teaching materials.
However, corpus evidence shows that semantic sets collocating with particular forms or lemmas come in all shapes and sizes, as the following examples may illustrate:

- the modifying noun in compounds with *recycling* (the semantic set of recyclable materials – *biosolids recycling, electronics recycling, packaging recycling, paper recycling*, etc.)
- the headword in compounds premodified by the adjective *biodegradable* (a semantic subset of waste substances – *biodegradable fluids, biodegradable organics, biodegradable slurry, biodegradable waste*, etc.)
- the graduating adverb modifying the adjective *acidic* (a semantic set of graduations – *extremely acidic, highly acidic, strongly acidic, moderately acidic, slightly acidic, weakly acidic,* etc.)
- the infinitive following *designed to* (more than half the 914 occurrences of *designed to* in my corpus are followed by an infinitive indicating a resultative action or a state – *designed to achieve, designed to capture, designed to carry, designed to contain, designed to control*, etc.)
- in the phrase *under _ conditions,* the slot accepts variants from a semantic set of process descriptors (*under acidic conditions, under (un-) aerobic conditions, under controlled conditions, under fuel-rich conditions, under laboratory conditions, under reducing conditions*, etc.)
- following the prepositional phrase *prior to*, we find two distinct sets: one of times (years and dates – *prior to 1942/1999/etc.*) and one of processes (*prior to chlorination/discharge/disposal/ filtration/injection/sampling/use* etc.)

This list is by no means exhaustive.

What about semantic prosody? If we look at traditional textbooks, we find various cases of semantic prosody, even if generally unnoticed. As words like *increase* and *decrease* occur frequently with words like *slightly* or *slowly,* they can be said to have a semantic preference for such qualifying adverbs. But if these word combinations also express something positive or negative, this constitutes a semantic prosody. It is evident from the corpus that the combination *dramatic* increase* tends to occur in negative contexts and the combination *effective* increase* in positive ones.

If someone were to make a corpus of texts discussing the issue of semantic prosody, the word *attitudinal* would probably be high on a keyword list. For Sinclair (1999) semantic prosody develops "when the usage of a word gives an impression of an attitudinal or pragmatic meaning". But can this definition be applied to domain-specific language? The question is whether there is evidence of attitudinal pragmatic meaning in specialist language, and whether semantic prosody plays a role in this.

In general language, Partington notes that items like *rightly, timely, excessive* and *flabby* have an "in-built favourable or unfavourable speaker evaluation" (2004: 131). The same seems true in specialist language for items like *hazardous, difficult, valuable* and *effective*. Positive or negative evaluation seems central to their meanings.

At first sight, other words are more neutral, but in actual use they acquire a positive or negative semantic prosody through their immediate linguistic co-texts, as in our *increase/decrease* example. Another example from the corpus regards the word *potential*. At first glance rather neutral, *potential* can acquire either positive meanings (such as *neutralization potential* and *methane-recovery potential*), or negative ones (such as *acid generation potential, potential for problems, potential to cause AMD or corrosion*).

Some morphological components also appear to possess semantic prosodies. One is the fashionable prefix *bio-,* which plays a prominent role in generating new words in environmental engineering English (*bioavailable, bioremediation, bioactive, biodegrade*) or the suffix *-able* (i.e. as in *biodegradable, recyclable, refillable*). None of these examples seem to get anywhere near "attitudinal meaning". But they definitely indicate positive or negative evaluations. While attitudinal meaning and evaluative meaning may be hard to distinguish in general English, in specialist language they are not. And that is because of the absence of attitudinal meaning in such a precise and stylistically neutral language as that of engineering.

In general language, the speaker can choose to use a certain semantic prosody for a special reason. Let us take Sinclair's example *set in* (cf. Sinclair 1987; Partington 2004: 135) The speaker decides to combine *winter* and *set in* in order to express a particularly negative attitude. As the verb *set in* has a semantic preference for words like *foot-rot* or *deterioration,* in *winter set in* it acquires an additional attitudinal meaning. It is a stylistic element exemplifying a creative use of language. But if I use a word like *cause* together with *erosion, damage, clogging* or *fouling* in engineering language (cf. Stubbs 1997 for a discussion of the semantic prosody of *cause* in general English), I do not choose this word for stylistic effect. The style is neutral and the words have only denotative meanings. When defining semantic prosody, care should be taken to distinguish between attitudinal and evaluative meaning.

Partington provisionally treats semantic prosody as a sub-category of semantic preference, stating that "the relation of the two phenomena as set and sub-set, probably works as rule of thumb in most cases" (2004: 149). However he goes on, citing evidence from Stubbs (2001) and Sinclair (1996a), to state that "the relationship is more complex and the difference more fundamental" in that "semantic prosodies are evaluative or attitudinal and are used to express the speaker's approval (good prosody) or disapproval (bad prosody) of whatever topic is momentarily the object of discourse" (Partington 2004: 150). For the purpose of describing a domain-specific language, I would argue that a view of semantic prosody as a sub-set of semantic preference is adequate. No functional interpretation of how speakers position themselves is necessary when language is used for conveying information. In such cases, Partington's claim that semantic prosodies are "independent of individual speakers" (2004: 152) holds true. Every native speaker has been primed by repeated encounters with lexical items which, according to Hoey (2005: 9), "leads to a speaker unintentionally reproducing some aspect of the language". Native speakers know intuitively that words such as *cause* or *set in* have negative prosodies, and consequently they can make use of the creative potential of language to achieve special effects. This is how attitudinal meaning is added, and for this reason we should think twice before treating attitudinal meaning as equivalent to semantic prosody at least in a specialist language

Partington also touches upon the reasons why it is important to signal whether some expressed idea is to be regarded as positive or negative. Investigating maximisers like *utterly, totally, completely*, etc. and their semantic preference for absence or change of state, he claims that these preferences seem to be connected with bad prosodies, and may be related to fundamentals of the human condition which go beyond language itself.

> In universal terms, in human psychology the presence of something is preferable to its absence (to have is better than to have not). In equally universal terms, change causes anxiety to the human psyche. (Partington 2004: 147)

This suggests that linguistics alone may not be in a position to explain the existence of semantic prosodies, and why it is not sufficient to understand from the word *fouling* on its own that it describes an unpleasant condition. The understanding of semantic prosody might be a fundamental of the human condition, not just of language. Why is it already inherent in the word *cause* that there is a link with *fouling* and that this signals negativeness? It may raise anthropological and philosophical questions to explain whether it is necessary to send preliminary signals to indicate that something positive or negative will follow.

4. More preferences and prosodies in specialist language

Before considering the place of semantic preferences and prosodies in the ESP classroom, I would like to examine some further examples of these features in environmental engineering as compared with general English.

Specific language displays specific semantic preferences. For instance in General English the word *pregnant* has semantic preferences for verbs such as *become, get* or *be*, and for time periods such as *three/four/five/... months*. In the colligation *pregnant with* it has a preference for a name, or an ordinal + *child/son/daughter* (*her first/second/third child*: BNC news section). In contrast, in environmental engineering *pregnant* has acquired a special meaning, where it has a semantic preference for specific liquid chemical substances used to dissolve metals out of ore (*liquors/lixiviants/solutions* – as in *pregnant (leach) solution*).

element	*attested collocations*	*semantic preference*	*semantic prosody*
-free	*debris-free product* *lead-free solder* *smercury-free equipment* *plastic-free organics*	products, devices or substances that are free from a contaminant	positive
-rich	*clay-rich tailings* *fuel-rich zones* *iron-rich barren solution* *ozone-rich gas* *soil-rich area* *grass-rich yardwaste*	locations or substances that are rich in a certain element or substance	positive
-prone	*erosion-prone silt/soil* *strike-prone area*	location that is prone to a negative influence	negative
-resistant	*abrasion-resistant materials* *corrosion-resistant alloys* *fire-resistant lubricants* *water-resistant surface*	material that is resistant to chemical or mechanical influences	positive
-borne	*airborne concentrations* *fluidborne species* *soilborne plant diseases* *wastewater-borne nitrogen* *waterborne pathogens* *windborne bacteria*	harmful substances or diseases carried by a certain medium	negative
-containing	*asbestos-containing soils* *carbon-containing materials* *chlorine-containing organics* *iron-containing zones* *oxygen-containing gas* *sulfide-containing rock* *clopyralid-containing feedstocks*	substance or location holding a chemical or another kind of impurity	negative only if chemical is a contaminant
-contaminated	*DNAPL-contaminated aquifer* *lead-contaminated soil* *pesticide-contaminated sites* *sewage-contaminated zone* *metal-contaminated biomass*	object or location contaminated by a substance	negative

Table 1. Semantic preferences and prosodies of suffixes in the environmental engineering corpus

Studies of morphology have taught us that some word-formation elements “appear in series of forms” (Adams 2001: 96). Environmental engineering has its own series-forming elements, such as *-free, -rich, -prone, -resistant, -borne, -containing* and *-contaminated*. These elements display their own specific semantic preferences and prosodies.

These examples show that the principles of semantic preference and semantic prosody are, if attitudinal meaning is left aside, the same in the specific language as in General English. They merely differ in their individual manifestations.

5. In the ESP classroom

These examples are but a selection of the instances of semantic preference and semantic prosody in a domain-specific language which can be unveiled by corpora. Although vocabulary work has attracted much attention during the past few years, materials designers and textbook authors have not yet focused on all the features of extended units of meaning. There is still a gap to be bridged by the ESP teacher who – with the help of a specialist corpus – can provide the kind of lexical and semantic information necessary to use specialist language in discourse. The corpus can serve as a source of information to improve course design as well as for classroom material.

According to Sinclair, a word *becomes associated with a meaning through its repeated occurrence in similar contexts* (1996b: 114). The aim of teaching should therefore be to create opportunities to encounter words in their typical contexts. Native speakers have an intuitive knowledge of which semantic preferences and prosodies a word possesses, while second language learners lack this kind of intuition. Up to now, the way they have acquired such knowledge has generally been through teacher corrections, stating that certain words cannot be used together or that one word should rather be replaced by another. But reactive teacher behaviour opens only a tiny window for the student to understand that the use of a certain word is restricted to a specific semantic set of other words. It is doubtful that a teacher will come up with all the members of a set, or know that the word should only be used in positive or negative prosodies. As teaching time is scarce, a more proactive approach is needed when teaching vocabulary, which confronts the learner with typical collocations and colligations along with the restrictions set by semantic preferences and semantic prosodies.

The natural approach of facilitating language learning through repeated encounters can be supplemented by conscious processing. Such processing can be triggered by teacher instruction, but with the help of a corpus and simple concordancing techniques, students can also explore language for themselves. Examples of simple exploratory exercises might involve elements like *-free, -rich, -resistant* or *-containing*. Students could thereby find that you can say *fuel-rich* and *clay-rich* but rather *pollutant-laden* and not *pollutant-rich*. Comparisons of a General English corpus with a specialist corpus can help them understand differences between different registers, as I tried to show with the *pregnant* example.

This can be done without even mentioning the terms "semantic preference" and "semantic prosody" to students. The point is that the learner should be sensitized to these phenomena with the help of corpus examples. The relation of a word to its semantic preference and prosody is at a higher level of abstraction, which can simplify parts of the language learning process by organising knowledge into semantic sets and cross-linking it. Conscious processing may shortcut the otherwise lengthy process of students being presented with language material, using it in their own discourse, and being corrected when they infringe these restrictions.

6. Conclusion

Investigations using my domain-specific corpus show that there certainly are semantic preferences and semantic prosodies in environmental engineering English, and that they are more frequent than engineering English textbooks generally suggest. Semantic prosody is like a special quality of semantic preference, where some lexical items choose their collocations from an even more restricted semantic field, displaying just or mainly positive or negative prosodies. Infringements of such restrictions may lead to misunderstandings, and language may become imprecise – a huge drawback in the engineering field.

Engineering language does not show any signs of attitudinal meanings. This paper provides support for the need to distinguish these from evaluative meanings, and to keep the notion of semantic prosody distinct from attitudinal meaning in creative language use. Only then can we maintain that semantic prosody is independent of the individual speaker.

As long as ESP material designers and textbook authors fail to do justice to the results of corpus linguistic research, it will remain the task of the teacher to prepare the ground for repeated encounters with suitable language material, and to raise students' awareness of phenomena such as collocation, colligation, semantic preference and semantic prosody which go beyond the single word level. This can be achieved by teacher instruction as well as by students exploring language themselves.

References

Adams V. (2001) *Complex words in English*. Harlow: Pearson Education.

Partington A. (1998) *Patterns and meanings*. Amsterdam: John Benjamins.

Partington. A. (2004) Utterly content in each other's company – semantic prosody and semantic preference. *International journal of corpus linguistics*, 9, 131–156.

Sinclair J. (1987) *Looking up*. London: Collins.

Sinclair J. (1996a) The search for units of meaning. *Textus*, 9, 75–106.

Sinclair J. (1996b) The empty lexicon. *International journal of corpus linguistics*, 1, 99–119.

Sinclair J. (1999) Tuscan Word Centre website. <www.twc.it/happen.html> Consulted 12 May 2007.

Stubbs M. (1997) Cause and provide. In G. Cook and B. Seidlhofer (eds.), *Principle and practice in applied linguistics*. Oxford: Oxford University Press, 247–256.

Stubbs M. (2001) *Words and phrases: corpus studies of lexical semantics*. Oxford: Blackwell.

Tognini-Bonelli E. (2002) Functionally complete units of meaning across English and Italian: towards a corpus-driven approach. In B. Altenberg & S. Granger (eds) *Lexis in contrast – corpus-based approaches*. Amsterdam: John Benjamins.

VIEW – British National Corpus interface, by Mark Davies. <http://view.byu.edu/> Consulted 13 May 2007.

JOSEF SCHMIED

Teaching and learning contrastive linguistics using an EU translation corpus with English, German, French and Spanish

Abstract

This paper uses two translation corpora, first the bilingual Chemnitz English-German Translation Corpus from the InternetGrammar of English and then the multilingual Chemnitz EU (Parliament) Translation Corpus with translations in four European languages, English, German, French and Spanish, to illustrate that multilingual corpora are worth exploring in detail. It argues that they are not only a reliable basis for complex contrastive linguistic analyses but that they bring an added advantage for language learners and teachers alike. They allow users to disambiguate polysemous forms and to discover fine similarities and differences in closely related languages, e. g. in causative constructions (like have*) and other grammaticalisation processes (like* help*).*

1. New learning options through new resources

Over the last few years, language learning and linguistics have changed considerably, not only because the World-Wide Web has given learners and linguists access to new authentic materials or real-language examples of various text-types (from email to on-line newspapers), but also because computer-assisted language learning (CALL) and language corpora are presenting new options and new challenges to language learners, teachers and language "explorers" in general. In this presentation, I will argue (and provide examples) that multilingual corpora may make not only more complex analyses possible, but paradoxically also make it easier to "see patterns" in a more complex comparison. However, finding the "right" input for the searches may be as difficult as finding the collocations (lexical patterns) and colligations (grammatical patterns) that enable the explorer-learners to conceptualise their own "meaning" or "grammar" from a corpus. To demonstrate my point, I will investigate learning options in a multilingual corpus for advanced learners of English who are not corpus-linguistic specialists, but open to corpus-linguistic methodologies. To them, corpus-driven autonomous learning, i.e. querying a simple untagged corpus with the help of a simple interface and seeing lexical and grammatical patterns in the search results, poses problems, which the teacher who introduces the learners to these new learning opportunities, may tend to underestimate.

In studying patterning, corpus-driven linguists concede that while collocation can be easily identified in KWIC (key-word-in-context) concordances of unannotated data, colligation is less obvious to spot unless a corpus is grammatically tagged. Yet any tagging is undesirable for strict descriptivist corpus-driven linguists, as grammatical tagging inserts patterns that are based on preconceived theories, and consequently may result in a distortion of the raw data or a one-sided interpretation. According to Firth (1968: 181), colligation refers to the relations between words at the grammatical level, i.e. the relations of "word and sentence classes or of similar categories" instead of "between words as such". Thus studying colligation in Firth's original sense necessitates a tagged or even a parsed corpus. To overcome this problem, Firth's definition of colligation is often applied in a loose sense, in spite of the claim that corpus-driven linguistics is deeply rooted in Firth's work. Nowadays the term colligation is used to refer not only to significant co-occurrence of a word with grammatical classes or categories (e.g. Hoey, 1997; Stubbs, 2001: 112) but also to significant co-occurrences of a word with function words (e.g. Krishnamurthy, 2000). The patterning of such function words like modal auxiliaries can, of course, be observed and computed even in an untagged corpus.

In this contribution, I will demonstrate how contrastive structures can be explored using a translation corpus with four European languages, English, German, French and Spanish. This approach is based on modern principles of corpus learning, which include computer literacy and autonomous learning. These principles have been discussed under various headings like explorative, investigative and inductive learning in general, or data-driven (Jones, 1991) and corpus-driven learning (e.g.

Tognini-Bonelli, 2001) more specifically. It is clear that this type of learning has certain advantages and disadvantages and is often seen differently from a learner and a teacher perspective (Schmied, 2006). It is also obvious that the contrastive explorers do not have to be fluent in all the languages included, but they have to be aware of major contrastive differences and be able to recognise similarities and patterns in lexicon and grammar.

This type of learning has only become possible relatively recently, when new resources have become available on the World-Wide Web. Most resources, however, can only be used on the intranet or are only available for bilingual contrastive research. The following list of URLs is certainly not exhaustive, but shows that related projects have been launched and used successfully in many European countries from Norway to Portugal:[1]

- http://www.hf.uio.no/iba/prosjekt/
- http://www.englund.lu.se/content/view/66/127/
- http://ell.phil.tu-chemnitz.de/search
- http://www.linguateca.pt

The only really multilingual corpora currently available on the Web are from Oslo and Chemnitz, which suggests that this valuable resource is underused. Since the corpus data are freely available (e.g. <http://ell/phil.tu-chemnitz.de/multiSearch/>), they can be used for various investigations and the examples offered here are only an illustration of the many possibilities.

Generally, this paper argues that multilingual corpora are not only relevant but bring an added advantage to contrastive linguistics for language learners and teachers alike (see also Hunston, 1995). This is in line with the contrastive linguistic trends in the last decade, where more attention has been paid to raising language awareness and to the gradient nature of contrastive phenomena. Corpus linguistics can certainly make an important contribution in this respect.

1 As of 01/06/07.

2. Learning contrastive research queries

In principle, we can distinguish between two methodological approaches to language learning based on a multilingual translation corpus. The deductive approach allows contrastive linguists to use the corpus to test rules or hypotheses by posing general search queries and checking the results to see whether they include all and only the examples predicted. The inductive approach allows language explorers to search a corpus to find numerous examples that can lead them to formulate rules in the form of collocational or colligational (i.e. lexical and grammatical), qualitative or quantitative patterns.

The following examples use modal auxiliaries to illustrate how contrastive corpus searches can be useful discovery procedures for language learners, first on the basis of the English-German Translation Corpus, and then the Chemnitz EU (Parliament) Translation Corpus. Fig. 1 shows the query interface, where investigators can not only search for strings in one language or the other but also for combinations of strings, and overlaps of prototypical or non-prototypical equivalents. In addition, the input and the output can be manipulated: if we have a hypothesis about the style value of a construction, we can watch the occurrences in academic texts, for instance; as they are considered relatively formal; if we anticipate that collocates may occur in a wider cotext of the (input string) node, we can widen the span from the usual 3 words left and right to the complete sentence. Occasionally, we may only want to test the hypothesis by looking at the statistics, disregarding the examples temporarily.

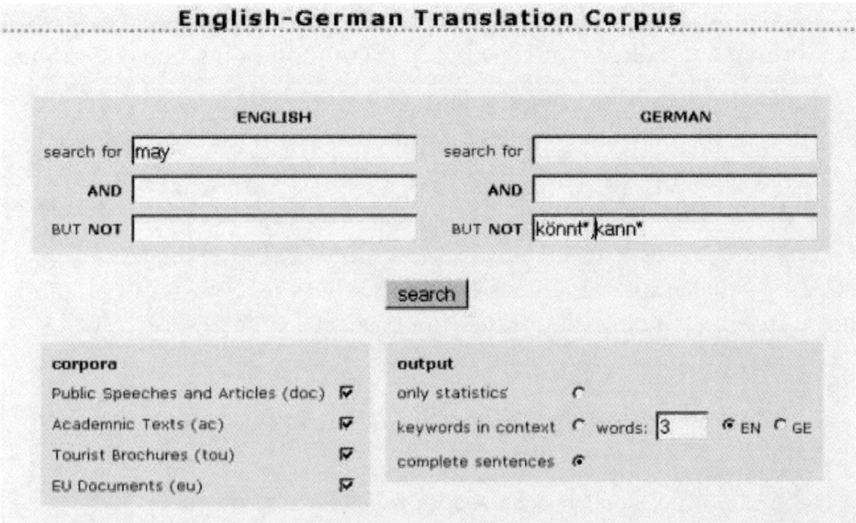

Fig. 1. Search interface of the English – German Translation Corpus comparing English *may* with its German equivalents, but not morphological variants of the prototypical equivalent *können* (etymologically *can*).

Thus the first task for investigators is to learn to submit good research queries by tailoring the input and the output, by including or excluding forms in the original or the translation. This is difficult for untagged corpora when languages with strong inflections are searched (like German). When comparing English and German modal auxiliaries, corpus explorers have to think of the German inflectional forms *mag, magst, mögen, mögt*, etc. and truncate them to *mög**, *mag** to include all present tense variants. However, *etymological* equivalents do not always correspond in the related language. This particularly applies to modal auxiliaries, where developments over the last thousand years have led to systematic shifts, so that, for instance, English *may* is not equivalent to German *mögen* any more but much closer to *können* (as in Fig. 1 above). But even these formal grammatical equivalents (like other modal auxiliaries) do not cover the whole spectrum. Students have to think of semantic equivalents, for instance, in the case of hedges where modal auxiliaries may also be rendered as modal adverbs (in many cases *may* can be translated as *vielleicht*).

To sum up, a comparison of the English modal auxiliary *may* with its German equivalents must be based on the following considerations:

- think of etymological equivalents: *mögen – mög*/mag**
- think of formal equivalents like modal auxiliaries, e.g. *können – könnt*/kann*
- think of semantic equivalents (e.g. hedges) like modal adverbs, e.g. *vielleicht*

The first few sample sentences that researchers receive as output of the query in Fig. 1 include the following cases:

(S1) **ac/decker:** **525**
Landslides ***may*** have helped form this cliff, but its origin is still a matter of lively debate.
Erdrutsche ***mögen*** zur Bildung dieser Klippe beigetragen haben, aber ihr Ursprung ist noch immer Anlaß für lebhafte Debatten.

(S2) **ac/decker:** **532**
Mars ***may*** once have had running water, but its present features show a barren land of ancient volcanoes swept by violent sandstorms.
Vielleicht gab es auf dem Mars früher einmal fließende Gewässer, aber heute besteht er aus einer kahlen Landschaft mit alten Vulkanen, über die gewaltige Sandstürme hinwegfegen.

(S3) **ac/decker:** **541**
The Russian radar has also mapped a 100-kilometer-wide oval depression on the northern continent, which ***may*** be a caldera.
Der russische Radar hat auch eine 100 Kilometer breite Senke auf dem nördlichen Kontinent ausgemacht, bei der es sich ***wahrscheinlich*** um eine Caldera handelt.

(S4) **ac/decker:** **546**
The gases in Venus's atmosphere – carbon dioxide, nitrogen, water vapor, and sulfur compounds - suggest that they ***may*** be of volcanic origin.
Die Gase in der Atmosphäre der Venus – Kohlendioxid, Stickstoff, Wasserdampf und Schwefelverbindungen – ***deuten*** auf einen möglicherweise vulkanischen Ursprung ***hin***.

Fig. 2. German equivalents of *may*; output of the query in Fig. 1.

Here the explorative learner discovers not only that besides *mögen* other modal auxiliaries (like *können*) play a role in translating *may*, but also that adverbs like *vielleicht* and *wahrscheinlich* occur – and occasionally, even totally different full verbs like *darauf hindeuten* (in S4).

Such equivalents can be found by looking through the results of queries for elements in the semantic field: e. g. the equivalents of German *vielleicht* (Fig. 3) include *possibly* on the English side, and in turn this may reveal further equivalents on the German side later, and so on. In this ping-pong style, central and peripheral, prototypical and non-prototypical members of the semantic field can be identified. However, frequency is not enough for describing overlapping contrastive fields; cotext, context, style and many other meaning elements play a role.

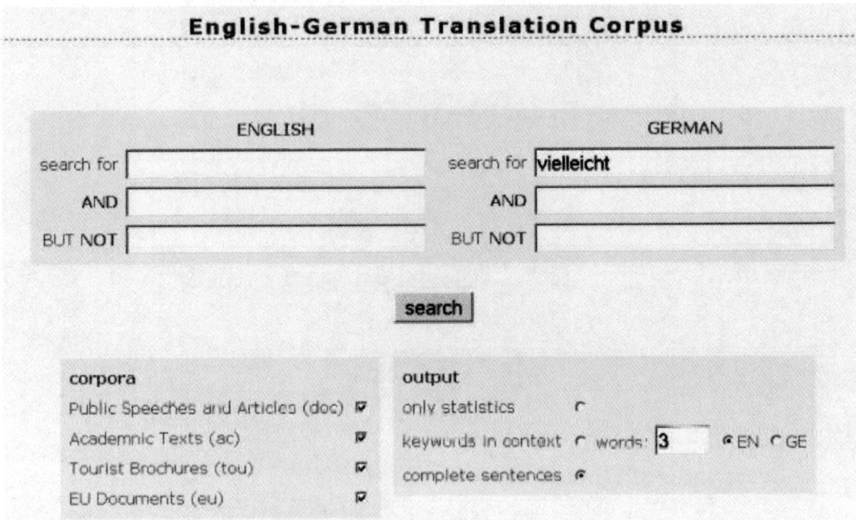

Fig. 3. Search interface of the English-German Translation Corpus querying *vielleicht* to discover more equivalents (like *possible*) or style-specific preferences.

The statistical output has to be studied in detail when style-specific constructions are investigated. Fig. 4 demonstrates clearly that *vielleicht* (like hedges in general) is particularly common in academic writing (thus the examples above are prototypical). This is true not only in absolute terms of the number of occurrences (there are more academic sentences in the database than sentences from political speeches), but also in relative terms, in proportion to the number of sentences in each subcorpus.

text type	*occurrences*	*sentences*	*absolute*	*relative*
ac	194	12265	1.58 %	69.78 %
doc	26	4612	0.56 %	9.35 %
eu	14	7058	0.20 %	5.04 %
tou	44	4524	0.97 %	15.83 %
total	278	28459	0.98 %	100.00 %

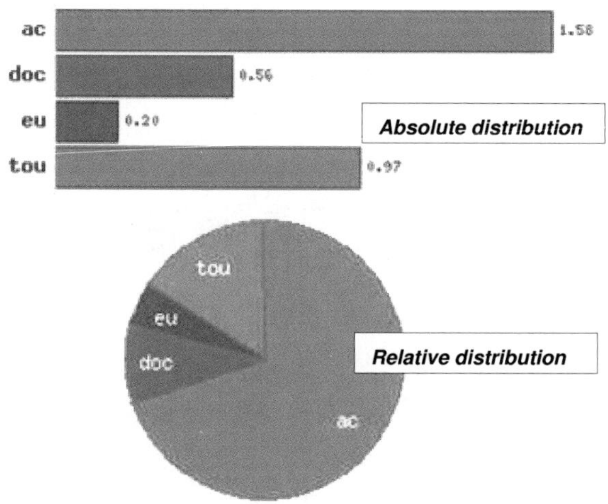

Fig. 4. Occurrences of German *vielleicht* with different absolute and relative occurrences (text type abbreviations are explained in Fig. 2).

Since the value of translation corpora in contrastive research has been demonstrated amply elsewhere (e.g. Johansson, 2005; Schmied, 1999), the following sections will try to illustrate the added value that can be gained by comparing not only bilingual but multilingual corpora using the same methodology.

3. The added value of multilingual corpora for contrastive studies

3.0 The EU (Parliament) Translation Corpus as a database

The following examples are taken from the English, German, French and Spanish versions of the same debates of the European Parliament between 1997 and 2004. The texts are easily available on the internet in machine-readable form and the translation quality of most texts is relatively high, since the parliamentary debates are considered important for the development of the European Union and are translated by experienced professionals. These advantages are however marred by some disadvantages of EU documents, which are often accused of containing a lot of unnecessary jargon and may thus not serve as good models for translations for advanced students of English. An additional (technical) problem of this pilot study was that the alignment provided was completely unacceptable.

The advantage of the EU multilingual corpus is that two Germanic languages (German and English) can be compared with two Romance languages (French and Spanish) and that the typological choices between modal auxiliaries and modal adverbs can be investigated. This may also provide a cline of constructions – for instance in German – English – French – Spanish, assuming that English has been heavily influenced by French and that French has more Germanic substrate influence than Spanish.

The search options in the multilingual corpus (Fig. 5) are essentially the same as in the bilingual corpus described above (Fig. 1), with the exception that the style comparison is replaced by the language comparison. There are however additional advantages in multilingual searches.

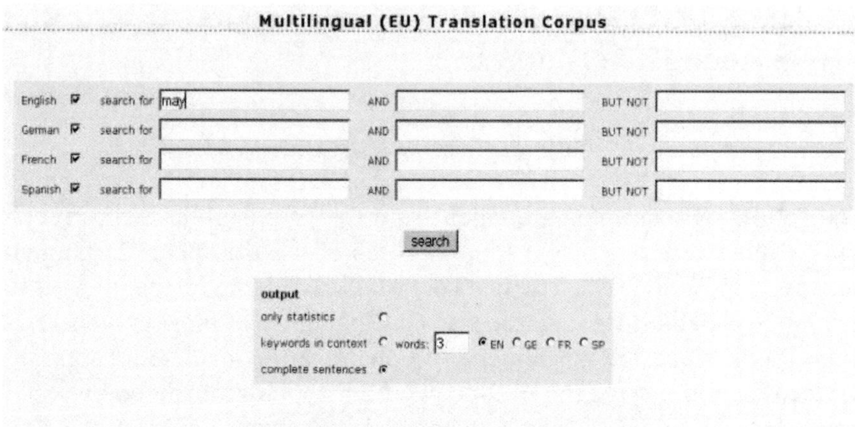

Fig. 5. Search interface with English, German, French and Spanish search option in the EU Translation Corpus comparing English *may* with its equivalents.

3.1 Disambiguation of ambiguous forms

A major problem of any form-based corpus linguistic approach is that many forms are ambiguous. This applies particularly to high-frequency forms like *have* in English. For bilingual corpora, this is usually a major reason for tagging. Therefore the following example illustrates how polysemous auxiliaries can be disambiguated in an untagged corpus.

An illustrative example here are the ambiguous auxiliaries expressing causativity, as for instance in the construction *I had him wash the car*. This construction with a full verb between the direct and the indirect object is difficult to isolate from the temporal auxiliary *have* in an untagged corpus, because the usual queries with *had* would render a vast number of past perfect constructions like *I had washed (him) the car*.

However, this problem of ambiguity of *have* in English can be overcome by including more than one language in the search query, since there is a simple equation of *have* = *lassen* = *faire* (despite the usual problems of inflections) and since German and French have other past perfect constructions. The English *have* construction presented in the results will only include the causative auxiliary *have* and not the temporal auxiliary *have*. However, what seems clear in theory is not always so easy in practice.

Simple searches involving primary auxiliaries are not easy, since *have*, *lassen* and *faire* have rather irregular forms in their respective languages. The causativity of English *have*, German *lassen* and French *faire* can, for instance, be expressed in the following complex search query:

English: *ha** + German: *la** + French *fai**

The result of such a query can be seen in S5 and S6 below (Fig. 6). Whereas S5 is a good example for causatives, S6 is definitely not, although it fulfils the search criteria formulated above. In order to avoid this over-collection, the corpus explorer can either add a search criterion for Spanish or look through all the research results critically (as long as there are not too many). Although such cases are exceptional and can easily be "weeded out" by hand, the example again illustrates that many quantitative comparisons cannot be done automatically, and it is always necessary to check the real examples before drawing wide-ranging conclusions.

(S5) ep-00-05-03: 2651

English: I **have** also noted that my dear friend, Mr Dell' Alba, **has had** his grumbles printed as an appendix to my opinion.

German: Ich habe auch zur Kenntnis genommen, daß mein spezieller Freund aus dem Parlament, Herr Dell ' Alba, seine Kritik als Anlage zu meiner Stellungnahme hat drucken **lassen**.

French: J'ai également noté que mon cher ami député M. Dell'Alba avait **fait** imprimer ses rouspétances en annexe à mes remarques.

Spanish: También he observado que mi querido amigo, el Sr. Dell' Alba del Parlamento, ha **logrado** ver impresas sus opiniones como anexo a mi dictamen.

(S6) ep-97-07-14: 39

English: Just eight days earlier, the European Parliament **had** adopted a resolution in the topical and urgent debate which runs to about three pages in length.

German: Das Europäische Parlament hatte genau acht Tage vorher eine Entschließung in der Dringlichkeitsdebatte verabschiedet, die ungefähr drei Seiten **lang** ist.

French: Huit jours auparavant, le Parlement européen avait adopté une résolution au cours du débat d'actualité, une résolution qui doit **faire** environ trois pages.

Spanish: Exactamente ocho días antes, el Parlamento Europeo aprobó una resolución en el debate de urgencia que abarca aproximadamente tres páginas.

Fig. 6. Equivalents of *have* in French, German and Spanish

3.2 Fine-tuning of similarities and contrasts

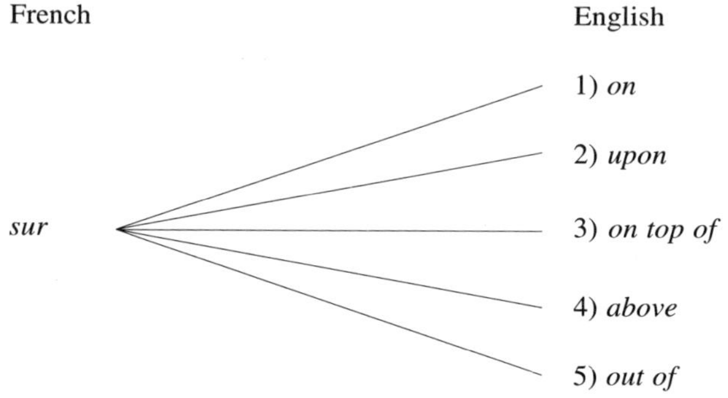

Fig. 7. Polysemy in prepositions: French *sur* and its English equivalents

In many translations, prepositions are a particularly tricky area because they constitute an overlapping system of polysemy that is not easily rendered in a foreign language. This can be seen in both monolingual and bilingual dictionaries, which are often not a great help for the translator who would like to distinguish prototypical from non-prototypical, and idiomatic from creative usages. For example, the French preposition *sur* can be translated by at least five English prepositions (Fig. 7 above). Thus the contrastive investigator has to go through many examples to distinguish the non-prototypical translations in S7 from the prototypical translations in S8 (Fig. 8 below). The juxtaposition of more than one language makes it easier for the autonomous learner to see the pattern in a vast number of examples even without an experienced instructor. The similarities and contrasts between the related West European languages English, German, French and Spanish allow a fine-tuning of semantic spaces in areas where this may be otherwise very difficult.

(S7) **ep-00-01-17.txt: 12**

English: My question **relates to** something that will come up on Thursday and which I will then raise again.

German: Meine Frage **betrifft** eine Angelegenheit, die am Donnerstag zur Sprache kommen wird und auf die ich dann erneut verweisen werde.

French: Ma question **porte sur** un sujet qui est à l'ordre du jour du jeudi et que je soulèverai donc une nouvelle fois.

Spanish: Mi pregunta se refiere a un asunto del que se hablará el jueves, día que en volveré a plantearla.

(S8) **ep-00-03-01.txt: 427**

English: We will be producing a communication shortly **on** an issue which this Parliament feels passionately about, that is, how we can ensure that election observation is conducted as comprehensively and sensibly as possible without diminishing the integrity of the institutions which do it.

German: In Kürze werden wir eine Mitteilung **zu** einem Thema veröffentlichen, das dem Parlament sehr am Herzen liegt, nämlich wie wir sicherstellen können, dass eine Wahlbeobachtung so umfassend und vernünftig wie möglich durchgeführt werden kann, ohne dass die Integrität der Institutionen, die sie vornehmen, geschmälert wird.

French: Nous publierons bientôt une communication **sur** un sujet qui passionne le Parlement, à savoir les actions que nous pouvons entreprendre pour que l'observation des élections soit menée le plus complètement et le plus judicieusement possible, sans atteindre à l'intégrité des institutions qui les organisent.

Spanish: Presentaremos en breve una comunicación **sobre** un tema que es de gran interés para este Parlamento, a saber, cómo podemos garantizar que el seguimiento de las elecciones se lleva a cabo de la manera más exhaustiva y más sensata posible sin restar por ello integridad a las instituciones responsables de su realización.

Fig. 8. Equivalents of *sur* in English, German and Spanish

3.3 Multilingual searches as discovery procedures

The following examples show that all contrastive corpus explorers, from advanced language learners to translators, can use multilingual corpora profitably. Johansson (2002:47) states: "if we want to gain insight into language and translation generally, and at the same time highlight the characteristics of each language, it is desirable to extend the comparison beyond language pairs".

In contrast to the bilingual comparison in 3.2 above, a multilingual comparison of grammaticalisation confirms the expanded function of

English *help* more clearly. In many sample sentences (Fig. 9 below) English *help* is not the equivalent of German *helfen*, French *aider* and Spanish *ajudar.*

(S9) ep-00-02-02.txt: 267
English: We also hope that the communication will **help to** build a better common understanding of how to manage risks and to dispel fears that the precautionary principle might be used in an arbitrary way or as a disguised form of trade protectionism.
German: Wir hoffen außerdem, daß die Mitteilung dazu **beitragen** wird, die Möglichkeiten des Risikomanagements besser zu verstehen und Befürchtungen auszuräumen, das Vorsorgeprinzip könnte willkürlich oder als versteckte Form des Handelsprotektionismus eingesetzt werden.
French: Nous espérons aussi que cette communication **contribuera** à instaurer une meilleure compréhension commune de la manière de gérer les risques et à dissiper les craintes selon lesquelles le principe de précaution pourrait être utilisé de façon arbitraire ou pourrait constituer une forme déguisée de protectionnisme commercial.
Spanish: Esperamos también que la comunicación **favorezca** un mejor entendimiento común de cómo deben gestionarse los elementos de riesgo y disipe los temores de que el principio de precaución pueda ser utilizado de manera arbitraria o como una forma encubierta de proteccionismo comercial.

Fig. 9. Equivalents of *help* in German, French and Spanish

A small statistical comparison demonstrates clearly that the correspondence of *help* is rather *beitragen/contribuer/contribuir*:

help to	30	*helfen*	*4*	*beitragen zu*	*23*
		aider	*4*	*contribuer à*	*26*
		ayudar	*9*	*contribuir a*	*17*

Fig. 10. Equivalents of English *help* in German, French and Spanish in the EU Translation Corpus

Generally, multilingual queries are innovative discovery procedures for contrastive linguistics. Close quantitative and qualitative inspection of search results helps investigators to:

- distinguish prototypical from non-prototypical forms,
- recognise idiomatic phrases as constructions that occur only in fixed co(n)texts,
- measure collocates of various strength,
- become aware of side effects of new discoveries in search results.

A final example (Fig. 11) will demonstrate this:

(S10) ep-96-09-19: 19
English: *Mr President, ladies and gentlemen, Mrs Gradin*, before coming to the individual requests I would like to situate this report within a wider framework, even if this **may** seem presumptuous to the eyes and in the ears of some Members.
German: *Herr Präsident, liebe Kolleginnen und Kollegen, liebe Frau Kommissarin Gradin!* Bevor ich zu unseren einzelnen Forderungen komme, möchte ich diesen Bericht in einen größeren Zusammenhang stellen, auch wenn dies in den Augen und Ohren der einen oder anderen **vielleicht** anmaßend erscheint.
French: *Monsieur le Président, chers collègues, Mme le commissaire,* avant que je n'en vienne à nos exigences, j'aimerais placer ce rapport dans un contexte plus large même si cela ***paraît*** prétentieux aux yeux de l'un ou l'autre.

Fig. 11. Address conventions in English, German and French

Discourse conventions are only rarely studied systematically using corpora because they do not occur often enough, and because many corpora do not include complete larger texts but only excerpts (usually not starting at the beginning). Here the search for equivalents of English may not only provide prototypical translations of the modal auxiliary in German and in French (*vielleicht, paraître*), but also interesting differences in address conventions. Of course, before we draw general conclusions the constructions discovered here have to be checked against similar occurrences, but the choice of names and titles in certain conventionalised contexts is something that we might not have become aware of so easily without a multilingual corpus.

4. Conclusion

In this contribution, I have tried to give introductory examples of how the EU Parliament Translation Corpus, a simple untagged corpus with texts in English, German, French and Spanish, can be used for explorative learning and teaching. The emphasis of our argumentation has been on autonomous learner-investigators, on discovering patterns and on raising awareness for structures and their dependencies.

I hope to have shown that apart from their practical applications (for language teaching and learning, lexicography and translation), multilingual corpora (like the EU Translation Corpus) can be a basic resource for contrastive linguists, since they can display differences between languages much more clearly than bilingual corpora. The use of multilingual corpora increases our knowledge of typological and language-specific features as well as of cultural differences and language universals. The contrastive perspective gives us moreover deeper insights into individual languages and allows the fine-tuning of qualitative and quantitative similarities and differences which are difficult to uncover through monolingual introspection.

Of course, the project sketched here could be expanded to include more complex quantitative comparisons, like analysing multiple overlaps and dependencies of forms or measuring "equivalents".

Generally, translation or parallel corpora are a basis for contrastive analyses as well as human and machine translations. Whereas translation specialists study translation through parallel corpora, contrastive analysts compare language structures. Incongruencies in multilingual translation corpora may be attributed to three reasons (which can not always be kept apart unambiguously):

- differences because the translator produced a different text consciously or unconsciously (translationese due to universal features of the translation process, which may lead to more explicit or more or less comprehensible texts:. Olohan & Baker, 2000);
- differences because structures are transferred from the source language to the target language (translationese due to interferences, which may lead to unnatural structures or preferences in the target language);
- differences because the target language prefers other structures naturally.

The first reason is particularly relevant for translation studies, the second for language learning and teaching, and the third for contrastive linguists.

Contrastive corpus-linguists need the input of corpus compilers and tool developers, just as corpus analysts supply an input for language service providers in the widest sense, from translators to teachers. For the results of corpus-linguistic studies cannot only be used in language descriptions, but also in applied linguistic areas. However so far, multilingual lexicology and lexicography (see also Teubert, 2001) seem to be particularly underdeveloped.

References

Firth J. (1968) A synopsis of linguistic theory 1930–1955. In Palmer F. R. (ed.) *Selected Papers from J. R. Firth 1952–59*. Bloomington: Indiana University Press, 1–32.

Hoey, M (1997) 'From concordance to text structure: new uses for computer corpora' in *PALC '97: Proceedings of Practical Applications of Linguistic Corpora Conference, University of Lodz* , 2–23.

Hunston S. (1995) Grammar in teacher education: the role of a corpus. *Language Awareness*, 4, 15–31.

Johns T. (1991) Should you be persuaded: two examples of data-driven learning. In Johns T. & P. King (eds) *Classroom concordancing. ELR Journal 4*. Birmingham: University of Birmingham, 1–16.

Krishnamurthy, R. (2000). Collocation: from silly ass to lexical sets. In Heffer J., H. Sauntson & G. Fox (eds) *Words in context: a tribute to John Sinclair on his retirement.* Birmingham: Birmingham University Press. 31–47.

Mukherjee J. (2002) *Korpuslinguistik und Englischunterricht. Eine Einführung*. Frankfurt am Main: Peter Lang.

Olohan M. & M. Baker (2000) Reporting *that* in translated English: evidence for subconscious processes of explicitation? *Across Languages and Cultures* 1, 141–172.

Schmied J. (1999). Applying contrastive corpora in modern contrastive grammars: the Chemnitz Internet Grammar of English. In Hasselgard H. & S. Oksefjell (eds) *Out of corpora. Studies in honour of Stig Johansson*. Amsterdam: Rodopi, 21–30.

Schmied J. (2006) Corpus linguistics and grammar learning: tutor versus learner perspectives. In Braun S., K. Kohn, & J. Mukherjee (eds) *Corpus technology and language pedagogy*. Frankfurt am Main: Peter Lang, 87–106.

Stubbs M. (2001) *Words and phrases: corpus studies of lexical semantics*. Oxford: Blackwell.

Teubert W. (2001) Corpus linguistics and lexicography. *International Journal of Corpus Linguistics* 6, 125–153.

Tognini-Bonelli E. (2001) *Corpus linguistics at work*. Amsterdam: John Benjamins.

Part two
Learner corpora

JUAN PABLO JIMENEZ-CAYCEDO & MEG GEBHARD

"Expert-like" elementary narratives: A genre- and corpus-based study of L2 writing development

Abstract

Research on early L2 writing is scarce worldwide. This study aims to contribute to this area by analyzing a micro-corpus of personal narratives written by an English language learner (ELL) and comparing these with larger reference corpora. The purpose was to identify whether and how this student developed his ability to write "expert-like" personal stories, using on the one hand genre analysis; and on the other corpus-based[1] *language analysis. The findings show how these approaches can be used to highlight development from a more spoken style to a more literate and expert written use.*

Introduction

Starting from an English for Specific Purposes (ESP) context, (Tribble, 2000: 1) states that "accounts of the linguistic contrast between written genres are of potential value to language teachers and apprentice writers". Extrapolating to English language learners (henceforth ELLs) in public elementary schools in the United States, we would argue that accounts of the contrast between expert and apprentice texts in a given genre can also be of value to teachers and apprentice writers here. In this paper we compare a micro-corpus of narrative texts produced by a

1 Tognini-Bonelli (2001) made a distinction between corpus-based and corpus-driven investigations on language. For him the former uses a corpus as a source of examples to check research intuitions about the language within a smaller data set, while in the later the corpus itself is the only data from which patterns in language are identified and analyzed.

single ELL with a larger corpus of more expert and locally-produced or used exemplars of narrative (MELPE corpus[2]: (Jiménez-Caicedo *et al.,* 2006) and the British National Corpus (BNC). The aim was to identify whether and how this learner developed an ability to write "expert-like" personal stories, tracing the development of his academic literacy in this respect.

The context of this study was a public urban school involved in an ACCELA[3] professional development project in Western Massachusetts, USA. At the time of data collection, there were 450 students in grades K-5, mostly low-income Puerto Ricans, struggling to pass state exams (in 2004, 44% failed the English Language Arts MCAS exam and 46% scored "needs improvement").

Observations were focused on a 4th grade class in the academic year 2004–2005. There were 22 students, 20 of whom the class teacher identified as "Puerto Rican" and 2 as "white". Only 9 of these 22 were officially designated as ELLs, but the teacher reported that all were having trouble with academic reading and writing. We examined the "literacy practices" (Barton *et al.*, 2000) of five of these ELLs during three curriculum units concerned with reading and writing personal narratives. The learner focused on in this paper, Eloy (pseudonym), was one of them.

2 To address the question of representativeness in this study, I draw on the work of Walker on the "ecology of language" which he describes as "the relation between particular uses of the language and the context in which they occur" (Hockey & Walker, 1993). Walker suggests that, as one of the approaches to tackle the issue of sample representation in a corpus, one could collect "all the kinds of language to which a particular individual might be exposed at any one time, or within some fixed period of time, like a day" (ibid.). Following this notion, I compiled a corpus of all the written texts to which students in a class were exposed to during a period of instruction. This is what I call a MELPE corpus (Jimenez-Caicedo *et al.,* 2006).

3 The ACCELA Alliance (Access to Critical Content and English Language Acquisition) is a federally funded professional development partnership between the University of Massachusetts Amherst, three local school districts, and various community organizations in Western Massachusetts. See <http://www.umass.edu/accela/>.

The following research questions were posed:

- Over the course of an academic year, do the written narratives produced by an ELL show more of the textual features associated with narrative proficiency (e. g. use of the past tense, use of the rhetorical structures associated with narrative as a genre)?
- Are there changes in the lexico-grammatical choices (lexical variety, complexity of sentences, temporal connectives, etc.) associated with the realization of the obligatory or optional moves in written narratives? If so, can we describe development using corpus analysis?
- Does learner data support the hypothesis that writing develops from an oral and context-dependent to a more literate and expert use ((Biber, 1988; Halliday 1989)?

2. Theoretical orientation

This pilot study is informed by socio-cultural perspectives of language, and language learning, in which literacy is primarily understood as a set of social and cultural practices enacted by a group (Barton et al., 2000; Bloome *et al.*, 2000; Dyson, 1997; Dyson & Freedman, 2003; Gee, 2000; Street, 1995). Regarding second language learning in particular, Gebhard (2002) points out that a sociocultural orientation of second language acquisition "takes as a starting point an understanding that the origin and structure of cognition are rooted in the daily social and cultural activities in which people participate (p. 19)." I draw specifically on the notion of genre as a socio-cultural unit of analysis; which Bathia (1993), departing from Swales' work (Swales, 1981, 1990), defines as

> a recognizable communicative event characterized by a set of communicative purpose(s) identified and mutually understood by the members of the professional or academic community in which it regularly occurs (p. 13).

For Swales (1990) genre is an abstraction that provides us with a framework for the production and interpretation of language in particular social and cultural contexts. Consequently, Bathia (1993: 11) asserts that genre analysis represents a "thick" description of language in use, in which

> It is necessary to combine socio-cultural (including ethnographic) and psycholinguistic (including cognitive) aspects of text construction and interpretation with linguistic insights in order to answer the question, Why are specific discourse-genres written and used by specialist communities the way they are?

3. Methods and results

The data examined here are drawn from a larger body regarding 4th grade English language learners' literacy practices. The latter includes multimedia longitudinal records of the texts produced by 5 ELLs. (Scanned and transcribed versions of the original handwritten texts, as well as audio and/or video recorded readings of them). In transcribing the texts, the recommendations of the Lancaster-Leverhulme Corpus of Children's (Smith & McEnery, 1998) Writing were followed. The texts were produced during three curriculum units on reading and writing personal narratives, mainly at school during the English language arts class, at three different times in the year (October, February and May). Contextual information regarding the teaching of narrative and students' processes of interpretation, production and distribution of the texts was collected through class video recordings, field notes, and teacher and student interviews.

Analysis aimed to combine qualitative and quantitative approaches, analyzing both process and product. For the "process" data, methods associated with ethnographic investigations of classroom literacy events were employed (Heath, 1983) while for the. "product" data, corpus linguistics methods developed for learner corpora were used (Biber *et al.*, 1998; Ghadessy *et al.*, 2001; Granger, 1998; Granger *et al.*, 2002).

The results presented here focus on two personal narratives written by Eloy in October, 2004 (Time 1) and in May, 2005 (Time 3).

3.1 Genre analysis

According to Hassan (1984, 1989), every text has a recognizable form or generic structure that is related to its social purpose. Anyone familiar with a letter of application can recognize this. Letters of application have identifiable elements of text structure (some obligatory, some optional), or moves of the genre, which can appear in various orders. Each move can be seen as fulfilling a partial purpose, and together they fulfill the overall communicative purpose of the application.

Scanned original final draft	*Typed text-only version*
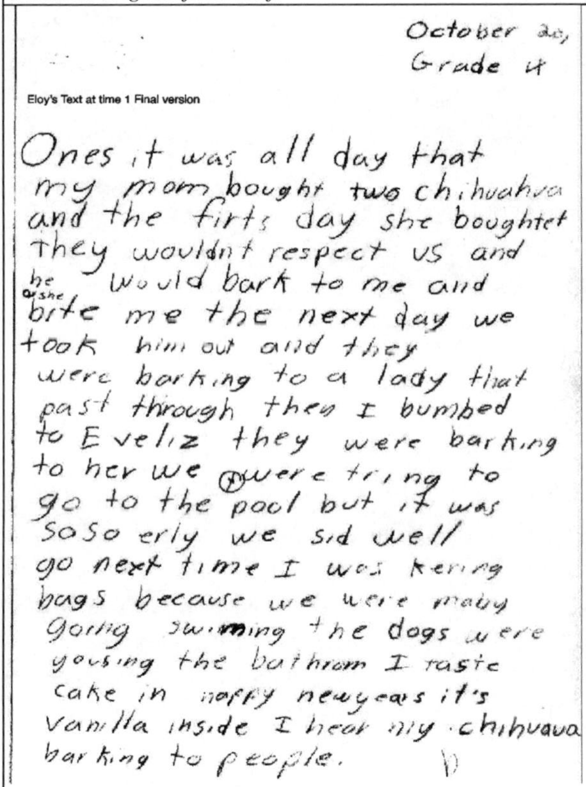 October 20, Grade 4 Eloy's Text at time 1 Final version Ones it was all day that my mom bought two chihuahua and the firts day she boughtet they wouldn't respect us and he or she would bark to me and bite me the next day we took him out and they were barking to a lady that past through then I bumbed to Eveliz they were barking to her we were tring to go to the pool but it was SoSo erly we sid well go next time I was kering bags because we were maby going swiming the dogs were yousing the bathrom I taste cake in happy newyears it's vanilla inside I hear my chihuvava barking to people.	Eloy – Time 1 (Oct. 2004) Ones it was all day that my mom bought two Chihuahua and the first day she boughtet they wouldn't respect us and he or she would bark to me and bite me the next day we took him out and they were barking to a lady that past through then I bumbed to Eveliz they were barking to her we were tring to go to the pool but it was so so erly we sid well go next time I was kering bags because we were maby going swimming the dogs were yousing the bathroom I taste cake in happy newyears it's vanilla inside I hear my Chihuahua barking to people.

Fig. 1. Eloy's first text (October 2004, Time 1).

Personal narrative also has obligatory and optional discursive moves. There is an obligatory *orientation* or setting move in which the writer refers to a specific place and time to situate the story, and where the main characters are introduced. Another obligatory move is the *series of events,* characterized by the sequence of actions that happened. This typically leads to the *complication* – a problem to be dealt with. The final obligatory move is the *resolution*, through which we learn how the problem was solved. In addition to these four obligatory moves, a narrative may contain two further optional elements. There may be an *abstract* or introduction – "I am going to tell you a story about when I first came to 4th grade", – and a final evaluative commentary, or *coda*, where the writer summarizes the final outcome or lesson learned (Derewianka, 2002; Paltridge, 2001).

3.1.1 Genre analysis of Eloys' first text

The social purpose of the expected text for this assignment was to describe or narrate a specific event in the life of the student, with teacher and classmates as audience. Thus the expected text type was a personal narrative. However, while we can identify moves corresponding to *orientation* and to *series of events* (the actions related to *Mom bought two Chihuahuas*), those of complication and resolution are absent. To conclude that the text cannot be characterized as a personal narrative would be misleading, however, as a corpus-informed microanalysis will demonstrate.

From a systemic-functional linguistics perspective (Halliday, 1978), an experiential analysis should provide answers to the question: "Who (participants) did what (processes) to whom (participants) under what circumstances regarding the thematic content of the studied text?" In Eloy's first narrative the major participants are *My mom* (also referred to as *she*), *two Chihuahuas* (*they*) and *I (we).* This suggests the text is about a personal event in Eloy's life. The processes are of two main kinds: relational (*being* verbs) and material (*doing* verbs). The relational processes (3/17) are found in the orientation move to locate characters and events in time, in the clauses "*Ones it was all day that my mom bought two Chihuahua*", "*... but it was so so erly*", while the material processes (the majority), are used in the series of events (14/17). Many of these material processes are in the past tense (*bought, took*), which is considered a primary marker of narrative discourse (Biber 1988: 223), and there is one use of projecting (verbal) processes (*we sid*), signaling narrated dialogue between participants. Circumstances are expressed using temporal connectives (*The first day, the next day, next time*).

Microanalysis of the experiential metafunction of Eloy's first text (see Table 1 below) thus confirms that the initial generic analysis may be misleading. The lexico-grammatical choices regarding participants, processes and circumstances suggest that this text may be an emerging narrative.

3.1.2 Genre analysis of Eloy's second text

Scanned Original final draft

Eloy's teacher-typed version: Peer-editted (05/19/05)

church dance

Ones my brother, sister and I were at the church dance. It was time to leave. The church dance ended at 11:45 P.M. up the stairs and we went to see a fight. But I didn't know that my sister was the one that was going to fitght. My sister went to the corner of Ninety Nine cents there were cops in the church dance. My sister stilld beging to fight my aunt was in a party is near were my sister if fighting so my aunt sall her my aunt jump at the cop punhed him and then they got arrested. They went inside the police car and they sat in the police back seat. They where riding to the police station. I tride to broke the window of the cops car. My brother to so they left we followed them running they went to the police station. Then the other morning the cops said you need 40 dollars to take her out so we did. I was kind of happy but my sister didn't come out of Juvenile Jail, the next morning My sister came back from Juvenile Jail I was so happy. I hug her she hug me back I took her home it was the happiest day. We did a picnic now we are happy she's back.

Typed text-only final version
church dance Ones my brother, sister and I were at the church dance. It was time to leave. The church dance ended at 11:45 P.M. up the stairs and we went to see a fight. But I didn't know that my sister was the one that was going to fight. My sister went to the corner of Ninety Nine cents there were cops in the church dance. My sister still began to fight, my aunt was at a party near were my sister was fighting. My aunt saw her and my aunt jumped at the cop punched him and then they got arrested! They went inside the police car. They sat in the back seat of the police car. The police drove them to the police station. My brother and I tried to brake the window of the cops car. They left and we followed them running. They went to the police station. Then the next morning the police said "you need 40 dollars to take her out" so we did. I was kind of happy but my sister didn't come out of juvenile jail. My sister came back from juvenile jail I was so happy. I hug her she hug me back I took her home it was the happiest day. We did a picnic now we are happy she's back.

Fig. 2. Eloy's second text (May 2005, Time 3).

As with the first text, the social purpose of the expected text at time 3 (May, 2005) was to describe or narrate a specific event in the life of the student, having the teacher and the student's classmates as the main audience. Thus the expected text type was again a personal narrative. A generic analysis shows us that this text is more 'narrative-like', since we can identify all the obligatory moves and some optional ones. Starting from the use of a title *(Church Dance),* the text begins with the formulaic *"Ones"*, which marks the text as a narrative and introduces the *Orientation*, using relational processes (*being* verbs) to introduce the participants, setting and time. Next, we find a *Series of events*, mostly presented through doing verbs (material processes) in the past tense (*went, fight, jumped, got arrested, sat, left, followed*). The series of events leads to a *Complication (they got arrested!)* and a few lines further down we find the *Resolution* (*My sister came back from juvenile).* We also find the optional move of *Evaluation* (*I was so happy... now we are happy*). Here the text features quite a sophisticated element, the temporal connective ***now*** to return to the present from the narrated past.

3.2 Tracing the student's capacity to produce "expert-like" narratives

The wordlist function of WordSmith Tools (Scott, 1996) was used to analyze salient words in Eloy's texts in comparison with the MELPE corpus and with the BNC.[4]

We find the typical pattern of function words as being the most frequent (cf. the BNC column). However when we compare the lists for Eloy's two texts we find a larger proportion of content words in the second (16/50) than in the first (10/50). What seems significant is not just this increased ratio, but also the greater frequencies of the content words contained in the second text. In the first text, only two nouns are used more than once (*day, Chihuahua*), while all the other eight are hapaxes. In the second text there are 11 content words used more than once, 8 of them three or more times each (*sister (7), police (6), back (4), church (4), dance (4), aunt (3), car (3) fight (3)).* Only four are hapaxes *(cents, cop, corner, day).* It is interesting to view these findings in the light of accounts of differences between written and spoken language in use (Biber, 1988; Halliday, 1989). Halliday for example, claims that in general, the more "written" the language being used, the higher will be the proportion of lexical words to the total number of words in a text. Thus, as shown in the previous analysis, we can conclude that Eloy's second text (Text 3), produced at the end of the school year, has several features that characterizes it as displaying a more "written" type of register. In other words, the tracing of genre specific features in both texts suggests that Eloy's capacity to produce "expert-like" narratives is increasing, and therefore his L2 writing is developing.

4 I used the wordlist of The British National Corpus provided with the WordSmith Tools suite.

4. Discussion

The analysis above shows how one can combine genre- and corpus-based tools in the analysis of an English language learner's academic literacy development. Comparing Eloy's texts from October 2004 and May 2005, it is clear that there is a shift to a more academic written register. For instance (as shown in the appendix), in the second text there were proportionally fewer instance of clauses initiated with *and,* and a greater use of conventional punctuation.

The second text also made greater use of expressions signaling the genre moves. It used more, and more varied, temporal connectives such as "*it was time to leave*" to highlight the complication, "*Then, the next morning*" within the series of events; and "*now*" to relate the series of events to the resolution, and again to introduce the (optional) *evaluation* move which brings the narrative to an end. While in the first text there is a very limited used of *doing* verbs (material processes) in the series of events, with an overuse of the past progressive, in the second text there is frequent use of the simple past to indicate a greater variety of processes.

We can see from the frequency data that Eloy's texts shifted from exhibiting features of spoken language to features of written discourse (e.g. a greater use of content-carrying words). The content words serve as an indicator of this student's growing ability to produce lexically denser narratives in a written narrative register (Biber, 1988; Halliday & Hasan, 1976; Tannen, 1982).

This is an exploratory analysis based on frequency data. Keyword analysis in comparison with other corpora may provide a fuller picture, by offering a means to establish which genre-specific words and phrases are important in a particular genre. In Tribble's words, identifying those words and phrases and exposing teachers and learners to them may help to "reduce the strangeness of a genre and its associated texts, and thereby the difficulty of writing in the new genre" (Tribble 2000: 11).

Authors' Note

We thank Amy Rivera, the teacher participating in the ACCELA Alliance professional development program, for opening the doors of her classroom to us. We are equally grateful to the anonymous TaLC7 reviewers for their insightful and constructive comments on an earlier draft of this paper, and to the Healey Foundation for supporting this study.

References

Barton D., M. Hamilton & R. Ivanic (2000) *Situated literacies: Reading and writing in context*. London: Routledge.

Bathia V. K. (1993) Analyzing genre: Language use in professional settings. New York: Longman Publishing.

Biber, D. (1988) *Variation across speech and writing*. Cambridge: Cambridge University Press.

Biber D., S. Conrad & R. Reppen (1998) *Corpus linguistics: Investigating language structure and use*. Cambridge: Cambridge University Press.

Bloome D., L. Katz, J. Solsken, J. Willett & J.-A. Wilson-Keenan (2000) Interpelations of family/community and classroom literacy practices. *Journal of Educational Research, 93*(3), 155–163.

Derewianka B. (2002) *Exploring how texts work*. Maryborough, Victoria: Primary English Teaching Association.

Dyson A. H. (1997) *Writing superheroes: Contemporary childhood, popular culture, and classroom literacy*. New York: Teachers College Press.

Dyson A. H. & S. W. Freedman (2003) Writing. In J. Flood, D. Lapp, J. R. Squire & J. M. Jense (eds), *Handbook of research on teaching the English language arts* (2nd. ed., pp. 967–992). Mahwah: Lawrence Erlbaum Assciates, Publishers.

Gebhard M. (2002) Fast capitalism, school reform, and second language literacy practices. *Canadian Modern Language Review, 59*(1), 15–52.

Gee J. P. (2000) The new literacy studies: From "socially situated" to the work of the social. In D. Barton, M. Hamilton & R. Ivanic (eds), *Situated literacies: Reading and writing in context*. London: Routledge.

Ghadessy M., A. Henry & R. Roseberry (eds) (2001) *Small corpus studies and ELT: Theory and practice*. Amsterdam: John Benjamins Co.

Granger S. (ed.) (1998) *Learner English on computer*. Harlow, England: Addinson Wesley Longman Limited.

Granger S., J. Hung & S. Petch-Tyson (eds) (2002) *Computer learner corpora, second language acquisition, and foreign language teaching*. Amsterdam: John Benjamins.

Halliday M. A. (1978) *Language as social semiotic*. London: Edward Arnold.

Halliday M. A. K. (1989) *Spoken and written language* (2nd ed.). Oxford: Oxford University Press.

Halliday M. A. K. & R. Hasan (1976) *Cohesion in English*. London: Longman.

Heath S. (1983). *Ways with words: Language, life and work in communities and classrooms*. Cambridge, England: Cambridge University Press.

Hockey S., & D. Walker (1993) Developing effective resources for research on texts: Collecting texts, tagging texts, cataloguing texts, using texts, and putting texts in context. *Literary and Linguistic Computing*, 8(4), 235–242.

Jiménez-Caicedo J. P., M. Gebhard & A. Rivera (2006) Combining ethnographic and learner corpora methods in critically analyzing the texts of English language learners in the context of high-stakes school reform in the United States. Paper presented at the *Seventh International Conference on Teaching and Language Corpora*. Paris, July 2006.

Paltridge B. (2001) *Genre and the language learning classroom*. Ann Arbor: University of Michigan Press.

Scott M. (1996) Wordsmith tools (Version 4.0). London: Oxford University Press.

Smith N., & T. McEnery (1998) Issues in transcribing a corpus of children's handwritten projects. *Literary and Linguistic Computing*, 13(4), 217–225.

Street B. (1995) *Social literacies*. London: Longman.

Swales J. (1981) *Aspects of article introductions. Aston ESP research report* (No. 1). Birmingham, UK: Language Studies Unit, University of Aston.

Swales J. (1990) *Genre analysis: English in academic and research settings*. Cambridge [England]; New York: Cambridge University Press.

Tannen D. (1982). *Spoken and written language: Exploring orality and literacy*. Norwood, N. J.: ABLEX Pub. Corp.

Tognini-Bonelli E. (2001). Corpus linguistics at work. *Studies in Corpus Linguistics*, 6. Amsterdam: John Publishing Co.

Tribble C. (2000) Genres, keywords, teaching: Towards a pedagogic account of the language of project proposals. In L. Burnard & T. McEnery (eds), *Rethinking language pedagogy from a corpus perspective: Papers from the third international conference on teaching and language corpora*. Hamburg: Peter Lang.

Appendix

Most frequent words in Eroy's first and second texts, the MELPE corpus and BNC wordlist

N	First text	Freq.	%	Second text	Freq.	%	MELPE	Freq.	%	BNC	Freq.	%
1	TO	7	6.31	THE	18	7.93	THE	181	5.46	THE	6,055,105	6.09
2	THE	5	4.5	MY	11	4.85	AND	132	3.98	OF	3,049,564	3.07
3	WERE	5	4.5	TO	9	3.96	I	78	2.35	AND	2,624,341	2.64
4	AND	4	3.6	WAS	8	3.52	TO	76	2.29	TO	2,599,505	2.61
5	I	4	3.6	I	7	3.08	A	68	2.05	A	2,181,592	2.19
6	WE	4	3.6	SISTER	7	3.08	IN	52	1.57	IN	1,946,021	1.96
7	BARKING	3	2.7	AND	6	2.64	OF	46	1.39	#	1,604,421	1.61
8	DAY	3	2.7	POLICE	6	2.64	WAS	44	1.33	THAT	1,052,259	1.06
9	THEY	3	2.7	OF	5	2.2	HER	37	1.12	IS	974,293	0.98
10	WAS	3	2.7	THEY	5	2.2	MY	35	1.06	IT	922,687	0.93
11	CHIHUAHUA	2	1.8	WE	5	2.2	AS	28	0.84	FOR	880,848	0.89
12	GO	2	1.8	AT	4	1.76	HIS	28	0.84	WAS	863,917	0.87
13	IT	2	1.8	BACK	4	1.76	ON	28	0.84	I	732,523	0.74
14	ME	2	1.8	CHURCH	4	1.76	OVER	28	0.84	ON	731,319	0.74
15	MY	2	1.8	DANCE	4	1.76	WE	27	0.81	WITH	659,997	0.66
16	NEXT	2	1.8	HER	4	1.76	IT	23	0.69	AS	655,259	0.66
17	SHE	2	1.8	WENT	4	1.76	WHO	23	0.69	BE	651,535	0.66
18	SO	2	1.8	#	3	1.32	HE	21	0.63	HE	593,609	0.6
19	THAT	2	1.8	A	3	1.32	SHE	21	0.63	YOU	588,503	0.59
20	A	1	0.9	AUNT	3	1.32	THEN	21	0.63	AT	524,075	0.53
21	ALL	1	0.9	CAR	3	1.32	MAMMA	20	0.6	BY	513,444	0.52
22	BAGS	1	0.9	FIGHT	3	1.32	YOU	19	0.57	ARE	458,368	0.46
23	BARK	1	0.9	HAPPY	3	1.32	UP	18	0.54	THIS	454,419	0.46
24	BATHROOM	1	0.9	WERE	3	1.32	GRANDMA	17	0.51	HAVE	448,684	0.45
25	BECAUSE	1	0.9	BROTHER	2	0.88	THEIR	17	0.51	BUT	446,783	0.45
26	BITE	1	0.9	BUT	2	0.88	THEY	17	0.51	NOT	431,075	0.43
27	BOUGHT	1	0.9	COPS	2	0.88	WITH	17	0.51	FROM	425,987	0.43
28	BOUGHTET	1	0.9	DID	2	0.88	ALL	16	0.48	HAD	413,144	0.42
29	BUMBED	1	0.9	DIDN'T	2	0.88	FOR	16	0.48	HIS	410,294	0.41
30	BUT	1	0.9	HUG	2	0.88	OMAR	16	0.48	THEY	376,289	0.38
31	CAKE	1	0.9	IN	2	0.88	ME	15	0.45	OR	370,166	0.37
32	DOGS	1	0.9	IT	2	0.88	PA	15	0.45	WHICH	366,196	0.37
33	ERLY	1	0.9	JAIL	2	0.88	WHEN	15	0.45	AN	338,743	0.34
34	EVELIZ	1	0.9	JUVENILE	2	0.88	HOME	14	0.42	SHE	325,351	0.33
35	FIRST	1	0.9	OUT	2	0.88	OUT	14	0.42	WERE	308,363	0.31
36	GOING	1	0.9	SO	2	0.88	RAIN	14	0.42	HER	304,311	0.31

N	First text	Freq.	%	Second text	Freq.	%	MELPE	Freq.	%	BNC	Freq.	%
37	HAPPY	1	0.9	STATION	2	0.88	THAT	14	0.42	WE	300,833	0.3
38	HE	1	0.9	THAT	2	0.88	HAD	13	0.39	ONE	290,466	0.29
39	HEAR	1	0.9	THEM	2	0.88	INTO	13	0.39	THERE	285,870	0.29
40	HER	1	0.9	THEN	2	0.88	OUR	13	0.39	ALL	277,566	0.28
41	HIM	1	0.9	ARE	1	0.44	WOULD	13	0.39	BEEN	260,360	0.26
42	IN	1	0.9	ARRESTED	1	0.44	GRANDMA'S	12	0.36	THEIR	254,603	0.26
43	INSIDE	1	0.9	BEGAN	1	0.44	OFF	12	0.36	IF	253,804	0.26
44	IT'S	1	0.9	BRAKE	1	0.44	WHOO	12	0.36	HAS	252,703	0.25
45	KERING	1	0.9	CAME	1	0.44	BUT	11	0.33	WILL	251,179	0.25
46	LADY	1	0.9	CENTS	1	0.44	RICARDO	11	0.33	SO	239,549	0.24
47	MABY	1	0.9	COME	1	0.44	SAY	11	0.33	WOULD	229,699	0.23
48	MOM	1	0.9	COP	1	0.44	THERE	11	0.33	NO	229,618	0.23
49	NEWYEARS	1	0.9	CORNER	1	0.44	WERE	11	0.33	WHAT	225,524	0.23
50	ONES	1	0.9	DAY	1	0.44	BACK	10	0.3	CAN	211,093	0.21

MARIA BELEN DIEZ BEDMAR & ANTONIO VICENTE CASAS PEDROSA

The use of prepositions by Spanish learners of English at University level: a longitudinal analysis

> One of the most common errors that people learning English make is to use the wrong preposition (Sinclair 1991: vii).

Abstract

Prepositions are a fuzzy word class due to their morphological, syntactic and semantic characteristics. They are difficult to use by foreign learners of English at all levels, as reported by various scholars using different methodological approaches which are not always comparable. In order to find out which prepositions pose problems to Spanish university students, a four-year longitudinal learner corpus was analysed a posteriori following Granger's Integrated Contrastive Model. Our findings show four patterns of development in the use of prepositions, and reveal the role of the mother tongue. These results lead to some suggestions to improve the design of EFL materials for Spanish university students.

1. Introduction

The last fifty years have seen a proliferation of studies analysing either errors in learners' production (Error analysis) or learners' entire production (Interlanguage analysis). These methodologies have recently benefited from the compilation of learner corpora such as the International Corpus of Learner English (ICLE, Granger et al. 2002), which have opened up possibilities for empirical research into learners' actual written or oral production (cf. papers in Granger 1998; Ghadessy et al. 2001; Granger et al. 2002; Ketteman & Marko 2002; Granger & Petch-Tyson 2003; Aston et al. 2004; Prat Zagrebelsky 2004; Sinclair 2004; Cosme et al. 2005; Gilquin et al. in press). The use of a common error tagset (Dagneaux et al. 1996) allows researchers to compare results, and facilitates comparison of the production by learners with different L1 backgrounds.

Furthermore, prepositions pose many problems to second or foreign language students at any level, Spanish students of English being no exception. To analyse the problems that Spanish students have with English prepositions so as to better address them in the classroom, we carried out a four-year longitudinal study.

2. Prepositions: a problem for many students

2.1 The importance and complexity of English prepositions

The fact that English prepositions are difficult for Spanish learners of English is evident from our own learning and teaching experience. This seems due to two main aspects: their relevance and their complexity (Casas Pedrosa 2005). The frequency of prepositions makes it essential for the teacher to raise students' awareness of their importance. There is at least one preposition in most English sentences, and the prepositions *of*, *to*, and *in* are among the ten most frequent words in the Bank of English (BoE) (Sinclair 1991: vi). The twenty most frequent words in the British National Corpus (BNC) (XML edition) also include *for, on, with, at, by* (in order of descending frequency).

Prepositions are complicated both in Spanish and English, so learning them is a long, hard process (Watcyn-Jones & Allsop 1990: 5). There is no standard list of the units that should be classified as English prepositions, and it is not even clear whether they should be considered a closed or an open class. One of their main features is their morphological fuzziness: many words can be analysed as prepositions, adverbs or conjunctions depending on their syntactic behaviour. Consider *before*, which behaves as a preposition, an adverb, and a conjunction respectively in *I shall arrive in Paris before you*; *I have never been in Paris before*; *I shall have read it before you return from Paris* (Merino 1982: 3).

Syntactically speaking, prepositions are best studied as parts of larger units rather than as isolated ones. They often follow adjectives (*aware of, suitable for*), nouns (*access to, comments on*) and verbs (*focus on, listen to*), where they bind the elements preceding and following them. In these cases their presence may be regarded as imposed by other word choices (which is why they are called "dependent"). They also play an important role in introducing idioms and frozen expressions, such as *in a stew*, *off the boil*, *on tenterhooks*, *under the weather*.

From a semantic viewpoint, most prepositions are polysemous (conveying not only place and time, but also other notions). *To*, for instance, may express a locative meaning (direction) in *To the airport, please* (Hall 1986: 11), time in *It's already a quarter to six, let's go home* (Hall 1986: 36), or one of transformation in *I'm going to change to a healthier margarine* (Hall 1986: 87). Many English prepositions present both literal and metaphorical meanings: *into* is literal in *The silent figure disappeared into the wood* (Hall 1986:11), but metaphorical in *She fell into a deep depression* (Lindstromberg 1998: 75). Needless to say, the polysemous nature of prepositions also affects their translation from and into English (Hall 1986).

Contrastive analyses of English and Spanish prepositions (Rivas 1981; Merino 1982; Rosset 1995) highlight the difficulties that Spanish learners of English encounter with prepositions in the foreign language. This is not surprising considering that Spanish students make mistakes with prepositions even in their mother tongue (Escarpanter 1992).

2.2 Use of prepositions by learners of English from different L1 backgrounds

English prepositions have been shown to be problematic for students from many different L1 backgrounds.

- Aarts & Granger's (1998) analysis of the Dutch, Finnish and French subcorpora of ICLE, tagged using the TOSCA-ICE tagset, revealed general underuse of patterns involving prepositions, including the four most common ones in a native-speaker corpus, the Louvain Corpus of Native English Essays (LOCNESS).[1] Only two patterns including prepositions were overused, in all three subcorpora.[2]

- Granger & Rayson (1998), who used a reduced version of the CLAWS4 tagset (Garside & Smith 1997) to profile French-speaking learners' written English, also found general underuse of prepositions in comparison to LOCNESS data.[3]
- Ringbom (1998), who compared wordlists from the Dutch, Finnish, Finnish-Swedish, French, German, Spanish and Swedish ICLE subcorpora, found that the prepositions *by* and *from* were underused by all seven learner groups when compared to LOCNESS.
- Tono's (2002) study, which used the CLAWS C7 tagset to examine the top trigrams in subcorpora of his *Japanese English as a Foreign Language Learner* (JEFLL) corpus, suggests that Japanese students also underuse patterns involving prepositions, since of the 9 trigrams present in LOCNESS but not in his learner data, 7 contained prepositions.
- Leńko-Szymańska (2004) also used CLAWS for her study of Polish students'use of English demonstratives based on The Polish English-Learner Corpus Research and Applications (PELCRA) corpus. She found that in postmodification structures used with these demonstratives, prepositional phrases were underused.
- Prat Zagrebelsky (2004) did not use part-of-speech tagging but did employ the error tagset devised for the ICLE project (Dagneaux et al. 1996) in her study of Italian learners. The error category Lexico-

1 This is a corpus of native-speaker English following the same design criteria as the subcorpora collected for ICLE. As a result, it is normally used as a comparable native-speaker corpus with the ICLE data.

2 The patterns are "preposition + pronoun + punctuation" and "adverb + adjective + preposition" (Aarts & Granger 1998: 138).

3 The specific prepositions underused were *after, along, amongst, by, despite, for, including, into, off, out, over, per, regarding, than, throughout, to, until, up,* and *upon. About, above, among, before, between, by means of, during, in front of, in spite of, of, on, thanks to, till, towards* and *without* showed the opposite tendency (Granger & Rayson 1998: 123–127).

grammar ranked in fourth position, with dependent prepositions[4] and the distinction between countable and uncountable nouns having the highest percentages of errors.

Many studies have suggested that such difficulties are largely due to the influence of the L1:

- Waibel (2002, cited in Prat Zagrebelsky 2004: 100) compared the German and the Italian ICLE subcorpora, finding that dependent prepositions were difficult for Italian learners, with more than 50% of the errors due to L1 influence.
- Cowan et al. (2003) highlight the problems that Korean students have with prepositions following verbs, preceding noun phrases and the unnecessary addition of prepositions after some verbs, which they claim stem from L1 influence.
- Tanimura et al.'s (2004) analysis of Japanese students' errors using prepositions in the National Institute of Information and Communications Technology Japanese Learner English (NICT JLE) Corpus (Tono et al. 2002) shows that the number of incorrect use of prepositions decreases as the level of the students increases. Particularly persistent across proficiency levels, despite a decrease from low to intermediate levels, are errors of omission, where *in* and *to* cause most problems because of L1 transfer.[5]
- Koosha & Jafarpour (2006), in a study of the effect of Data-Driven Learning on Iranian students' production of prepositions, analysed errors on a translation task on the collocation of prepositions, finding that 68.4% of errors were due to L1 interference.

The problems that various groups of learners have with prepositions have also been considered in analysing collocations (Nesselhauf 2003, 2005) and signalling nouns (Flowerdew 2006). Prepositions also seem to be a problem when learning languages other than English, as a study

4 By "dependent prepositions", the UCLEE (Dagneaux et al. 1996) and Lindstromberg (1998) mean prepositions which depend on an adjective, noun or verb.

5 In speaking of 'influence', 'interference' or 'transfer', we have maintained the terminology used by the authors.

of English, German, Japanese, Polish, Swedish and Thai students of Spanish has shown (Alonso Alonso & Palacios Martínez 1994).

2.3 Use of prepositions by Spanish students of English

The use of prepositions by Spanish learners of English has been analysed at various levels.

Primary school students

- Benítez Pérez & Simón Granda (1990) compiled a corpus of free essays and completion tasks in English and French, finding an underuse of prepositions, with clear interference from the L1 and a tendency to associate them in a one-to-one correspondence.

Secondary school students

- In a cross-sectional study of written production, Bueno González (1992) found that prepositions were the word class with the highest percentage of errors, accounting for 26.56% of all errors in his corpus. Errors with prepositions were ranked first in all the years of secondary education but the second.
- Jiménez Catalán (1996), using a surface taxonomy (Dulay et al. 1982: 150–163), found that addition and omission of prepositions came in the sixth and seventh positions respectively, stemming from literal translation from the L1.[6]
- Alonso Alonso (1997), who divided errors into overextension of analogy, transfer of structure, interlingual/intralingual and substitution errors, found that problems with prepositions were caused by transfer of structure and, to a lesser extent, overextension of analogy.
- Bazo Martínez (2001) suggests that incorrect preposition use by students at this level in the Canary Islands is due to negative interference.

The use of prepositions in the written production by Spanish students at years 2, 3 and 5 in Official Language Schools was studied by Moreno

6 Data for the substitution of prepositions is not provided in the article, only the percentages for the top ten errors being given.

Ibáñez and Ruiz Gracia (1985), who concluded that overgeneralization is the main reason for errors, preposition errors among them.[7]

University students

- García Gómez & Bou Franch (1992) focused on errors due to L1 interference in second year university students. Syntactic errors were the most frequent (63 %), prepositions amounting to 26.47 % of the errors in this category and, therefore, 16.66 % of all errors in their corpus (García – Gómez & Bou Franch 1992: 282). González Cruz (1996) analysed the role of transfer in essays written by students in her university.[8] Preposition errors accounted for 20 % of the errors in her corpus, 80 % of these being due to transfer from the L1.
- Valero Garcés (1997) analysed the written production of first-year university students using a different error tagset, divided into spelling, morphology, syntax, vocabulary, omission, addition and others. Syntactic errors were the most frequent, prepositions scoring 28.5 %. Further preposition errors were categorised as omissions.[9]
- Navarro i Ferrando & Tricker (2000–2001) gave first and third year students elicitation tasks such as sentence generation and analysis with the central and radial senses of *at*, *in* and *on*. Notwithstanding the students' familiarity with all the senses, they were unable to use them fluently or creatively.
- In a study of empty categories (i.e. omissions) in the oral production by Spanish immigrants in London and students at three levels at the Universidad de Santiago de Compostela, Cebreiros Álvarez (2004, 2005) noted that preposition omissions due to transfer were less common in immigrants than students, and that the percentage of preposition omissions due to transfer increased with proficiency.[10]

7 At the time of publication of the paper, courses at the Official Language Schools in Spain consisted of five years divided into two stages (3 + 2 years).

8 Unfortunately, the year the students are taking at university is not stated.

9 Percentages are not given for errors with prepositions in the omission category.

10 The author explains that this increase stems from cases of overgeneralization and the production of more complex structures, including preposition stranding (Cebreiros Álvarez 2004: 44).

- Díez-Bedmar (2004, 2005) conducted an analysis of the written production of first-year students in her UCLEE error-tagged learner corpus. Lexical selection was one of the main problematic areas, and within this error category prepositions accounted for 25 % of the errors, outnumbered only by the instances of misuses of verbs (39 %).[11]

The Spanish subcorpus of the ICLE project has also been used to describe Spanish university students' production in English.

- The use of prepositions by fourth-year university students, as reflected in a part of the SPICLE corpus, is described in Martínez Osés & Neff Van Aertselaer (2001), who tagged it with TOSCA and compared it with LOCNESS. It was evident that native speakers used a wider variety of prepositions, even though the first ten items were very similar in both corpora. Unlike the students of the L1s analysed in Granger & Rayson (1998), Spanish students did not significantly underuse prepositions as a whole, but they did underuse *on* and *out of*, overused *according to*, *between*, *in*, *inside*, *of*, and *thanks to*,[12] and misused *in* (Martínez Osés & Neff Van Aertselaer 2001).
- In a study of grammatical collocations, lexical collocations and idiomatic expressions in SPICLE, Ballesteros et al. (2005) found that wrong use of prepositions was the most frequent grammatical collocation error (65 %).

To sum up, Spanish students of English also have problems with prepositions when using the foreign language, which seems largely to stem from L1 influence. However, the different error taxonomies used, the lack of information concerning students' proficiency level and indeed the methodology employed, do not provide a clear picture of the problems that Spanish learners of English have with this word class. To the best of our knowledge, there are no longitudinal analyses of the prepositions which pose most problems at university level, and the pattern(s)

11 The prepositions in this error category are independent ones.

12 This overuse was also noticed in French students' production (Granger & Rayson 1998).

in the acquisition and improvement of preposition use (if any) have not been explored yet. Hence the need for a study to provide better insight into Spanish university students' use of prepositions, so that we can design and use appropriate graded materials in teaching them.

3. Methodology

A longitudinal learner corpus was compiled at the University of Jaén during the academic years 2002–2003 to 2005–2006. It consists of English compositions produced for exams or in exam-like situations by 28 student volunteers who began their degree course in English Studies (*Filología Inglesa*) in 2002–2003. As expected in any longitudinal study, there was drop out: only 13 of the 28 finished their degree in the four years. As a result, the number of samples varied from one year to another.

For this study only part of this corpus has been used, consisting of 164 compositions (mainly descriptive) totalling 69,980 words (Table 1). In the first two years these were written for the annual courses in English usage, *Inglés Instrumental Intermedio* and *Inglés Instrumental Avanzado*. In the third and fourth years, where there are no such courses, they were written during classes kindly offered by other lecturers for the purpose. To ensure comparability, the same time limits were always imposed, and no access to reference materials was permitted.

	Number of essays	*Number of words*
year 1	67	26,259
year 2	43	16,465
year 3	29	15,874
year 4	25	11,382
Totals	164	69,980

Table 1. Part of the corpus used in the present study.

In order to find out which prepositions were the most problematic ones, we followed Granger's Integrated Contrastive Model *a posteriori* (1996: 44).

First, we compared students' use of prepositions in the four years by means of a CIA. The corpus had been previously error tagged using UCLEE (Hutchinson 1996) and the error-tagging manual version 1.1 (Dagneaux et al. 1996). Instances of misused prepositions were retrieved from the general error category Lexical Selection (LS) using *WordSmith Tools* (Scott 1999). The error categories Word Missing and Word Redundant were also checked for cases of prepositions.[13] This enabled us to shortlist 27 prepositions which had caused problems to these students (Table 2), and to retrieve all the instances of their correct use, again using *WordSmith Tools*. Numbers of correct and incorrect uses each year were calculated for each preposition, to see whether there was any overall statistically significant development pattern.

About	*Behind*	*In*	*Since*
Across	*Besides*	*Inside*	*Throughout*
Along	*Between*	*Instead of*	*To*
Around	*By*	*Into*	*Under*
As	*During*	*Like*	*Up to*
At	*For*	*Of*	*With*
Back	*from*	*On*	

Table 2. Problematic prepositions in the longitudinal learner corpus.

Second, we conducted contrastive analyses of those prepositions for which the proportion of errors showed statistically significant differences (either negative or positive), using Sinclair's (1991) and Merino's (1982) works on English prepositions and examples from the BNC and the Corpus de Referencia del Español Actual (CREA) corpus of Spanish.

13 The other categories which involve incorrect use of prepositions in the Error Editor (XNPR, XVPR, XADJPR) were not considered, since they deal with dependent prepositions (cf. Dagneaux et al. 1996).

4. Results

Comparing the percentages of correct and incorrect uses of prepositions over the four years, four patterns can be seen.

- Positive evolution, or a decrease in the percentage of errors over time. Prepositions following this pattern are *around*, *as*, *at*, *between*, *by*, *during*, *for*, *in*, *inside*, *like*, *of* and *to*.
- Negative evolution, or an increase in erroneous use over time. Prepositions following this pattern are *on*, *since* and *with*.
- The use of two prepositions, *along* and *from*, followed an irregular pattern, with fluctuations from one academic year to the next. For instance, the errors with *from* increased from year 1 to year 2, then fell in year 3, to rise again in year 4.
- Finally ten prepositions, *about*, *across*, *back*, *behind*, *besides*, *instead of*, *into*, *throughout*, *under* and *up to*, presented no errors in three out of the four academic years.

The accuracy with which students use prepositions thus shows four different patterns of development, not all of them desirable. Table 3 lists the prepositions in each:

Pattern	*Prepositions*
Positive evolution	*around*, *as*, *at*, *between*, *by*, *during*, *for*, *in*, *inside*, *like*, *of and to* (12)
Negative evolution	*on*, *since* and *with* (3)
Irregular evolution	*along* and *from* (2)
Frequency 0	*about*, *across*, *back*, *behind*, *besides*, *instead of*, *into*, *throughout*, *under* and *up to* (10)

Table 3. Prepositions within each pattern of development.

The highest number of prepositions is found in the positive evolution pattern, which shows that our students managed to make more appropriate use of those twelve prepositions as they studied for their degrees. Nevertheless, three prepositions showed the opposite trend, with a growing proportion of errors as time progressed. Finally, the use of two prepositions fluctuated from year to year, yielding unexpected results, while other prepositions showed no instances of erroneous use.

A chi-square analysis was carried out to see where the differences between the proportions of correct and incorrect uses of each preposition were statistically significant. This showed that the differences for *in*, *like* and *on* were statistically significant at the <0.05 level (*p*-values 0.0021, 0.0395 and 0.0428 respectively).[14] A binomial proportion for these three prepositions for the four years was then performed (Table 4):

	years					
Prepositions ($p < 0.05$)	1–2	1–3	1–4	2–3	2–4	3–4
In	X	✓	✓	✓	✓	X
Like	X	X	✓	X	X	X
On	✓	X	X	✓	✓	X

Table 4. Statistical significance of changes in error rates for *in, like* and *on.*

If we focus on consecutive years, only the differences between the second and the third for *in* and *on* are significant. It seems that there is a crucial stage, positive for *in* and negative for *on*, from the second to the third year. Between the first and the second years no significant differences were found apart from the preposition *on*, this lack of significant difference also being the pattern between the third and the fourth years. Differences between the first and the last year were present for *in* and *like*,[15] which was to be expected. However, the difference between the second and the fourth years was also significant for *in* and *on*.

After conducting a contrastive analysis of these three prepositions, we decided to focus on the preposition *in*, since it is the one which students used most frequently, both correctly and incorrectly (42% and 35% respectively). Following Lindstromberg (1998), we divided its senses into locative, temporal, and others. Out of the 104 incorrect instances, we found that most occurred in the expression of locative meanings (72%), followed by temporal ones (24%) and by other meanings (4%). Table 5 shows the prepositions that should have been used.

14 Attention should also be paid to the preposition *of*, whose *p*-value was ($p<0.0583$).
15 This was also the case of the preposition *of*.

	Along	*At*	*By*	*From*	*Of*	*On*	*Round*	*With*	Total
Place	1	21		3		49	1		75 (72 %)
Time		22				3			25 (24 %)
Others			1		2			1	4 (4 %)
Total	1	43	1	3	2	52	1	1	104 (100 %)

Table 5. Target prepositions when incorrectly using the preposition *in*.

The main reason for our students making so many mistakes with this preposition is the existence of a single preposition in Spanish (*en*) which conveys the spatial meanings of at least three English ones (*at*, *by* and *on*), as can be seen in examples (1)–(3) and their translations (our own).

(1) I think it was (LS) **in** Christmas' Eve. (1-b-23)
Creo que fue ***en*** *Nochebuena.*

(2) I had never travelled (LS) **in** plane [...] (1-a-13)
Yo nunca había viajado ***en*** *avión [...]*

(3) [...] he came and saw me sleeping (LS) **in** the floor. (2-a-14)
[...] él vino y me vio durmiendo ***en*** *el suelo.*

Whether *en* should be translated into English as *at*, *by* or *on* depends on the specific notion it refers to and on the context in which it is found. Examining the incorrect uses of these three prepositions in the corpus, 89 % were translatable using *en* (95 % for locative meanings, 80 % for temporal ones, and 50 % for others).

In order to understand why these students had problems with the preposition *in*, we analysed all 104 erroneous instances to see what Spanish preposition would have been an appropriate translation (see examples (4)–(7) below). *En* clearly outnumbers the other two possible prepositions, *de* and *por*, along with cases where no preposition is needed in Spanish.

	De	*En*	*Por*	(No translation)	Total
Place	2.67%	94.66%	2.67%	–	100 %
Time	12 %	80%	8%	–	100 %
Others	50%	50%	–	–	100 %
Total	3.85%	89.42%	3.85%	2.88%	100 %

Table 6. Breakdown of Spanish prepositions.

(4) I live in the center of the city (LS) **in** Sao Paulo. (2-c-20)
Yo vivo en el centro ***de*** *la ciudad de Sao Paulo.*

(5) They had to send us our things (LS) **in** the next flight. (2-a-8)
Ellos tenían que mandarnos nuestras cosas ***en*** *el vuelo siguiente.*

(6) I was walking alone (LS) **in** a long street. (1-c-23)
Yo estaba caminando sólo ***por*** *una calle larga.*

(7) It is what I do (LS) **in** the weekends. (1-b-10)
Eso es lo que yo hago ***Ø*** *los fines de semana.*

Needless to say, the presence of a single preposition in Spanish and three or more in English means students have to decide among a greater number of prepositions and are more likely to make mistakes. Even though they are told not to translate from Spanish into English when producing the foreign language, they clearly tend to do so.

5. Conclusions

Our research provides a shortlist of twenty-seven English prepositions which were problematic to our Spanish university students. Scholars using various methodologies have already mentioned the problems that some of these pose (*between*, *from*, *of*, *on*, and *thanks to*) to students from various L1 backgrounds, including Spanish (cf. Pavesi 1987; Granger & Rayson 1998; Ringbom 1998; Martínez Osés & Neff Van Aertselaer 2001). Comparing students' preposition use over the four years of the degree, it appears that:

- Prepositions following a positive evolution pattern, with progressive improvement, include six of the eight most frequent prepositions in the BNC (Leech et al. 2001), namely *of*, *in*, *to*, *for*, *by* and *at* (in frequency order). This may be due to the extensive reading and listening input that students receive at university.
- The prepositions *on*, *since* and *with* show a negative pattern of evolution, i.e. the proportion of errors in their use increases over the four years. This suggests that these prepositions should be singled out in teaching, focussing on those uses students have difficulty with.

- The other patterns identified, i.e. irregular evolution and frequency 0, deserve further research. They may include cases of avoidance (Schachter 1974), with changing percentages of errors being due to the limited number of examples in the corpus.
- The high number of occurrences of *in* (both correct and incorrect) may be due to overgeneralization, with *in* being preferred to other prepositions. *In* is, after all, the second most common preposition in the BNC. The proportions of incorrect uses could also be consequences of overuse or underuse of other prepositions. This would call for more detailed analysis, and comparison with a native speaker corpus such as LOCNESS.
- The influence of the L1 seems both positive and negative. It helps learners in those cases where we find a one-to-one correspondence between English and Spanish preposition use (e.g. *As a conclusion/Como conclusión*), and confuses them where a single English preposition conveys different senses in Spanish or the other way round. For instance, the English preposition *by* can be translated into Spanish as *en, junto a*, *por* and *tras*: *by car/en coche, the girl by the window/la chica junto a la ventana*, *a book written by Hardy/un libro escrito por Hardy*, *year by year/año tras año* etc. Therefore, students should be taught not to disregard the similarities and differences between languages.
- Students seem to get familiar first with the prototypical meanings of prepositions and only later with secondary ones, since mistakes concerning the former are rarer than those concerning the latter. In this respect their learning process seems quite similar to that of native speakers (Lindstromberg 1998).

In terms of pedagogical implications, our study supports the view that prepositions should not be taught as isolated items but in meaningful contexts. As we are in favour of the explicit teaching of prepositions, we would suggest that language awareness exercises and remedial work focus on the phrase level rather than on the word level. Many mistakes could be avoided if students noticed that particular prepositions are often imposed by the elements which precede or follow them. If students were taught phrases or "chunks", they would make fewer mistakes: if, for example, they learnt that the prepositions which usually precede the nouns *moment* and *floor* are *at* and *on*, respectively, they would improve their use of these two prepositions, which accounted for 12.5 % and 17.3 % of all errors. These features should be taken into account when designing teaching materials, as well as dictionaries specialised in the translation of prepositions from English into Spanish such as Rosset (1995).

While most attention has been given to quantitative analysis of this corpus, it is hoped to carry out an in-depth qualitative analysis of all prepositional uses (both correct and incorrect) in the future, looking for particular learning trends (if any) and particular problems relating to specific senses. It would be interesting to compare findings with the ICLE subcorpora to see if students with other L1s struggle with the same prepositions.

Acknowledgments

The authors would like to thank Sonia Castillo Gutiérrez, from the Department of Statistics at the University of Jaén, for her help with statistical analysis.

References

Aarts J. & S. Granger (1998) Tag sequences in learner corpora. In Granger S. (ed.) *Learner English on computer*. London and New York: Addison Wesley Longman, 132–141.

Alonso Alonso M. R. (1997) Language transfer: Interlingual errors in Spanish students of English as a foreign language. *Revista Alicantina de Estudios Ingleses* 10, 7–14.

Alonso Alonso M. R. & I. M. Palacios Martínez (1994) Expresión escrita y transferencia: análisis de errores en la lengua escrita de estudiantes de español como segunda lengua. *REALE* 2, 23–37.

Aston G., S. Bernardini & D. Stewart (eds) (2004) *Corpora and language learners*. Amsterdam: John Benjamins.

Ballesteros F., J. P. Rica, J. Neff Van Aertselaer & M. Díez Prados (2005) The ICLE error tagging project: analysis of Spanish EFL writers. In Mourón Figueroa C. & T. I. Moralejo Gárate (eds) *Studies in contrastive linguistics. Proceedings of the 4th International Contrastive Linguistics Conference, September 2005*. Santiago de Compostela: Servizo de Publicacións e Intercambio Científico, 89–97.

Bazo Martínez, P. (2001) A qualitative analysis of the interlanguage found in compulsory secondary education students in the Canary Islands. *Revista Canaria de Estudios Ingleses* 43, 209–218.

Benítez Pérez P. & J. Simón Granda (1990) Adquisición de la preposición en la primera y segunda lengua. *RESLA* 6, 139–148.

Bueno González A. (1992) Errores en la elección de palabras en inglés por alumnos de Bachillerato y C. O. U. In Bueno González A., J. A. Carini Martínez & Á. Linde López *Análisis de errores en inglés: tres casos prácticos*. Granada: Servicio de Publicaciones de la Universidad de Granada, 39–105.

Casas Pedrosa A. V. (2005) Teaching English prepositions to Spanish speakers: some aspects to bear in mind. *Greta* 13(1–2), 94–101.

Cebreiros Álvarez R. (2004) The operation of transfer and interlanguage principles: the case of empty categories in the interlanguage of Spanish learners of English. *VIAL* 1, 33–54.

Cebreiros Álvarez R. (2005) The operation of transfer and interlanguage principles: the case of empty categories in the interlanguage of Spanish learners of English. In Calvo García de Leonardo J. J., J. Tronch Pérez, M. del Sanz Rubio, C. Manuel Cuenca, B. Pennock Speck & M. J. Coperías Aguilar (eds) *Actas XXVIII Congreso Internacional AEDEAN*. Valencia: Servicio de Publicaciones de la Universidad de Valencia, 132–139.

Cosme, C., C. Gouverneur, F. Meunier & M. Paquot (2005) *Proceedings of the phraseology 2005 conference*. Louvain-la-Neuve.

Cowan, R., H. E. Choi & D. H. Kim (2003) Four questions for error diagnosis and correction in CALL. *CALICO Journal* 20(3), 451–463.

Dagneaux E., S. Denness, S. Granger & F. Meunier (1996) *Error tagging manual version 1.1*. Louvain-la-Neuve: Centre for English Corpus Linguistics, Université Catholique de Louvain.

Díez-Bedmar M. B. (2004) *Approaches to the interlanguage evolution of first-year students at the University of Jaén*. Unpublished MA Dissertation. University of Jaén.

Díez-Bedmar M.B. (2005) Struggling with English at university level: error patterns and problematic areas of first-year students' interlanguage. In Danielsson, P. & M. Wagenmakers (eds) *The corpus linguistics conference series* (available online at <http://www.corpus.bham.ac.uk/PCLC/>, last accessed on 07/05/2008).

Dulay H. C., M. K. Burt & S. Krashen (1982) *Language two*. Oxford: Oxford University Press.

Escarpanter J. (1992) *Eso no se dice. El rompecabezas de las preposiciones*. Madrid: Playor.

Flowerdew J. (2006) Use of signalling nouns in a learner corpus. *International Journal of Corpus Linguistics* 11, 209–226.

García Gómez E. & P. Bou Franch (1992) Estudio experimental sobre interferencias lingüísticas. In Losada Durán, J. R. & M. Mansilla (eds) *Actas VIII Congreso Nacional de Lingüística Aplicada, 2–4 mayo 1990*. Vigo: Sevicio de Publicaciones de la Universidad de Vigo, 279–291.

Garside R. & N. Smith (1997) A hybrid grammatical tagger: CLAWS4. In Garside R., G. Leech & T. McEnery (eds) *Corpus annotation: Linguistic information from computer text corpora.* Harlow: Addison Wesley Longman, 102–121.

Ghadessy M., A. Henry & R.L. Roseberry (eds) (2001) *Small corpus studies and ELT. Theory and practice.* Amsterdam and Philadelphia: John Benjamins.

Gilquin G., S. Papp & M.B. Díez-Bedmar (eds) (in press) *Linking up contrastive and learner corpus research.* Amsterdam and New York: Rodopi.

González Cruz M.I. (1996) The role of Spanish transfer: the need to include contrastive analysis in EFL teaching. In González Fernández-Corugedo S. (ed.) *Some sundry wits gathered together.* A Coruña: Servicio de Publicacións da Universidade da Coruña, 55–71.

Granger S. (1996) From CA to CIA and back. An integrated approach to computerized bilingual and learner corpora. In Aijmer K., B. Altenberg & S. Johansson (eds) *Languages in contrast.* Lund: Lund University Press, 37–51.

Granger S. (ed.) (1998) *Learner English on computer.* London and New York: Addison Wesley Longman.

Granger S., E. Dagneaux & F. Meunier (eds) (2002) *The International Corpus of Learner English. Handbook and CD-ROM.* Louvain-la-Neuve: Presses Universitaires de Louvain.

Granger S., J. Hung & S. Petch-Tyson (eds) (2002) *Computer learner corpora, second language acquisition and foreign language teaching.* Amsterdam and Philadelphia: John Benjamins.

Granger S. & S. Petch-Tyson (eds) (2003) *Extending the scope of corpus-based research. New applications, new challenges.* Amsterdam and New York: Rodopi.

Granger S. & P. Rayson (1998) Automatic profiling of learner texts. In Granger, S. (ed.) *Learner English on computer.* London and New York: Addison Wesley Longman, 119–131.

Hall D. (1986) *Working with English prepositions.* Surrey: Nelson.

Hutchinson J. (1996) *UCL error editor.* Louvain-la-Neuve: Centre for English Corpus Linguistics, Université Catholique de Louvain.

Jiménez Catalán R.M. (1996) Frequency and variability in errors in the use of English prepositions. *Miscelánea: A Journal of English and American Studies* 17, 171–187.

Ketteman B. & G. Marko (eds) (2002) *Teaching and learning by doing corpus analysis.* Amsterdam: Rodopi.

Koosha M. & A.A. Jafarpour (2006) Data-driven learning and teaching collocation of prepositions: the case of Iranian EFL Adult Learners. *Asian EFL Journal* 8(4), 192–209 (available online at <http://www.asian-efl-journal.com/Dec_06_mk&aaj.php>, last accessed 07/05/2008).

Leech G., P. Rayson & A. Wilson (2001) *Word frequencies in written and spoken English: based on the British National Corpus.* London: Longman (word lists available online at <http://www.comp.lancs.ac.uk/ucrel/bncfreq/>, last accessed 07/05/2008).

Leńko-Szymańska A. (2004) Demonstratives as anaphora markers in advanced learners' English. In Aston, G., S. Bernardini & D. Stewart (eds) *Corpora and language learners*. Amsterdam and Philadelphia: John Benjamins, 89–107.

Lindstromberg S. (1998) *English prepositions explained*. Amsterdam: John Benjamins.

Martínez Osés F. & J. Neff Van Aertselaer (2001) Corpus analysis of prepositional patterns in native and non-native university writing. In Muñoz C., M.L. Celaya, M. Fernández-Villanueva, T. Navés, O. Strunk & E. Tragant (eds) *Trabajos en lingüística aplicada*. Barcelona: Univerbook, 139–147.

Merino J. (1982) *Las preposiciones inglesas y sus ejercicios*. Madrid: C.E.E.I.

Moreno Ibáñez C. & C. Ruiz Gracia (1985) Aplicación de las teorías del análisis de errores a un caso práctico. In Fernández F. (ed.) *Pasado, presente y futuro de la lingüística aplicada en España*. Valencia: Servicio de Publicaciones de la Universidad de Valencia, 371–377.

Navarro i Ferrando I. & D. Tricker (2000–2001) A comparison of the use of *at*, *in*, and *on* by EFL students and native speakers. *RESLA* 14, 295–324.

Nesselhauf N. (2003) The use of collocations by advanced learners of English and some implications for teaching. *Applied Linguistics* 24, 223–242.

Nesselhauf, N. (2005) *Collocations in a learner corpus*. Amsterdam: John Benjamins.

Pavesi M. (1987) Variability and systematicity in the acquisition of spatial prepositions. In Ellis R. (ed.) *Second language acquisition in context*. Englewood Cliffs, NJ: Prentice-Hall, 73–82.

Prat Zagrebelsky M.T. (2004) *Computer learner corpora. Theoretical issues and empirical case studies of Italian advanced EFL learners' interlanguage*. Alessandria: Edizioni dell'Orso.

Ringbom H. (1998) Vocabulary frequencies in advanced learner English: a cross-linguistic approach. In Granger S. (ed.) *Learner English on computer*. London and New York: Addison Wesley Longman, 41–52.

Rivas D.J. (1981) *Prepositions in Spanish and English: A contrastive study and sample thesaurus based on the Spanish word count taken at the University of Puerto Rico. 1952*. Montevideo: Géminis.

Rosset E.R. (1995) *Dictionary of English to Spanish prepositions*. Irún: Stanley.

Schachter J. (1974) An error in error analysis. *Language learning* 27, 205–214.

Scott, M. (1999) *WordSmith Tools, Version 3.0*. Oxford: Oxford University Press.

Sinclair J.M. (ed.) (1991) *Collins COBUILD English guides 1. Prepositions*. London: HarperCollins.

Sinclair J.M. (ed.) (2004) *How to use corpora in language teaching*. Amsterdam: John Benjamins.

Tanimura M., K. Takeuchi & H. Isahara (2004) From learners' corpora to expert knowledge description: Analyzing prepositions in the NICT JLE (Japanese Learner English) Corpus. *IWLel 2004: An Interactive Workshop on Language e-Learning*, 139–147.

Tono Y. (2002) *The role of learner corpora in SLA research and foreign language teaching: the multiple comparison approach*. Unpublished doctoral dissertation. Lancaster University.

Tono Y., T. Kaneko, H. Isahara, T. Saiga & E. Izumi (2002) The Standard Speaking Test Corpus. *Studies in Lexicography* 11(2), 7–18.

Valero Garcés C. (1997) The interlanguage of Spanish students beginning English Philology. *GRETA* 5(2), 74–78.

Waibel B. (2002) *A corpus-based approach to learner language: a comparative study of Italian and German learners of English*. Unpublished MA thesis. Freiburg (Germany).

Watcyn-Jones P. & J. Allsop (1990) *Test your prepositions*. London: Penguin.

Part three
Resources and tools: Creation

SARA CASTAGNOLI, DRAGOS CIOBANU, KERSTIN KUNZ,
NATALIE KÜBLER & ALEXANDRA VOLANSCHI

Designing a Learner Translator Corpus for Training Purposes

Abstract

This paper presents the development of the MeLLANGE corpus, a multilingual, aligned and annotated learner tranlsator corpus (LTC). Unlike other learner corpora, MeLLANGE focuses on translation-related rather than language acquisition issues. The corpus contains thus students performance into their mother tongues. Moreover, the intention is not to deliver a repository od students errors, but rather give both trainers and trainees the opportunity to identify possible translation problems, as well as possible solutions, in a multilingual, corpus-based environment. The information attached to the corpus is divide into metadata regarding the soruce text, the translator and the translation situation, lingusitic annotation, and erro-annotation according to an error typology developed in the project. We show examples of how the MeLLANGE corpus can be exploited in teaching translation from a data-driven point of view, and from a data-based point of view.

1. Introduction

This article sets out to present the development of a multilingual annotated Learner Translator Corpus (hereafter LTC) – a corpus whose core is composed of translations produced by trainee translators and whose primary purpose is to provide insights into the most significant characteristics of such texts in order to inform translation pedagogy. The LTC was designed in the framework of the EU-funded Leonardo da Vinci project called MeLLANGE (*Multilingual e-Learning in LANGuage Engineering*) which aims at devising a methodology for the collaborative creation of eLearning teaching content in the fields of translation and translation technology, producing corpus-based teaching materials and, more ambitiously, establishing a framework for a European Master in Translation Technologies.[1]

The MeLLANGE LTC collects student translations of selected texts in all the language pairs commonly taught in the translation departments of the project's partners. In addition to these, the corpus contains some reference translations, namely translations produced by professional translators. Detailed information on how source texts (STs) were selected, on available language pairs, as well as on the whole collection procedure is provided in §3 below. In order to enhance the analysis of the student translations, a subset of the corpus was annotated with metadata and linguistic information, as well as error categories from an error typology specifically designed for the MeLLANGE project (see §4 below). A query tool was developed to take into account the exceptional structure of the LTC and enable queries involving error, metadata and linguistic categories – examples follow in §5.

The article concludes by presenting some statistics derived from the first analyses carried out on the LTC. Besides illustrating how the data were used for the immediate purposes of the MeLLANGE project, suggestions are made as to how these data can inform and support the "customisation" of teaching programmes and the development and improvement of (traditional and eLearning) teaching materials.

2. Project background and current research involving learner translation corpora

The idea that collecting and studying the output of trainee translators can provide useful information for translation teaching and research was first put forward at the end of the 1990s in pioneering projects such as Bowker and Bennison's *Student Translation Archive* (STA, Bowker & Bennison 2003) and the PELCRA project (Uzar & Waliński 2001).

1 Further details on MeLLANGE are available on the project's official website: <http://mellange.eila.univ-paris-diderot.fr>.

These principally aimed at identifying common problems in student translations – i.e. difficulties and errors – in order to improve teaching contents and materials. Similar objectives have been stated in the framework of recent studies, such as Florén's ENTRAD (2006; this volume) and Sosnina's *Russian Translation Learner Corpus* (RuTLC, Sosnina 2006). Overall, research of this type can be seen as standing at the crossroads between the translation corpora and the learner corpora research traditions, with translation students representing a special type of language learners whose *interlanguage* is the focus of investigation. Error analysis appears to be the most frequent type of analysis conducted on these learner translation corpora, even though they might also enable research on successful translation strategies and correct retextualisations.[2]

The four above-mentioned corpora differ mainly in terms of the languages involved, the translation direction, and the techniques/technology employed for corpus creation and querying. Most studies focus on translations into the students' native language in order to research translation-related phenomena, with the exception of the the PELCRA corpus, which was conceived as a tool for foreign language teaching (Uzar & Waliński 2001), and therefore includes student output in the foreign language. Table 1 summarises the main features of the four corpora referred to in this §as they relate to the MeLLANGE *Learner Translator Corpus*.

2 While pursuing a rather different goal, a corpus of student translations was also designed by Popescu-Beliş et al. (2002) for the automatic evaluation of Machine Translation systems. The authors' starting point was that MT evaluation tools would benefit from the existence of a set of reference translations against which to compute the similarity/difference of a further candidate translation, and that a corpus of student translations could be employed in order to have access not only to presumably gold-standard translations – produced by professional translators – but also to lower-quality, and even "imperfect", translations. This corpus has also been reported to be potentially helpful in "extract[ing] statistics about the types of translations mistakes, and the correlation between the distribution of mistakes in a translation and the grade scored by that translation" (2002: 18), which makes it resemble the objectives set by MeLLANGE and the other corpora previously mentioned. However, its stated purposc, dcsign and application set it apart and for the purpose of the present discussion it will not be analysed further.

Corpus	*SL(s)*	*TL(s)*	*TL status*	*Error*	*Availability annotation*
STA	FR, ES	EN	native	no	no
PELCRA LTC	PL	EN	foreign	yes	no
RuTLC	EN	RU	native	yes	no
ENTRAD	EN	ES	mixed	yes	online
MeLLANGE	DE, EN, FR, ES	CA, DE, EN, ES, IT, FR	native	yes	online

Table 1. Corpora details.

Being the result of a large-scale European project assembling partners from 7 countries, the MeLLANGE LTC is unique in terms of language coverage and number of students involved. What further distinguishes it from the other corpora under examination is its composite structure: it includes reference professional translations alongside student translations, with all texts being aligned at context level (see § 5 below). Compared to the only other corpus available online – ENTRAD – it enables complex queries – e. g. queries involving error types – and allows users to display different competing translations for a given sentence.

3. Building the LTC

The MeLLANGE LTC, which is being extended constantly, comprises originals of four different text types together with translations of these texts done by students and professional translators. The text types selected are: legal, technical, administrative, and journalistic.

This choice was motivated by the need to cover a spectrum of text types that professional translators handle most frequently, as well as to provide texts with various degrees of difficulty. The chosen materials were selected as being of a reasonable size to be put to pedagogic use – i.e. 350 words on average – and as available in at least all of the languages regularly used in the project partners' translation classes. Consequently, the legal text was offered for translation out of *da, de, el, en, es, fi, fr, it, nl* and *pt*, the technical and administrative ones out of *de, en, es, fr* and *it*, and finally the journalistic text out of *ca, de, en, es, fr* and *it*.

Following consultations with industry partners, in order to mirror real-life translation projects we provided translators with supporting information alongside the written material to be translated. This led to the building of *translation kits* containing a translation brief, the source text, and the longer passage from which the source text was extracted, which also contains additional background information. These translation kits were published on a collaborative content management system (CMS) – a Plone platform also used for project internal communication and collaboration purposes.

Students and professionals have translated under various conditions and using different methods: the translation tasks were either integrated into curricular translation courses offered at the partner institutions – as in-class or home assignments – or carried out as voluntary exercises. Translators could use various tools and resources –dictionaries, the Internet, corpora, translation memories, terminological databases, etc. Their translations were submitted to the MeLLANGE project through a customised upload mechanism implemented on the Plone platform, consisting of an HTML collection form linked to a MySQL database, which also recorded information related to the translation conditions mentioned above, as well as other metadata such as the duration of the translation task, the translator's native, second (and third) languages, and his/her university qualifications.

Before moving any further, we would like to stress that the MySQL database should not be confused with the MeLLANGE *Learner Translator Corpus* proper. While the former is an invaluable mechanism for storing translations and information about the author of the translation and the circumstances in which he/she produced it, the latter combines this information with tokenisation, lemmatisation, POS tagging and translation error annotation according to the MeLLANGE error categories (see §4), and also provides a complex and user-friendly query interface to all these data.

The MySQL database currently stores 152 translations into Italian, 74 into French, 62 into English, 49 into Catalan, 22 into Spanish, 15 into

German, 2 into Romanian and 1 into Slovak, the overwhelming majority of which were produced by trainee translators and a small minority by professional translators. Both students and professionals were required to provide translations into their own native language because the purpose of the LTC is to provide insights into the characteristics of texts translated by trainees, and not into how well learners master a second (target) language.

The next step in building the LTC after receiving the students' and professional translators' contributions was storing metadata related to the translator and to the conditions under which the translation was done. Having the translations stored in a MySQL database enables the easy retrieval of metadata together with the content to be post-processed and optimised for the LTC query tool. Annotators wishing to enrich the LTC with either or both linguistic information such as part-of-speech (POS) and lemma tags, and translation error categories, can download subsections of the LTC from the MySQL database which meet criteria relating to the text type, source and target languages and institutional affiliation of the translator.

Several POS taggers and lemmatisers have been used to generate the linguistic level of annotation, and a specialised tool – MMAX – was adapted within the project partnership to enable translation tutors teaching at the partner universities and having native knowledge of the target language to create the MeLLANGE error annotation level (see §4 below).

Within the LTC, professional translations are used as reference translation solutions. This allows a direct comparison of translation equivalents with and without errors thanks to a functionality of the LTC query tool which displays relevant corresponding contexts in the source and target languages – including any reference and student alternative translations available (see §5 for more details).

4. Annotating the LTC

4.1 Linguistic Annotation

The linguistic annotation of the translations stored in the LTC – i.e. tokenisation, POS tagging and lemmatisation – was performed automatically at each partner institution using either publicly-available or locally-developed tools. In order to ensure the coherence between the linguistic and error annotations, tokenisation of the translations to be included in the corpus was performed prior to both types of analyses. This operation is essential since tokens are the minimal units to which errors may be associated, i.e. the minimal markable elements (also known as "markables"). Thus, the tokenised files were also used as input files for the error annotation tool (see §4.2).

Table 2 provides a summary of the tools used for each language and of the size of the tagsets used by each partner:

	Tagger	*Tagset size*
EN	Tree-tagger	49 tags (Tree-tagger EN tagset)
DE	TnT-tagger	54 tags (Stuttgart-Tübingen-Tagset)
FR	In-house probabilistic tagger	43 tags (selected from the 300 tags used in the Paris 7 "Le Monde Corpus")
IT	Tree-tagger	52 tags (Tree-tagger IT tagset)
ES	Connexor tagger	36 tags (Connexor Tagset for Spanish)
CA	Catcg (Constraint Grammar formalism)	380 tags

Table 2. Tools and tagsets used for linguistic annotation.

As the table above suggests, the tagsets used (apart from the one used for annotating translations into Catalan) are of a similar size. Partners agreed that, given the specificity of each of the 6 languages involved, designing a common tagset would not be a realistic expectation. Nevertheless, partners agreed on a "reasonable" size that would be appropriate for the main purpose for which the LTC was built, namely concordancing involving translation errors made by trainee translators. This resulted in the simplification of existing tagsets – for instance, in the case of a highly inflected language such as French, the tagset used only distinguishes between *common* and *proper nouns*, instead of a richer variant which also distinguishes between *masculine*, *feminine*, *singular* and *plural nouns*. For the purposes of the LTC query mechanism – i. e. in order to enable users to search for parts of speech in a more user-friendly way than by studying the tagsets for each language – various tags were grouped under more generic categories such as *verb*, *adverb*, etc.

4.2 Error Annotation

While the lack of a common tagset could be easily bypassed by using more generic and transparent categories, the partnership was aware that allowing annotators to mark errors within translations using their own conventions would considerably complicate the coherence and uniformity of the annotation – and, consequently, the retrieval and analysis of error types. Before starting the process of collecting translations, therefore, the consortium researched and defined an error typology which would include all the categories of errors expected to be found in student translations in all the languages involved. The underlying assumption was that providing pre-defined error categories would enhance consistency across translations, language pairs and annotators, while being aware that this could not result in the complete absence of subjectivity in the interpretation and annotation of "erroneous" parts.

The survey of existing translation evaluation models, tools and schemes carried out by Secară (2005), which takes into account both academic and professional contexts, was used as a starting point to reflect on principles and useful error categories for our purposes. It must be noted, however, that contrary to the models which were considered, the MeLLANGE error typology is not meant to contribute to any evaluative process, the focus being on *describing* and studying specific translation phenomena rather than giving any quality judgment. Therefore, it does not provide for the encoding of the perceived "seriousness" or errors. Following the first annotation tests, the typology has undergone a process of intensive discussion, with modifications being suggested also by translation teachers at partner universities.

The result is a hierarchical scheme (*Fig. 1*) based on the fundamental distinction between content-related and language-related errors. These two main categories are further divided into subcategories, such as *SL Intrusion* or *Terminology and Lexis*, which in turn group more specific error types, such as *Too Literal* and *Inappropriate Collocation*. Each error type is marked by a code which is attached to erroneous words/phrases/sentences during the annotation process.

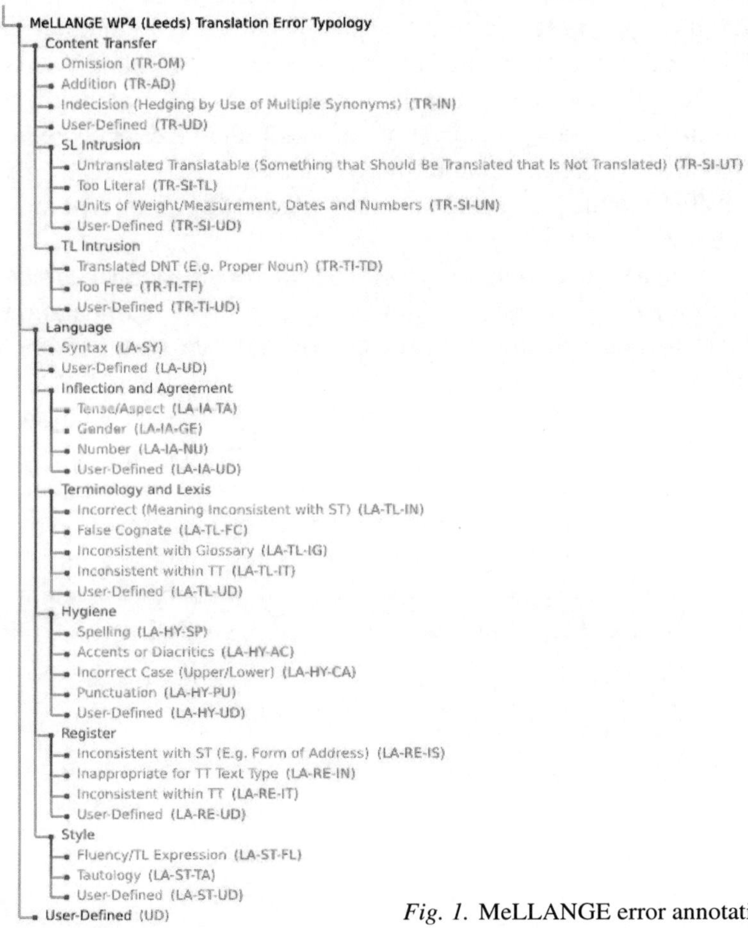

Fig. 1. MeLLANGE error annotation scheme.

The taxonomy also includes *User-Defined* categories that annotators can resort to in case they find that the error they wish to mark does not belong to any of the other categories. It is also possible for annotators to assign more than one category to given text parts, as well as to provide explanatory notes and/or suggest correct solutions.

Error annotation is performed through a customised version of the manual annotation tool MMAX2, originally developed by Mark-Christoph Müller at the European Media Laboratory, Heidelberg (2006). The tool has an XML-based representation format and makes use of multi-layer stand-off annotation, which means that information about the annotation project is stored in different files. Our error annotation consists of four different levels: the Paragraph, Sentence, Content Transfer and Language Levels. While the Paragraph and Sentence levels are created automatically, the Content Transfer and Language levels were designed specifically for the annotation of the MeLLANGE LTC and reflect the different categories and subcategories of the error typology described above.

In order to create an annotation project, annotators do not need to be aware of such technical details, but simply have to save the translation in .txt UTF-8 format and drag-and-drop it on the "start_annotation" application. The annotation process is carried out using the MMAX4-MeLLANGE graphical interface, which consists of several windows (see Fig. 2). The main window displays the text of the translation to be annotated. In this window annotators select the part(s) of the translated text which represent(s) either a Content Transfer or a Language error. The attribute window allows then for further specificity where annotators can select one or more of the pre-defined error categories or create a user-defined one, and leave appropriate feedback to students.

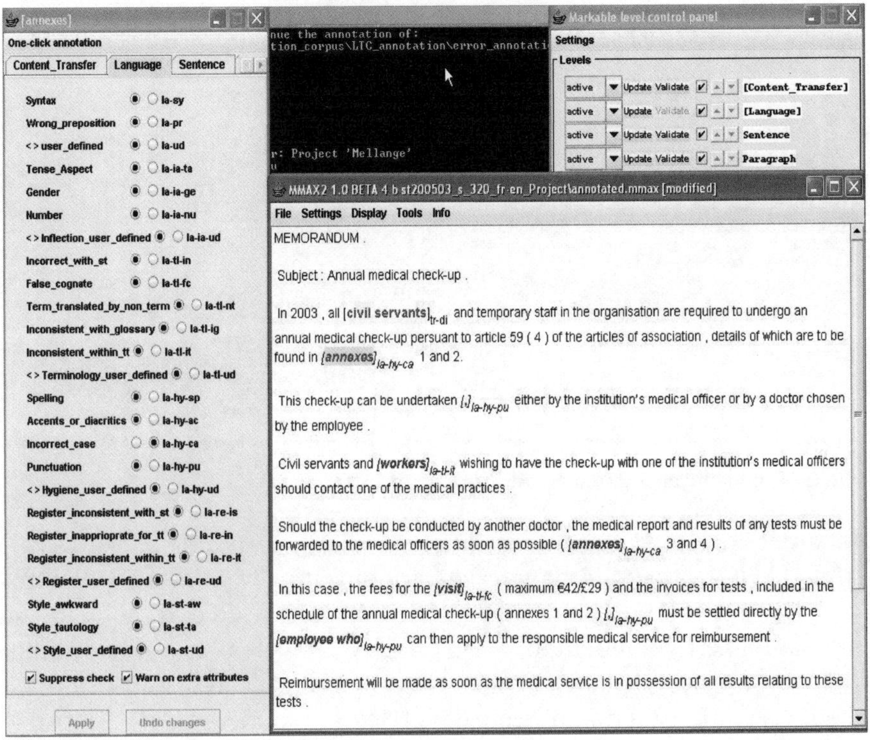

Fig. 2. The MMAX4MeLLANGE interface.

5. Exploiting the LTC

Once translations from the MySQL database have been downloaded, tagged with linguistic information and also annotated using the MeLLANGE error typology, the final stage of post-processing is performed before they can be used by the LTC query tool. This stage consists of a normalisation of the output of linguistic taggers for the 6 languages involved in the project. As already illustrated in §4, several taggers and tagsets were used in the linguistic tagging process, with results such as those illustrated by Fig. 3.

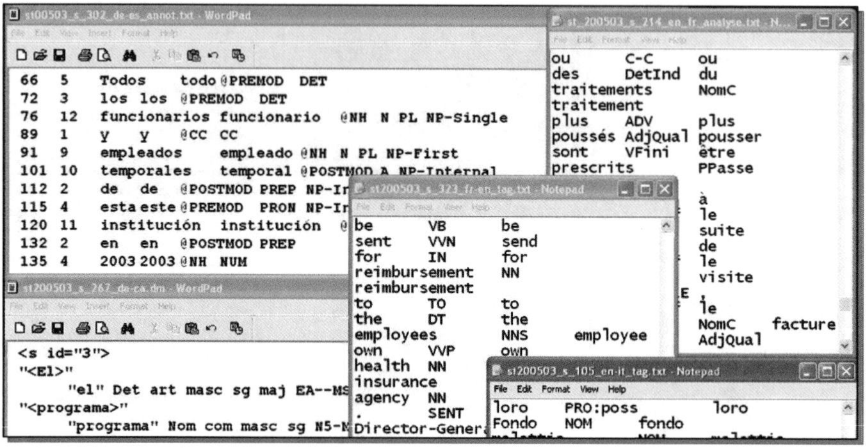

Fig. 3. Linguistic annotation output.

In order to integrate this information with the output of MMAX4-MeLLANGE a certain degree of harmonisation was needed. Figures 4–6 illustrate the final formats in which the tokenised output, linguistic annotation, error annotation on the Language level (§4 has already highlighted that there is also a Content Transfer level) and metadata associated with a translation are respectively stored in the LTC. We chose to use stand-off annotation – i. e. storing each level of annotation in a separate XML file – because of the numerous advantages of this approach in terms of information management and maintenance.

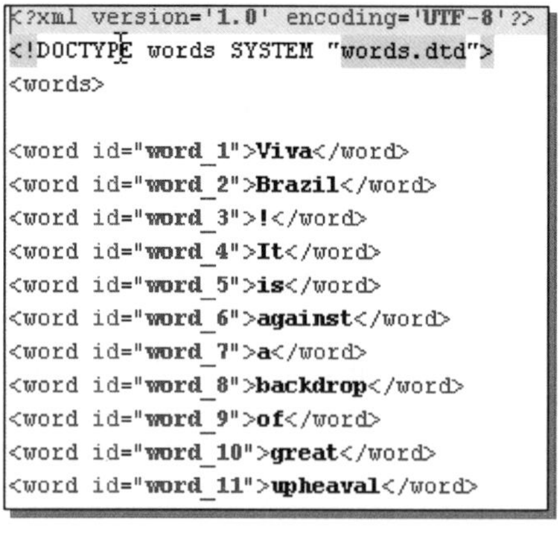

```
<?xml version='1.0' encoding='UTF-8'?>
<!DOCTYPE words SYSTEM "words.dtd">
<words>

<word id="word_1">Viva</word>
<word id="word_2">Brazil</word>
<word id="word_3">!</word>
<word id="word_4">It</word>
<word id="word_5">is</word>
<word id="word_6">against</word>
<word id="word_7">a</word>
<word id="word_8">backdrop</word>
<word id="word_9">of</word>
<word id="word_10">great</word>
<word id="word_11">upheaval</word>
```

Fig. 4. Extract from the tokenised version of a translation stored in the LTC.

```
<?xml version='1.0' encoding='UTF-8'?>
<ling_annot>
    <tokposlem id="1" span="word_1" pos="NP" lem="Viva" />
    <tokposlem id="2" span="word_2" pos="NP" lem="Brazil" />
    <tokposlem id="3" span="word_3" pos="SENT" lem="!" />
    <tokposlem id="4" span="word_4" pos="PP" lem="it" />
    <tokposlem id="5" span="word_5" pos="VBZ" lem="be" />
    <tokposlem id="6" span="word_6" pos="IN" lem="against" />
    <tokposlem id="7" span="word_7" pos="DT" lem="a" />
    <tokposlem id="8" span="word_8" pos="NN" lem="backdrop" />
    <tokposlem id="9" span="word_9" pos="IN" lem="of" />
    <tokposlem id="10" span="word_10" pos="JJ" lem="great" />
    <tokposlem id="11" span="word_11" pos="NN" lem="upheaval" />
```

Fig. 5. Extract from the linguistic annotation of a translation stored in the LTC.

```
<?xml version="1.0" encoding="UTF-8"?>
<!DOCTYPE markables SYSTEM "markables.dtd">
<markables xmlns="www.eml.org/NameSpaces/language">
<markable id="markable_18" span="word_58" la-st-aw_feedback="the"  style_awkward="la-st-aw" />
<markable id="markable_26" span="word_323" la-hy-sp_feedback="plummetted"  spelling="la-hy-sp" />
<markable id="markable_21" span="word_128" punctuation="la-hy-pu"  la-hy-pu_feedback="." />
<markable id="markable_24" span="word_200" la-re-in_feedback="unusual"
register_inappriopraté_for_tt="la-re-in" />
<markable id="markable_28" span="word_356" la-st-aw_feedback="reduced by a factor of 10? hit
extremely hard"  style_awkward="la-st-aw" />
<markable id="markable_25" span="word_291" la-hy-sp_feedback="employment"  spelling="la-hy-sp" />
<markable id="markable_23" span="word_175" la-st-aw_feedback="no real need for
sentence-initial and here, no real effect of style"  style_awkward="la-st-aw" />
</markables>
```

Fig. 6. Extract from the MeLLANGE error annotation (Language level) of a translation from the LTC.

This modular structure of the LTC has enabled the building of a complex query tool, publicly available at <http://corpus.leeds.ac.uk/mellange>. The query tool enables users to explore resources produced in the MeLLANGE project, as well as one of its predecessors, the eCoLoRe project.[3]

3 <http://ecolore.leeds.ac.uk>.

```xml
<?xml version="1.0" encoding="utf-8"?>
<?xml-stylesheet type="text/xsl" href="metadata.xsl"?>
<translation>
<user_info>
 <affiliation>Paris 7</affiliation>
<first_languages>en,pt</first_languages>
<second_languages>de,fr,it</second_languages>
<status>student</status>
<uni_level>postgraduate</uni_level>
<study_programme>Translation studies</study_programme>
<translation_studies_years>1</translation_studies_years>
<work_experience_as_translator>yes</work_experience_as_translator>
<work_years_as_translator>2</work_years_as_translator>
</user_info>
<text_info>
<source_text>ST200504</source_text>
<sl>fr</sl>
<tl>en</tl>
<years_using_sl>15</years_using_sl>
<years_using_tl>0</years_using_tl>
<reference_resources>yes</reference_resources>
<software_tools>yes</software_tools>
<local_peer_collaboration>no</local_peer_collaboration>
<remote_peer_collaboration>no</remote_peer_collaboration>
<expert_teacher_collaboration>no</expert_teacher_collaboration>
<assessed_translation>no</assessed_translation>
<had_time_limit>no</had_time_limit>
<time_spent>0</time_spent>
<ref_used_advice>no</ref_used_advice>
</text_info>
</translation>
```


Fig. 7. Extract from the metadata linked to a translation stored in the LTC.

While the interface to the eCoLoRe TMX corpus gives access to bilingual translation memories in 37 language pairs created from technical and financial translations, the MeLLANGE query interface also allows users to search the MeLLANGE LTC for examples of student errors, original and reference contexts, as well as student alternatives that meet various linguistic and/or metadata criteria (*Fig. 8*). A total of 232 annotated translations have been incorporated into the LTC (12 into *ca*, 13 into *de*, 54 into *en*, 49 into *es*, 48 into *fr*, and 56 into *it*).

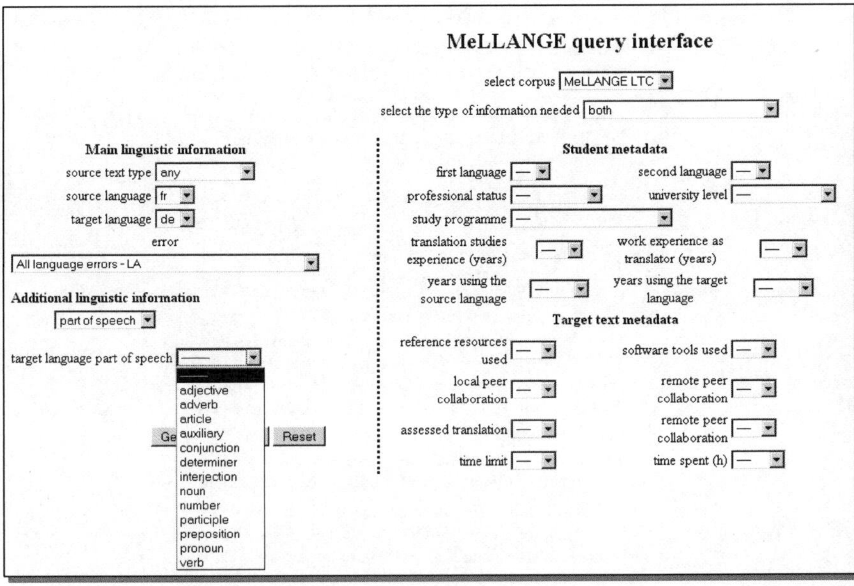

Fig. 8. Query interface to the MeLLANGE LTC.

After using some of the available search criteria, the user is likely to be presented with a result such as the one illustrated by *Fig. 9*, which presents a typical answer to a query such as "display all sentences translated from *fr* into *en* which contain language errors as identified by the annotators using the MeLLANGE error typology". First of all the user would be presented with the source context, then the target sentence which meets the criteria, followed by a reference context and alternative students translations if available.

1	Language	Context	Source
Original context	fr	Accès à l'emploi Tout ressortissant d'un État membre a le droit d'accéder à une activité salariée et de l'exercer sur le territoire d'un autre État membre, conformément à la réglementation nationale pertinente applicable aux travailleurs nationaux. Il bénéficie sur le territoire d'un autre État membre de la même priorité que les ressortissants de cet État dans l'accès aux emplois disponibles.	Full text
Target sentence	en	Every national of a Member State has the right to [undertake]$_{LA-TL-IC}$ gainful employment within the borders of any other Member State , according to the respective national [laws]$_{TR-DI}$ for [workers]$_{TR-OM}$.	Full text
Reference context	en	Focus on the employment Every national of a Member State has a right to work for a salary and to be employed on the territory of another Member State, as per the pertinent national regulations applicable to national workers. On the territory of another Member State, he/she is entitled to the same priority conditions as the nationals of this State to access to available jobs.	Full text
Alternative student context	en	Any citizen of a Member State has the right to access to employment within the territory of another Member State in respect of the relevant national [regulation]$_{LA-IA-NU}$ applicable to national workers . Wthin the territory of another Member State he is entitled to the same priority as national workers to access any available employment . He must be treated in the same way as national workers [looking for jobs]$_{LA-RE-IN}$ [through employment offices]$_{TR-DI}$.	Full text
Alternative student context	en	Any citizen of a Member State has the right to [access to]$_{LA-PR}$ employment within the territory of another Member State in respect of the relevant national regulation applicable to national workers . Within the territory of another Member State he is entitled to the same priority as national workers to access any available employment . He must be treated in the same way as national workers [looking for jobs]$_{LA-RE-IN}$ through employment offices .	Full text

Fig. 9. Query results from the MeLLANGE LTC.

Given the short length of the texts to be translated and the limited probability of translators joining or splitting many sentences, for the time being the LTC is not aligned at sentence level. Instead, once a sentence produced by a trainee translator is identified as meeting the search criteria, its sentence id number (*X*) is extracted and a context of three sentences (*X-1, X, and X+1*) is returned from the source text, as well as the reference translation and student alternative translations.

Hovering with the mouse over tokens in the target sentence and alternative student contexts reveals POS and lemma information. The same procedure applied to the error codes reveals the feedback left by the annotators.

In the near future we plan to adapt this query tool to support the output of statistical information about the LTC, so that data such as those presented in Fig. 10 and Fig. 11 will be available just like the query results presented above.

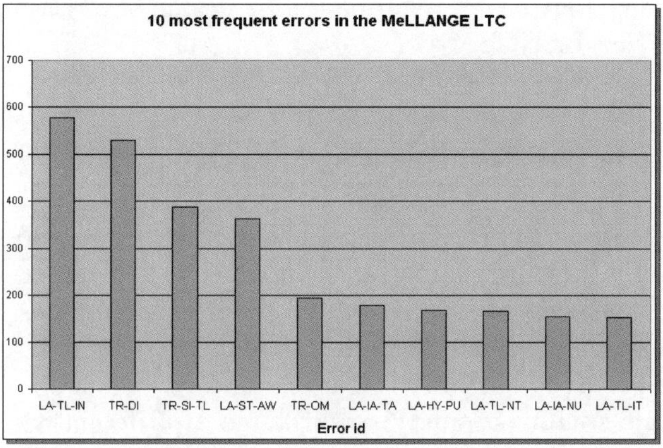

Fig. 10. 10 most frequent errors in the MeLLANGE LTC.

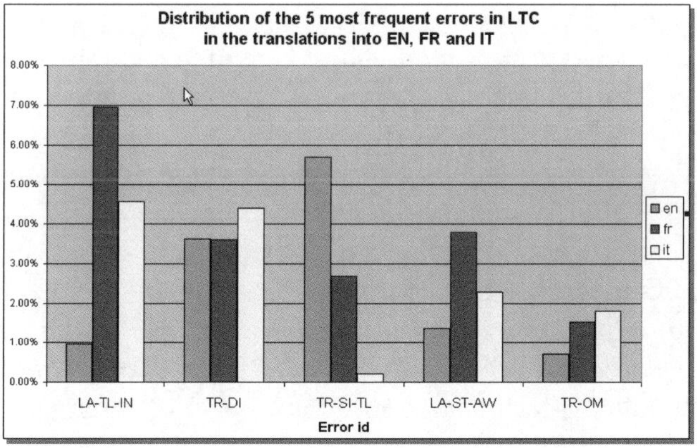

Fig. 11. Distribution of the 5 most frequent errors in the MeLLANGE LTC (translations into EN, FR and IT)

6. Possible applications of the LTC

Having introduced the two basic ways of consulting the corpus, namely by making parallel concordances and extracting statistics about error types, we will now provide practical examples of how the LTC data could be exploited in translation teaching and research, as well as of ways in which they have been used for the design of e-learning materials within MeLLANGE.

6.1 Using the LTC for didactic and research purposes

As far as the research into the quality and process of translation, as well as the teaching of translation, are concerned, the Learner Translator Corpus can – thanks to its different layers of annotation, associated to student metadata – enable researchers and teachers to look for specific types of errors in conjunction with particular word/lemma/pos sequences, and evaluate solutions found by translators of different backgrounds/ levels of expertise to translation problems associated with particular text types. For instance, statistical analyses of the LTC could provide answers to questions such as:

- *what are the most common errors in the whole corpus* vs *in translations into a specific target language?* – which could highlight trends associated to the translation process itself or to specific language pairs (see Fig. 10–11 above);
- *are language errors equally frequent in students with different degrees of familiarity with the field of Translation Studies?* (see Appendix 1) – which would enable assessment of the influence of pedagogy on competence development;
- *do terminology errors tend to disappear in translations for which students had access to resources such as dictionaries, the web etc.?* – which could offer insights into the impact of reference resources on the quality of translations.

On the other hand, the concordancing function can display examples of, for instance:

- *content-transfer errors in EN-FR translations* (e.g. Fig. 12);
- *language errors made by undergraduate students*,

together with the ST sentence the errors are associated with, the reference translations available, as well as all alternative student translations for the same segment the error was found in (as discussed in §5 and shown in Fig. 9).

EN	He is entitled to the same social and tax benefits as **national workers**. A national of one Member State working in another **is entitled to** equal treatment in respect of the exercise of trade union rights, including the right to vote and to be eligible for the administration or management posts of a trade union.
FR	Il bénéficie des mêmes avantages sociaux et fiscaux que les [**travailleurs**]**TR-OM** . Un citoyen d'un État membre travaillant dans un autre État membre [[**peut**]**TR-TI-TF** **exercer** les mêmes droits syndicaux]**TR-TI-TF** [**que les travailleurs nationaux**]**TR-AD** , ce qui inclut le droit de vote et [d'éligibilité au sein de l'administration ou de la gestion]**TR-OM** d'une organisation syndicale .
REF	Il y bénéficie des mêmes avantages sociaux et fiscaux que les **travailleurs nationaux**. Le travailleur ressortissant d'un État membre occupé sur le territoire d'un autre État membre **bénéficie** de l'égalité de traitement en matière d'exercice des droits syndicaux, y compris le droit de vote et l'accès aux postes d'administration ou de direction d'une organisation syndicale.

Fig. 12. Content-transfer errors in an EN-FR student translation (edited) TR-OM = omission, TR-TI-TF = too free, TR-AD = addition.

While the statistical approach can help trainers identify the most common difficulties within a given group of learners, thus indicating areas of the learning curriculum where teaching is most needed, the concordancing functionality can provide teachers/researchers with authentic examples of the relevant error categories, which can then be used to produce either corpus-driven or corpus-based learning materials.

The term *corpus-driven* refers to learning content based/focusing on assessed difficulties – i.e. materials developed taking real student errors into account in order to better anticipate the problems that other trainees may face. This approach is based on the assumption that errors made by the students included in the corpus may be used to predict difficulties that other students translating into the project languages will have, and to build translation exercises accordingly.

By *corpus-based* materials, on the other hand, we mean materials which contain examples from the LTC. For instance, teachers might decide to tackle specific translation problems by providing students with concordance lines which show cases of those problems, asking them to spot the errors and think of alternative solutions. Or they might prepare exercises on translation revision using texts taken from the LTC, possibly exploiting the multiple alignment functionality to help student reflect on acceptable vs unacceptable variation. Some practical suggestions for developing corpus-based materials using LTC data are provided in Appendices 2 and 3.

6.2 Other scenarios

We would like to conclude by illustrating the usefulness of the LTC in two further scenarios: the teaching of other translation-related subjects, and autonomous learning. In the first case we will draw directly on the MeLLANGE experience of designing e-learning courses in translation-related disciplines, while the second is a suggestion whose applicability and usefulness still need to be assessed following empirical testing.

As was previously mentioned in the introduction to this paper, one of the aims of the MeLLANGE project was to produce e-learning teaching materials which would then serve as a basis for a European Master in Translation Technologies. One of the subjects that were identified by the partnership as essential for the translator curriculum was the use of corpora for translation. While most of the tools and subjects presented in other MeLLANGE courses (e. g. Translation Memory, Terminology, Localisation, Machine Translation) are likely to be well-known among translation students (and professionals) already, awareness of corpora and their usefulness for the practice of translation is unfortunately still scarce; therefore, we felt the need to first provide motivation for introducing these tools into the translation curriculum. To convince trainees and professionals that corpora could help them produce better texts, we built an exercise in which we asked them to revise a translation into English taken from the Learner Translator Corpus – focusing on the sentence below, which contains a lexical problem (underlined):

> English TT: *He shall be entitled to the same social and fiscal benefits as national workers.*
> Spanish ST: *Se beneficiará de las mismas ventajas sociales y fiscales que los trabajadores nacionales.*

The exercise consisted of various steps which aimed at showing – with the use of a specialised target language corpus – that the adjective *fiscal* is not usually employed to qualify *benefits*, and lead students to conclude that the expression *tax benefits* would have represented a much better choice in this context. Since the LTC contains authentic texts produced by trainee translators, we believe it can represent a very good source of data for any course dealing with language issues, as it offers examples of problems encountered by 'real' students in 'real' communicative situations.

Lastly, we also believe the LTC can be a powerful tool in situations of *blended* or *autonomous learning*, i.e. in cases where students are required/recommended to practice individually to supplement or replace traditional classroom teaching. Since learning to translate is not a matter of just "right" or "wrong" answers, translation is not a discipline which can be easily taught online. Very often students need guidance in order to understand errors and/or reflect on different translation options. However, we believe the LTC can contribute in a self-learning direction because:

- the reference translations produced by professionals represent "gold standard" versions against which students can assess the quality of their work;

– the translations of the same texts produced by other trainees give students the possibility to compare their translations with others in which errors have been marked and (often) corrected, thereby allowing them to see a range of translation solutions whose acceptability has been evaluated.

The possibility to query source texts, reference and trainee translations, aligned at a small-scale context level and enriched with several layers of annotations, resembles very closely the typical translation classroom situation, where several students are asked to suggest alternative solutions for an expression or sentence, which are then compared, discussed and evaluated by the teacher. Whether the Learner Translator Corpus can effectively be used as a tool for totally autonomous learning, however, still needs to be empirically tested.

References

Bowker L. & P. Bennison (2003) Student translation archive: design, development and application. In Zanettin F., S. Bernardini & D. Stewart (eds.) *Corpora in Translator Education*. Manchester: St Jerome, 103–117.

Florén C. (2006) ENTRAD, an English Spanish parallel corpus created for the teaching of translation. Paper presented at the *7th Teaching and Language Corpora conference (TALC 2006)*, Paris, 1–4 July 2006.

Müller C. (2006) Representing and Accessing Multi-Level Annotations in MMAX2. *Proceedings of the workshop on multi-dimensional markup in Natural Language Processing (NLPXML-2006)*, EACL, Trento, April 2006.

Popescu-Beliş A., M. King & H. Benantar (2002) Towards a corpus of corrected human translations. In King M. (ed.) *Machine translation evaluation – human evaluators meet automated metrics, Workshop proceedings*, LREC 2002, 17–21.

Secară A. (2005) Translation Evaluation – a State of the Art Survey. *eCoLoRe/MeLLANGE Workshop Proceedings*, 39–44. (<http://www.leeds.ac.uk/cts/research/publications/leeds-cts-2005-03-secara.pdf>).

Sosnina E. P. (2006) Development and application of Russian Translation Learner Corpus. Presented at *Corpus Linguistics – 2006*, St. Petersburg, 10–14 October 2006.

Uzar R. & J. Waliński (2001) Analysing the fluency of translators. *International journal of corpus linguistics*, 6, 155–166.

Appendix 1. Using the LTC to explore research hypotheses

A first type of activity that can be performed using the MeLLANGE LTC is researching how the quality of trainee translations can be influenced, among others, by time, resources, experience and level of training.

Fig. 13, for instance, presents the difference between the work of a trainee translating into his/her mother tongue but with less than 2 years' experience in the field of Translation Studies. and that of another trainee with between 2 and 5 years of experience. Although we are guarded about generalising our results – mainly because we are currently expanding the coverage of the LTC – the initial results returned by the MeLLANGE query interface can already inform the drawing of research hypotheses.

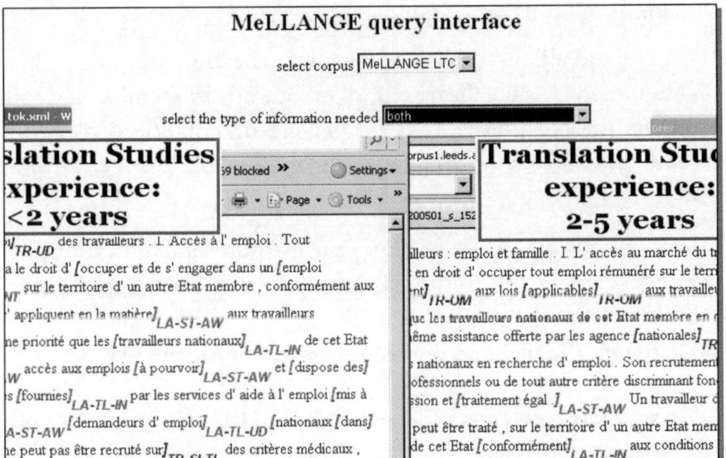

Fig. 13. Two translations produced by learners with different experience of Translation Studies.

Appendix 2. Translation error analysis using the LTC

Error-annotated excerpts from the LTC can be shown to students to raise their awareness of specific error types. Students may be asked to discuss the errors from different perspectives – such as possible causes (e.g. ambiguities in the source text) and seriousness (i.e. the extent to which the source text meaning is affected) – and suggest corrections.

EN	Exercising an occupation and equal treatment. A worker who is a national of a Member State may not, in the territory of another Member State, be treated differently from national workers as regards working and employment conditions (dismissal and **remuneration in particular**) because of his nationality.
FR	[Un]$_{LA-UD}$ travailleur d'un État membre [ne doit pas]$_{LA-TL-IT}$ être traité différemment [, sur le territoire d' un autre État membre ,]$_{LA-SY}$ des travailleurs [de cet État]$_{LA-TL-NT}$, en matière de conditions d'emploi et de travail [(licenciement , [[salaire inégal]$_{TR-AD}$]$_{LA-TL-IN}$)]$_{TR-OM}$ [en raison de sa nationalité]$_{LA-ST-AW}$.
REF	Le travailleur ressortissant d'un État membre ne peut être traité différemment, sur le territoire des autres États membres, des travailleurs nationaux, en raison de sa nationalité, pour toutes conditions d'emploi et de travail (licenciement, **rémunération notamment**).

Fig. 14. "Less serious" content transfer errors. Edited LTC query interface results.

Example 1. Content transfer errors can distort the meaning of the source text (ST) to a lesser or greater degree. Fig. 14 shows an example in which the genuine meaning of the ST is slightly different in the target text (words in the ST that are concerned with the error are in boldface; content-transfer errors are tagged with a code starting with *TR*). The first error, tagged *TR-AD* (addition), indicates that an unnecessary word has been added to the target text: EN: *remuneration* – FR: *salaire* ***inégal.*** Here, the adjective *inégal* is not necessary and alters the meaning of the ST, in which inequalities of treatment are implied, but not explicitly expressed. The second error *TR-OM* indicates that some parts of the ST have been omitted in the translation process: the equivalent of the English *in particular* does not appear in the French translation.

Example 2. In the following example (Fig. 15), no word has been added nor omitted. Part of the meaning of the ST however, has disappeared in the translation process. Here, the complex preposition *on the grounds of* has been translated into *basés sur*, which is closer to *based on*. There is a loss in semantic substance in the target text, where *en raison de* would much more precisely yield the original meaning.

EN	His recruitment may not be dependent on medical, occupational or other criteria which discriminate **on the grounds of** nationality.
FR	Son [embauche]$_{LA-TL-IG}$ [ne doit pas dépendre]$_{LA-TL-IT}$ de facteurs médicaux , professionnels ou [d' autres critères]$_{LA-ST-AW}$ discriminatoires [basés sur]$_{TR-TI-TF}$ sa nationalité .
REF	Son recrutement ne peut dépendre de critères médicaux, professionnels ou autres, discriminatoires **en raison de la** nationalité.

Fig. 15. "Too-free" content-transfer error. Edited LTC query interface results.

Example 3. This example shows an occurrence of a serious content-transfer error, namely distortion. Distortion stands for a modification of the ST's meaning in the target text. Here, the distortion scope extends to the whole sentence. The prepositional phrase *under public law* is attached to the head noun *bodies* and further on in the text, to the head noun *office*. The French translation shows the prepositional phrase to be governed by the verb *excluded*, which completely changes the meaning of the sentence.

EN	He may be **excluded** from the management of **bodies** under public law and from the exercise of **an office under public law**.
FR	[Il]$_{LA-HY-PU}$ peut être exclu de la gestion d' [organismes]$_{TR-OM}$ et [être démis de ses fonctions [au nom du droit public]$_{TR-DI}$]$_{TR-TI-TF}$.
REF	Il peut être exclu de la participation à la gestion d'organismes de droit public et de l'exercice d'une fonction de droit public.

Fig. 16. Serious content transfer error.

Appendix 3. Example of a revision exercise using the LTC

It is also possible to use translations from the LTC without any annotation and ask students to spot errors and suggest revised translations (errors appear in boldface in Fig. 17 to facilitate reading, but they do not appear as such in the real exercise). As mentioned in § 6.1, the multiple alignment functionality can also be used for triggering reflection on variation and translation acceptability, as students are allowed to analyse pros and cons of different translation solutions at the same time.

EN	Exercising an occupation and equal treatment A worker who is a national of a Member State may not, in the territory of another Member State, be treated differently from national workers as regards working and employment conditions (dismissal and remuneration in particular) because of his nationality.
FR	**Un** travailleur d'un État membre **ne doit pas** être traité différemment , **sur le territoire d'un autre État membre,** des travailleurs **de cet État**, en matière de conditions d'emploi et de travail (**licenciement, salaire inégal**) **en raison de sa nationalité** .
FR	Exercice d'une profession et **traitement égal**. Un travailleur dont la nationalité est celle d'un Etat membre ne peut être traité, sur le territoire d'un autre Etat membre, différemment des travailleurs nationaux de cet Etat **conformément** aux conditions de travail et d'embauche (plus particulièrement en matière de **refus** et de rémunération) à cause de sa nationalité .
FR	Exercice d'une profession et égalité de **rémunération**. Un travailleur, **citoyen** d'un Etat Membre **,** ne peut pas être traité différemment des travailleurs **du pays d'accueil** en ce qui concerne les conditions de travail et d' emploi (en particulier licenciement et rémunération) du fait de sa nationalité
FR	Exercice d'une profession et **traitement égal**. Un travailleur dont la nationalité est celle d'un Etat membre ne peut être traité, sur le territoire d'un autre Etat membre, différemment des travailleurs nationaux de cet Etat **conformément** aux conditions de travail et d'embauche (plus particulièrement en matière de refus et de rémunération) à cause de sa nationalité.

FR	Exercer une activité professionnelle et recevoir un **traitement égal**. **Un travailleur qui est** ressortissant d'un Etat membre ne peut pas, sur le territoire d'un autre Etat membre, être traité différemment des travailleurs nationaux **par rapport** aux conditions de travail et d'embauche (en particulier pour le licenciement et la rémunération) à cause de sa nationalité .

Fig. 17. A corpus-based exercise on translation revision.

Students can then be shown the reference text so that they can compare it with their suggestions for revision. Fig. 18 is the reference text for the student translations shown above:

REF	Exercice de l'emploi et égalité de traitement. Le travailleur ressortissant d'un État membre ne peut être traité différemment, sur le territoire des autres États membres, des travailleurs nationaux, en raison de sa nationalité, pour toutes conditions d'emploi et de travail (licenciement, rémunération notamment).

Fig. 18. Reference French translation.

MOJCA PECMAN

How awareness of lexical combinatorion can improve second language learning: A model for analysing collocations in scientific discourse

Abstract

The paper illustrates a method for investigating phraseology in specialised fields of knowledge for the purposes of second language learning. We attempt to illustrate this method through a contrastive French-English corpus-based study of general scientific language. The underlying assumption is that different scientific discourses have, alongside their specific terminologies, certain common linguistic features which can be observed essentially on the lexico-syntactic level in relation to the expression of a number of general scientific ideas. We first discuss the role of combinatorion in second language acquisition, then illustrate a model for analysing collocational frameworks in specialized corpora. The analysis is based on an onomasiological approach and gives rise to a set of combinatorial conceptual frameworks whose specificity lies in the regrouping of semantically related collocations. This method ensures an efficient transfer of the collocational profile of lexical items from a source language to a target language.

1. Introduction

This paper presents a model for analysing collocations in specialised fields of knowledge for the purposes of second language learning. It focuses on General Scientific Language (GSL), taking a contrastive point of view involving English and French (Pecman 2004, 2005a, 2005b, 2007). The underlying assumption is that different scientific discourses may have, alongside their specific terminologies, certain common linguistic features on the lexico-syntactic level used to express specific discourse functions and general scientific notions, such as exemplifying, reformulating, discussing background knowledge, presenting contrasts with past findings, introducing hypotheses, describing methods, tools, research motives, goals, results, discoveries, etc. Our approach draws on knowledge from various fields: collocation studies, phraseology, semantics, discourse analysis, corpus linguistics and languages for specific purposes.

2. Raising combinatorial awareness among language learners in a scientific setting

In order to explore ways in which awareness of lexical combinatorion could improve foreign language learning, we will first discuss their role in second language acquisition, and more specifically in acquiring skills in specialised language.

Studies by Granger (1998), Howarth (1993, 1996), Mel'čuk (1993), Pawley & Syder (1983) and Weinert (1995) all recognize the importance of word combination in linguistic competence, albeit with differences in their approach. While Mel'čuk essentially concentrates on the analysis of native speaker corpora, Howarth, Granger, Weinert and Pawley & Syder perform comparative studies of native and non-native data. Their work shows that non-native production tends to involve so-called "collocational blends", namely the use of collocations that bear strong resemblances to their native language counterparts. As Howarth (1996: ix) points out, such collocational errors can lead to lack of precision, and thus obscure the clarity required for scientific communication. For learners of scientific English, acquiring phraseological proficiency should therefore be an integral part of second language learning.

2.1 The role of combinatorion in second language learning

The question of phraseological competence is related to one of the fundamental mechanisms that govern language evolution and function: combinatorion. According to Pinker language is "a combinatorial system, in which a small inventory of elements can be assembled by rules into an immense set of distinct objects" (1999: 7). Combinatorial systems obey an exponential principle; that is, the number of possible combinations grows exponentially with size. Inconceivably vast numbers of objects can thus be generated through combination of a limited number of elements.

Language, nevertheless, is not a free combinatorial system but restricted. Were it a free system, its items would not be distinctive. To assure this distinctiveness, it has developed a mechanism which governs combinations through the two complementary principles which Sinclair (1991: 109–110) has termed the "open-choice principle" and the "idiom principle". The open-choice principle relates to the "slot and filler" model of language, based on the notion that language users manipulate sentence frames, while "the principle of idiom is that a language user has available to him or her a large number of semi-preconstructed phrases that constitute single choices, even though they might appear to be analysable into segments" (Sinclair 1991: 110).

To acquire the combinatorial properties of lexical units is a very complex task for adult learners. Collocations do not present themselves to the mind as minimal units of the language, and traditional teaching methods do not pay attention to the combinatorial properties of words. The role of combination is all the more important in that different languages display different combinatorial paradigms. Children acquire the combinations of their native language through high exposure, but for an adult second language learner this process requires an early introduction to it. Thus it is important to raise combinatorial awareness in the early stages of second language study. This can perhaps be achieved by providing teachers and learners with tools and methods for probing lexical combinations within a language, especially within languages for specific purposes, since the latter generally display high degrees of conventionality and idiomaticity.

2.2 Second language acquisition in a scientific setting

Native-like proficiency is all the more important in scientific settings, where conventional style is highly valued in communication. In French universities, we find that students of scientific disciplines are very soon confronted with the need to master the English of their domain. Scientific literature is overwhelmingly published in English, and students in master and doctoral programmes have to present their work in English, both in spoken or written form. Deviations from conventional style can reduce the intelligibility of their discourse. It is hoped that our model for analysing general scientific language will contribute to improving their phraseological competence and developing their feel for idiomaticity.

In our research into various scientific discourses (Pecman 2004, 2005b), we have found that certain general features are shared across disciplines. These features relate both to the lexico-grammatical level and to the rhetorical one. Different scientific discourses tend to use many of the same phraseologies to express basic scientific notions, and in much the same way they construct their argumentation using the same linguistic tools. Terminology, on the other hand, remains specific to different disciplines.

Only a decade ago, only a few linguists had explored such invariants across scientific discourses in English (e.g. Granger 1998, Howarth 1996), but recently interdisciplinary features have begun to attract greater interest (cf. Coxhead 2000, Kübler 2005, Pecman 2004, Tutin 2007). While the study of what Phal called "Vocabulaire Général d'Orientation Scientifique" in France began more than 30 years ago (Phal 1971), this approach was purely lexical and did not investigate phraseology. Other linguists studying collocation within specific scientific discourses have pointed out the existence of features that have cross-linguistic usage. Thus Gledhill (2000: 206) coined the term "generic collocations" to distinguish those items which can be found in various scientific discourses from those specific to the field he was working on. Here we use the term General Scientific Language (GSL) (Pecman 2004: 124–147) to refer to interdisciplinary language, hypothesising that GSL can be efficiently analysed through an onomasiological and phraseological approach to scientific discourse.

3. The onomasiological analysis of scientific discourse

The reason why an onomasiological approach can offer us an efficient method for probing the combinatorial properties of words is simple. An approach to collocations based on their formal constituents often implies grouping together multi-word units that have nothing but the node word in common. If we instead offer learners access to collocations on a semantic basis, all the combinatorial conventions used to express a given notion can be compared.

We constructed an English-French parallel corpus (82800 words) containing scientific texts (articles, abstracts, activity reports, communications) taken from a number of disciplines (biochemistry, life sciences, earth and planetary sciences, food and agriculture sciences, physics, astrophysics, astronomy and mechanics). From this corpus we extracted over 2000 bilingual multi-word units, such as *mettre la théorie en pratique* ↔ *put theory into practice, en attachant une attention particulière à* ↔ *with special reference to*, *voir ci-après* ↔ *see hereafter*. Selection of these units was based on their frequency and diffusion across different scientific disciplines.

A preliminary semasiological analysis was performed to identify the main semantic areas involved. Each multiword unit was linked to a condensed representation of its dominant meaning (cf. Pecman 2004, 2005a). For example, *in order to*, *ultimate goal*, *so as to*, *the purpose was to* were all labelled as |GOAL|. Subsequently, onomasiological analysis was carried out in order to identify the ways in which these general scientific ideas were lexicalized within the discourse. Decomposing and recomposing meanings in this way is unquestionably risky. Nevertheless, it is sufficient to think about translation to realise that such processes play a decisive role in putting ideas into words, especially in a second language.

Altogether, 125 semantic categories were identified. Each category was linked to one of four broad conceptual spheres – scientific, universal, modal and discursive – which seem to form the backbone of general scientific knowledge. The resulting database thus provides an overview of the semantic organisation of this knowledge.

One of the characteristics of scientific phraseology is that multiword units can vary in wording to some extent. Completely frozen units are rare. In order to be able to take such variation into account we developed a descriptive model based on the concept of collocational frameworks.

4. Collocational frameworks in scientific discourse

Contrary to earlier work that stressed the fixedness of phraseological units, an increasing number of studies have concluded that most such units are likely to involve variation (cf. Altenberg 1998: 105–106, Moon 1998: 92, Howarth 1996). Many linguists now hypothesise units allowing variability in their realisations, variously termed collocational frameworks (Renouf & Sinclair 1991), sentence builders (Granger 1998: 154), phrase-frame (Stubbs 2004), lexicogrammatical frames (Moon 1998), semi-prepackaged phrases (Francis 1993).
While generally defined as grammatical or lexical collocations with a variable lexical 'slot', there is little consensus about how they should be represented. For example Gledhill (2000: 133) uses a linear representation to display the structure of such units:

'in _ to' and *'in _ with'*

Fig. 1. A collocational framework (Gledhill 2000).

Gledhill explains that this framework serves to construct the lexical sets *in response to, in addition to, in contrast to*, etc., and *in agreement with, in combination with, in concurrence with, in conjunction with*, etc. The lexical slot is presented as void and the items destined to fill the slot are listed separately.

Oakey (2000) uses a linear representation which instead incorporates potential realisations in the framework:

it is/has been (often) asserted/believed/noted/argued/claimed that X.

Fig. 2. A collocational framework (Oakey 2000).

Granger (1998: 154) indicates lexical, grammatical and semantic slots in her "sentence-builders":

it + (modal) + passive verb (of saying/thinking) + that-clause,

Fig. 3. A sentence builder (Granger 1998).

She explains that this framework can be used to generate a series of clauses: *it is said that …*, *it is thought that …*, *it can be claimed that …*, *it can be assumed that …*, etc.

Gentilhomme (1995) adopts much the same approach for mathematical collocations in French, where these are fixed frames with slots that can be filled by either symbols or words.[1]

$^{p}C_{m}$	which can be read: *combinaison de m [objets] p à p*
$^{b}\int^{``}_{a}$	which can be read: *somme de a à b de...*

Fig. 4. Collocational framework (Gentilhomme 1995).

An alternative representation found frequently in the literature is the table. For example Menac (1970: 4) illustrates variation within the collocational framework *mesti/čistiti pred/ispred svoj kuća/prag/vrata* (lit. broom/clean in front of one's own house/doorway/door) as follows:

mesti	pred	svoj	kuća
čistiti	ispred		prag
			vrata

Fig. 5. Example of collocational framework (Menac 1970).

Such tables are logically identical to the linear representations outlined previously, though perhaps easier to interpret.

As can be seen from these examples, representations of collocational frameworks are primarily designed to capture lexico-syntactic features.

1 "Il y a comme un moule linguistique figé, dans lequel peuvent prendre place des symboles et des mots: *combinaison de* □ […] □ *à* □, les carrés et les crochets représentant des emplacements vides susceptibles d'être occupés respectivement par des symboles ou par des mots." (Gentilhomme 1995: 24)

In our opinion, it is possible to go further and also include semantic properties.

4.2 Combinatorial conceptual frameworks

In our research we have replaced the concept of collocational frameworks with one that also accounts for semantic features, for which we use the term *combinatorial conceptual frameworks*. The purpose is to state the combinatorial properties of words belonging to the same semantic category (e.g. *aim, target, goal, purpose*, etc.). Such semantically-related words often display similar distributions, with a tendency to occur in similar lexico-grammatical contexts (e.g. *to achieve a goal, to achieve an aim, to achieve a target; to reach a goal, to reach an aim, to reach a target; to pursue a goal, to pursue an aim*). The notion draws principally on the work of Altenberg (1998).

Altenberg's representation of collocational frameworks is illustrated in Fig. 6, which shows the lexical structures used to express gratitude in spoken English:

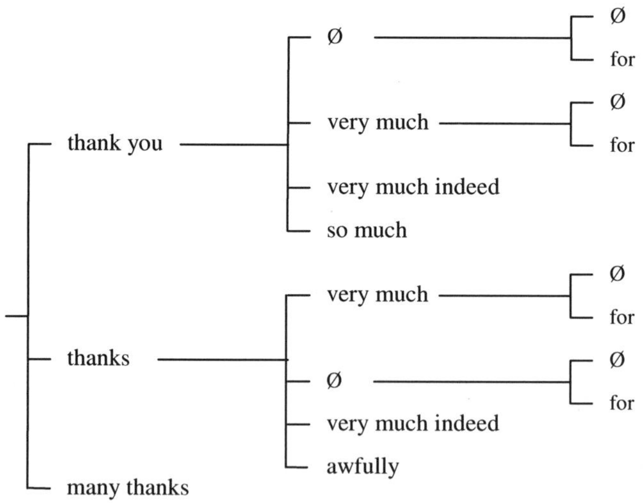

Fig. 6. Collocational framework (Altenberg 1998).

This representation is particularly suitable for complex lexico-grammatical structures. Fig. 7 illustrates a conceptual collocational framework for expressing the notion "hypothesis" in French.

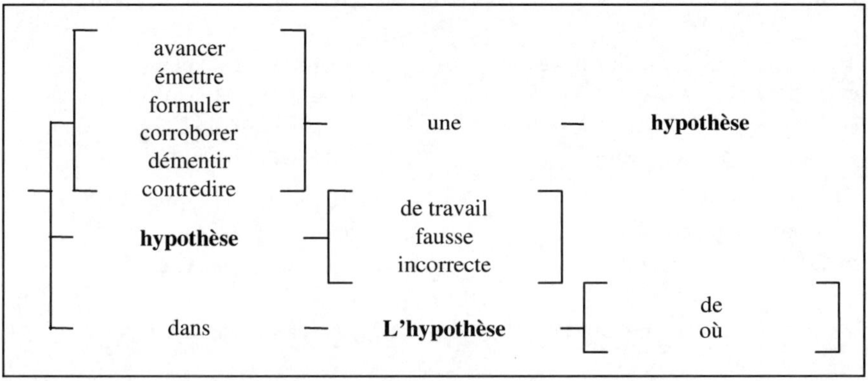

Fig. 7. A conceptual collocational framework.

Instead of constructing a framework around a single node, different lexical items can be grouped to illustrate the various patterns for expressing a given notion. Dashed brackets indicate alternative realizations:

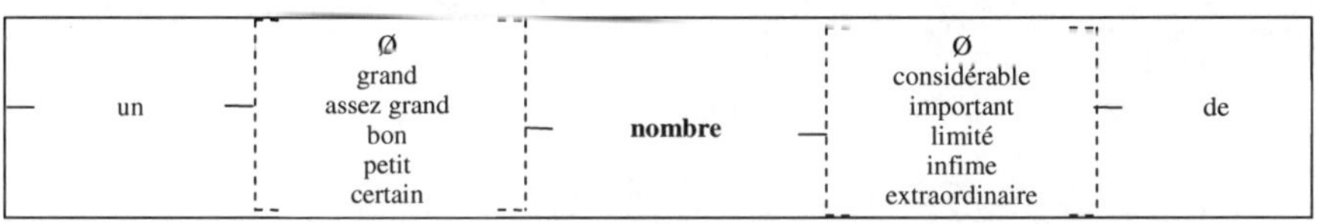

Fig. 8. Alternative realizations within a conceptual collocational framework.

while full brackets indicate compulsory elements:

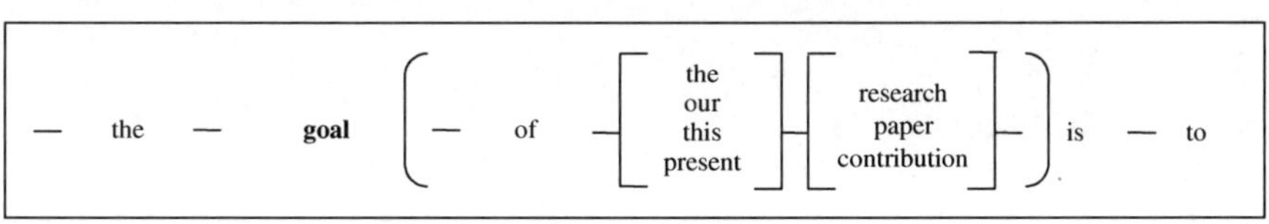

Fig. 9. Compulsory realisations within a framework.

Such representations highlight differences in combinatorial properties across languages, clearly showing the collocational structures related to a specific semantic category. These representations can however be transposed to linear ones in order to assemble language equivalents:

[avancer/émettre/formuler/suggérer] une hypothèse	↔	[advance/formulate/put forward/suggest] a hypothesis
[contredire/démentir] une hypothèse	↔	[invalidate/refute] a hypothesis
corroborer une hypothèse	↔	consolidate a hypothesis
hypothèse [fausse/incorrecte]	↔	[false/incorrect] hypothesis
hypothèse de travail	↔	working hypothesis
dans l'hypothèse [de/où]	↔	in case of, in the event of

Fig. 10. Bilingual representations of conceptual combinatorial frameworks.

The linear mode of representation is more redundant, but cannot be avoided where equivalences between languages are multiple. It may still therefore be useful when contrasting phraseology.

The notion of combinatorial conceptual frameworks is similar to Francis' "semi-prepackaged phrases" (1993). Under this label Francis presents collocating semantic sets such as:

the faintest idea
the least idea
the slightest idea
the foggiest idea
the remotest idea
the slightest conceptions
lightest notion
the foggiest notion
the remotest notion
the foggiest

Fig. 11. Semi-prepackaged phrases (Francis 1993).

Semi-prepackaged phrases are sequences which behave as variants of one another, but in which "there is no single lexical item which is essential" (Francis 1993: 144). Conceptual collocational frameworks go further, as they group not only cognates within a single type of lexico-grammatical frame but from a variety of frames. Our "hypothesis" example includes adjective-noun frames (*false/incorrect hypothesis*), verb-noun frames (*to advance/formulate/put forth/put forward/suggest a hypothesis*) and prepositional phrases (*in case of, in the event of*). Equivalent bilingual frames may thus be grammatically different (*hypothèse de travail* ↔ *working hypothesis*). In this manner, combinatorial conceptual frameworks provide an interface between the semantic and formal structure of a lexicon.

5. Conclusion

The specificity of combinatorial conceptual frameworks lies in grouping semantically-related collocations. The advantage of such frameworks is that they highlight the variational capacities of units playing similar semantic roles. This should ensure efficient transfer of the collocational profile of lexical items from the source language to the target language. Such an approach seems particularly suitable for general scientific knowledge, since the linguistic features shared by different scientific discourses can be observed in relation to the notions they express. We thus believe that combinatorial conceptual frameworks can be useful in foreign language teaching and learning, particularly where this aims at developing native-like communicative skills in a scientific environment.

References

Altenberg B. (1998) On the phraseology of spoken English: the evidence of recurrent word-combinations. In Cowie (1998), 101–122.

Cowie A.P. (ed.) (1998) *Phraseology: Theory, Analysis, and Applications*. Oxford: Oxford University Press.

Coxhead A. (2000) A new academic word list. *TESOL quarterly* 34, 213–238.

Francis G. (1993) A corpus-driven approach to grammar. In M. Baker, G. Francis & E. Tognini-Bonelli (eds), *Text and technology: in honour of John Sinclair*. Amsterdam/Philadelphia: John Benjamins, 137–156.

Gentilhomme Y. (1995) Contribution à une réflexion sur les locutions mathématiques. *Cahiers de lexicologie* 66, 5–37.

Gledhill C.J. (2000) *Collocations in science writing*. Tübingen: Gunter Narr.

Granger S. (1998) Prefabricated patterns in advanced EFL writing: collocations and formulae. In Cowie (1998), 145–160.

Howarth P. A. (1993) A phraseological approach to academic writing. In G.M. Blue (ed.) *Language, learning and success: studying through English*. London: Macmillan, 58–69.

Howarth P. A. (1996) *Phraseology in English academic writing: some implications for language learning and dictionary making*. Tübingen: Niemeyer.

Kübler N. (2005) Phraséologie verbale transdisciplinaire et spécifique: essai de classification en sciences de la terre. In C. Cosme, C. Gouverneur, F. Meunier & M. Paquot (eds) *Phraseology 2005. The many faces of phraseology: an interdisciplinary conference*. Louvain-la-Neuve :Université de Louvain, 223–225.

Martinet A. (1974) *Eléments de linguistique générale*. Paris: A. Colin.

Mel'čuk I. A. (1993) La phraséologie et son rôle dans l'enseignement/apprentissage d'une langue étrangère. *Etudes de linguistique appliquée* 92: 82–113.

Menac A. (1970) O strukturi frazeologizma. *Jezik* 18(1). Zagreb: Hrvatsko filološko društvo, 1–4.

Moon R. E. (1998) *Fixed expressions and idioms in English: a corpus-based approach*. Oxford: Clarendon.

Oakey D. (2000) A corpus-based study of the formal and functional variation of a lexical phrase in academic writing in social science, medical and technical disciplines. *Professional issues meetings reports* 6. <http://www.baleap.org.uk/pimreports/2000/uh/oakey.htm>.

Pawley A. & F. H. Syder (1983) Two puzzles for linguistic theory: nativelike selection and nativelike fluency. In J.C. Richards & R.W. Schmidt (eds) *Language and Communication*. London: Longman, 191–227.

Pecman M. (2007) Compilation, formalisation and presentation of bilingual phraseology: problems and possible solutions. In S. Granger & F. Meunier (eds) *Phraseology in language learning and teaching*. Amsterdam/Philadelphia: John Benjamins, 203–222.

Pecman M. (2005a) Systemizing the notation and the annotation of collocations. *Jezikoslovlje* 6(1), 79–93.

Pecman M. (2005b) Les apports possibles de la phraséologie à la didactique des langues étrangères. *Apprentissage des langues et systèmes d´information et de communication (ALSIC)* 8(1), 109–122.

Pecman M. (2004) *Phraséologie contrastive anglais-français: analyse et traitement en vue de l'aide à la rédaction scientifique*. Thèse de doctorat. Nice: Université de Nice Sophia-Antipolis.

Phal A. (1971) *Vocabulaire général d'orientation scientifique (V.G.O.S.): part du lexique commun dans l'expression scientifique*. Paris: CREDIF.

Pinker S. (1999) *Words and Rules: the ingredients of language*. New York: Basic Books.

Renouf A. & J. M. Sinclair (1991) Collocational frameworks in English. In K. Aijmer & B. Altenberg (eds) *English corpus linguistics*. London: Longman, 128–143.

Sinclair J. M. (1991) *Corpus, concordance, collocation*. Oxford: Oxford University Press.

Stubbs M. (2004) On very frequent phrases in English: distribution, functions and structures. Paper presented at *ICAME 25*, Verona.

Tutin A. (2007) Traitement sémantique par analyse distributionnelle des noms transdisciplinaires des écrits scientifiques. <http://w3.u-grenoble3.fr/tutin/taln_tutin_final_avril.pdf>.

Weinert R. (1995) The role of formulaic language in second language acquisition: a review. *Applied Linguistics* 16, 180–205.

Olympia Tsaknaki

Recognizing proverbs: A method and its applications

Abstract

This paper illustrates a method for recognizing automatically proverbs and deals with the challenges this task presents. Taking 2500 Modern Greek proverbs, a library of finite state transducers (FSTs) was constructed to represent canonical forms, variants and truncated forms. It was then applied to a large corpus of newspaper texts. Applications of FSTs and their concordance outputs in fields such as foreign language teaching and learning, cultural studies, and translation are discussed.

1. Introduction

Multiword expressions (MWEs) are generally acknowledged to be a central problem in Natural Language Processing (NLP). As they are of different kinds and have distinct properties, they should be analysed by means of the most appropriate method in each case.

This paper focuses on paremiology. Proverbs have their own specificities. They do not have free elements, and in this they differ from frozen expressions where the main verb is constrained and one or more noun phrase arguments is distributionally free. Also, they are semantically non-compositional: the meaning of a proverb is not deducible from the individual meanings of its component elements, though the degree of opacity may vary.

Merely to focus on proverbs may seem over-restricted. However, they constitute a challenge to NLP. The goal of this paper is to illustrate the problem, to present a method for locating proverbs in large text corpora and to propose applications not only to NLP but also to other domains.

In Section 2 we explain the reasons why we created a finite state transducers (FSTs) library in order to recognize proverbs. Section 3 briefly presents the FSTs, and Section 4 describes their application to a corpus. Section 5 evaluates our method while Section 6 focuses on its potential uses in other fields, particularly in foreign language teaching and learning.

2. A FST library of proverbs

Proverbs are generally considered to be entirely fixed. At first glance, they seem not to be affected by transformations on a morphological, semantic or syntactic level. Nevertheless, Conenna (1998) has shown that we should not be categorical in this respect. As in Conenna's work on French and Italian (2000a, b), we have found that Modern Greek proverbs present graphic, orthographic, morphological, lexical and morphosyntactic variations (Tsaknaki 2005). Such variations cannot be viewed as a marginal phenomenon.

In creating an electronic dictionary of proverbs we took into consideration the fact that almost every proverb has its own specific structure and potential variants. Methods for locating proverbs will consequently yield good results to the extent that these variants are exhaustively represented. Given the limited paradigms of the components, all these variants can be included in a dictionary. Otherwise, inadequately detailed descriptions may affect the results.

It is impossible or impractical to group proverbs in classes with shared syntactic properties, to create lexicon-grammar matrices, or to establish a simple list of entries (contrary to fixed expressions, compound nouns or frozen adverbs where these methods can be applied: De Gioia, 2000; Fotopoulou, 1993; Gross, 1984; Monceaux, 1993). For these reasons an approach using FSTs – finite state automata which produce some output – seemed more appropriate to identify proverbs. These devices are not a new method and are broadly applicable to many languages. They offer readability, precision and efficiency. We built a library of FSTs for 2500 Modern Greek proverbs, drawing on general language dictionaries of Modern Greek, proverb collections, and instances from the Press or the Internet or uttered by native speakers.

Each FST aimed at the recognition of one and only proverb and its variants.[1]

This method offers many advantages. Dealing with variants which are not listed in any dictionary, even dictionaries of proverbs, is one of them. The exhaustive character of the library provides very few errors due to silence or to noise. In addition, whenever we find a variant not yet included, we can easily add it, since FSTs are easily revised and updated. On the other hand, FSTs have the disadvantage that they need full descriptions of possible variants, which is a time-consuming task.

3. Recognition of proverbs in texts

A FST has an initial state, nodes representing transitions, and a final state. It then produces an output. Each input symbol in the FST is inside a node. In the case of proverbs, parallel transitions and the empty symbol <E> represent different variants. The output is the label "PROV". Fig. 1 shows an FST of the proverb

> *Αν η ζήλια ήταν ψώρα, Θα κολλούσε όλη η χώρα*
> *If jealousy was scabies, would get it all the country*[2]

where the variants of the proverb are clearly visible.[3]

1 Proverbs can also be grouped semantically.

2 Literal translation.

3 This proverb allows several types of variation. A graphic variation is the comma between the two parts. An orthographic variation resulting from a phonological variation is *όλη* (*whole*) and the oral form *όλ'*. A morphological variation is *ήταν* (*was*) and *ήτανε*. Restricted lexical variation is also possible e.g. *θα ψώριαζε* (*would get scabies*), *θα κολλούσε* (*would get*), *θα γέμιζε* (*would be full*), *θα είχε* (*would have*). Finally, we find syntactic variations, e.g. *η ζήλια αν ήταν* (*jealousy if it was*), *αν ήταν η ζήλια* (*if it was jealousy*), *αν η ζήλια ήταν* (*if jealousy was*). The above translations are literal.

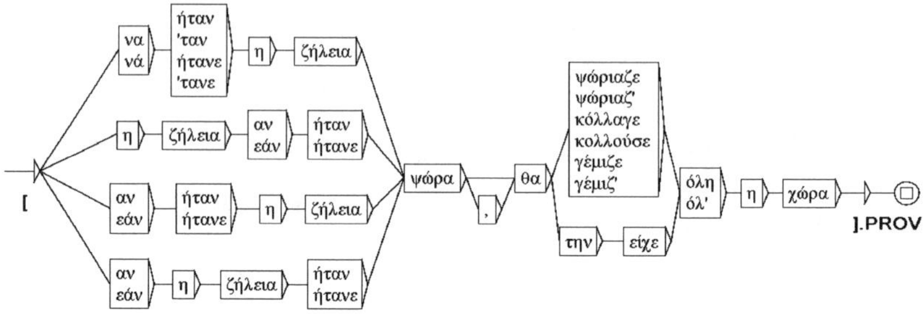

Fig. 1. FST representing a proverb and its variants.

To manage our data we used Unitex, a platform created by Paumier (2003) and developed in the Institut Gaspard-Monge at the Université de Marne-la-Vallée for the analysis of texts in natural languages. It is an effective means of creating a library of FSTs incorporating all the necessary information for our recognition task.

Additionally, we tried to identify cases where a proverb is truncated, a part of their canonical form being omitted. An example of such a FST is given below. It can recognize either the first part:

Αν η ζήλια ήταν ψώραή
If jealousy was scabies...

or the second:

...θα κολλούσε όλη η χώρα
...would get it all the country.

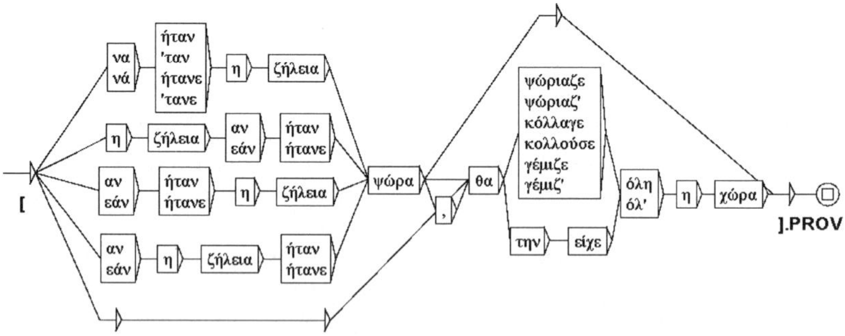

Fig. 2. FST to locate a truncated proverb.

4. Application to a corpus

To test the method, we applied it to a corpus. Corpora offer a number of advantages over other types of resources (e. g. dictionaries, printed texts, subject field experts, intuition) and can therefore be useful complements to such resources:

> – Their electronic form means that corpora can be larger and more up-to-date than printed resources, and they can be reached more easily.
> – Corpora consist of authentic texts that can be used to find out what people do and do not say, as well as how often they say it.
>
> Corpora can be used to conduct new investigations or to test existing hypotheses. (Bowker & Pearson 2002: 21)

The material used was a large newspaper corpus taken from the Greek newspaper *TA NEA* over the years 2001–2003, and totaling over 130 million words.[4] The reasons for this choice were that *TA NEA* has a wide reading public and it contains texts belonging to different genres which are written by many different authors.

From the 2500 canonical forms in our dictionary we selected a random sample of 250. The proverbs in the sample were lexically and semantically diverse. Table 1 lists the 12 most frequent in the corpus (in descending order of frequency) accompanied by their literal translation and their equivalent proverb(s) or fixed expression(s) in English:

4 Year 2001 = 255 MB (Unicode), 2104662 sentence delimiters, 54644602 tokens (367125 types); Year 2002 = 232 MB (Unicode), 1934654 sentence delimiters, 49190336 tokens (339765 types); Year 2003 = 153 MB (Unicode), 1195789 sentence delimiters, 30352569 tokens (280730 types).

	Proverb	*Literal translation*	*English equivalent(s)*
1	Ποτέ δεν είναι αργά	Never is late	It is never too late It is never too late to mend
2	Κάλλιο αργά παρά ποτέ	Better late than never	Better late than never
3	Ο σκοπός αγιάζει τα μέσα	The end hallows the means	The end justifies the means
4	Και την πίτα ολόκληρη και το σκύλο χορτάτο	The pie entire and the dog stuffed	You can't have your cake and eat it
5	Περασμένα, ξεχασμένα	Passed, forgotten	Let bygones be bygones
6	Έχει ο καιρός γυρίσματα	Time has turns	
7	Ποτέ μη λες ποτέ	Never say never	Never say never
8	Μ' έναν σμπάρο δυο τρυγόνια	With one shot two turtledoves	Kill two birds with one stone
9	Η σιωπή είναι χρυσός	The silence is gold	Talking is silver, silence is gold Silence is golden Speech is silver, silence is golden
10	Στερνή μου γνώση να σ' είχα πρώτα	My late knowledge, if I only could have you earlier	Repentance comes too late
11	Μπρος γκρεμός και πίσω ρέμα	Ahead a cliff and behind a river	Between the devil and the deep sea Caught between the devil and the deep blue sea
12	Τρώγοντας έρχεται η όρεξη	By eating comes the appetite	Eating whets the appetite

Table 1. Most frequent proverbs in the entire corpus.

We then processed the corpus with UNITEX to generate concordances showing the occurrences in their immediate context.[5] Results for the 12 proverbs in Table 1 are shown in Table 2:

5 The user can specify the number of characters to be displayed to the left and right of the search proverb. Clicking on an occurrence provides access to a wider context.

Proverb	*Occurrences/year (canonical form)*			*Total occurrences (canonical form)*	*Total occurrences (truncated form)*
	2001	2002	2003		
1	23	28	17	68	0
2	14	17	12	43	5
3	14	9	13	36	0
4	10	15	9	34	1
5	11	10	11	32	1
6	9	14	5	28	0
7	11	10	6	27	0
8	9	11	1	21	2
9	4	10	6	20	0
10	7	7	6	20	12
11	6	5	4	15	0
12	5	7	1	13	0
Total	123	143	91	357	21

Table 2. Occurrences of the 12 most frequent proverbs in the corpus.

Truncated forms were relatively rare overall, but it is worth noting that for the proverb No 10 the truncated form was during these three years more frequent than it was its canonical form each year separately.

5. Evaluation

In order to evaluate our method and estimate its performance we used precision and recall rates. Precision is the ratio of occurrences correctly retrieved by the system to the total number of incorrect and correct occurrences retrieved. Recall is the ratio of occurrences successfully identified to the total number of correct occurrences in the corpus.

For canonical forms, precision was 100 %. For truncated forms, precision was 100 % for all proverbs except one: the system incorrectly recognized the word *Περασμένα* (*passed*) as a proverb component. Due to this error, which was repeated 24 times for the proverb No 5, overall precision for truncated forms was only 46,6%. Because of the complete linguistic description, noise was non-existent. And due to the complexity of the structure of proverbs, there was no ambiguity between the sequences retrieved and other word combinations.

The size of the corpus did not permit an exact calculation of the recall, so this was estimated using a sample of 4.447 texts containing 2.005.786 words (29448 KB (Unicode)), in which proverb occurrences were marked up manually. All were retrieved by the system except one case which was not recognized due to an orthographic error (Ο σκοπός αγιάζει *το* μέσα). Considering that our data was relatively homogenous, we assume global recall in the corpus was similar to that in the sample.

6. Further applications

The tools we developed are not limited to NLP. They can also be used in other ways, meeting the criteria and needs of other fields, for instance in foreign language teaching and learning. The use of corpora in this area is not new, and even if it is no panacea, offers many possibilities.

Language relates to culture. In the foreign language class, it is essential to introduce students to the culture of the community whose language they are learning. Proverbs are closely tied to culture: in Modern Greek they are used both in oral and written discourse. The application of FSTs to a corpus allows the system to locate:

- examples of proverbs in canonical and/or truncated form;
- all the occurrences of proverbs in a text.

Flexible and easy to use, FSTs can thus allow teachers and learners to:

- exploit authentic texts;
- group and classify data retrieved by the system;
- locate specific linguistic features and learn vocabulary;
- study context: concordances of proverbs can provide information as to their pragmatic value, showing how they are inserted and used in discourse;

- develop activities to highlight linguistic and cultural similarities and differences;
- practice translation techniques;
- use search patterns as stimuli to understand and produce texts;
- experiment with computer-assisted learning.

FSTs and their concordance output may also be useful in other fields, for instance to assist translation or the investigation of literary data.

7. Conclusions

Our study on Modern Greek proverbs allowed us to confirm that their form is not necessarily fixed. The creation of a library of FSTs representing all variants allowed us to successfully retrieve proverbs from a large newspaper corpus. This study was limited to the recognition of canonical or truncated forms. However, proverbs can be creatively modified in texts. They can be defrozen, they can occur discontinuously, and parts of proverbs can occur by themselves. In some cases their constituents may be dispersed over wide contexts (Tsaknaki 2005). Future research will need to elaborate tools which can handle this flexibility.

References

Bowker L. & J. Pearson (2002) *Working with specialized language: A Practical Guide to Using Corpora.* London: Routledge.

Conenna M. (1998) Le proverbe, degré ultime de figement? In Mejri S., G. Gross, A. Clas & T. Baccouche (eds), *Le figement lexical.* Tunis: Actes des 1ères rencontres linguistiques Méditerranéennes, 361–371.

Conenna M. (2000a) Classement et traitement automatique des proverbes français et italiens. *BULAG*, Numéro spécial, Mélanges Gaston Gross, 285–294.

Conenna M. (2000b) Structure syntaxique des proverbes français et italiens. *Langages* 139, 27–38.

Conenna M. (2004) Principes d'analyse automatique des proverbes. *Lexique, Syntaxe et Lexique-grammaire: Papers in honour of Maurice Gross., Linguisticae Investigationes: Supplementa* 24, 91–104.

De Gioia M. (2000) Sur un lexique-grammaire comparé d'adverbes figés. *Lingvisticae Investigationes* 23, 327–346.

Fotopoulou A. (1993) *Une classification des phrases à compléments figés en grec moderne*. PhD Thesis. Paris: Université de Paris 8.

Gross M. (1984) Une classification des phrases figées du français. In Attal P. & C. Muller (eds), *De la syntaxe à la pragmatique*. Amsterdam/Philadelphia: John Benjamins, 141–180.

Kleiber G. (1994) Sur la définition du proverbe. *Nominales*. Paris: A. Colin, 207–224.

Michaux C. (1999) Proverbes et structures stéréotypées. *Langue française* 123, 85–104.

Monceaux A. (1993) *La formation des noms composés de structure Nom Adjectif. Élaboration d'un dictionnaire électronique*. PhD Thesis. Paris: Université de Paris 7.

Norrick N. (1985) *How proverbs mean: semantic studies in English proverbs*. Berlin: Mouton.

Paumier S. (2003) *De la reconnaissance de formes linguistiques à l'analyse syntaxique*. PhD Thesis. Marne-la-Vallée: U.F.R. d'Informatique, Université de Marne-la-Vallée.

Tsaknaki O. (2005) *The proverb in translation: Usage in Modern Greek and automatic treatment*. PhD Thesis. Thessalonica: Aristotle University.

PHILIPPE MARTIN

A language teaching software program using spontaneous speech corpora

Abstract
WinPitch Corpus (www.winpitch.com) is a software program specialized in speech analysis and dedicated to the teaching of a second language using audio examples of spontaneous speech. The underlying principle associates lexical or syntactic units not only to their translation in the learner language, but also to audio examples taken from various contexts. The program works as a complex database engine, extracting text and audio segments from any aligned corpus. This arrangement is particularly useful when using spontaneous speech corpora, as it allows the learner to acquire features of spoken language not normally available from textbooks or from CD-ROM materials. The software also allows teachers to comment specific speech segments.

1. Introduction

WinPitch (downloadable from www.winpitch.com) is a software tool integrating a large number of functionalities for teaching both written and oral language material. With this tool, the instructor can prepare various lessons based on corpora of transcribed and aligned spontaneous speech, and include aspects of oral style not easily integrated in standard curricula. The software can be used in presentia or absentia. If present, the instructor can base complete lessons on linguistic and stylistics aspects of the recorded material. If absent, the learner can discover at his/her own pace pertinent speech and pronunciation characteristics helped by a set of bookmarks and text comments elaborated by the instructor.

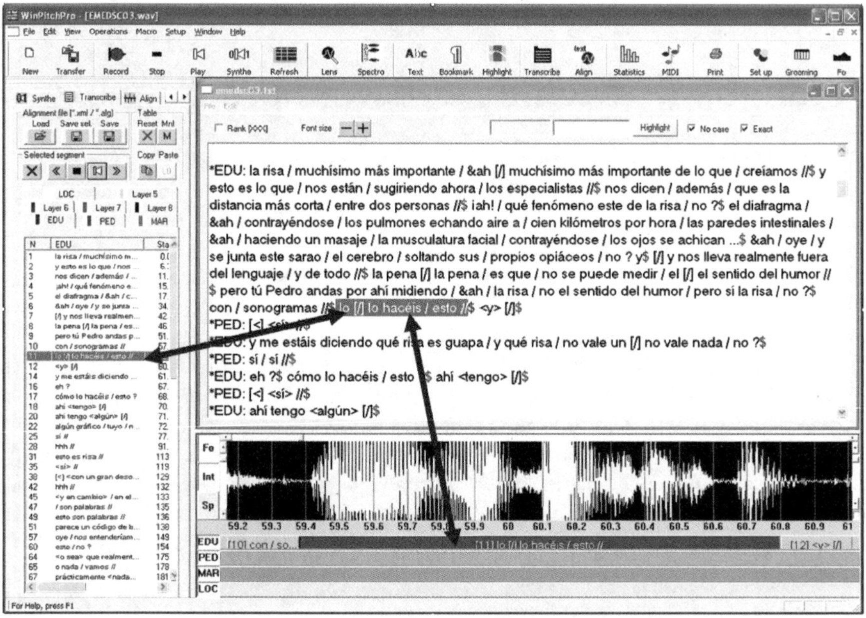

Fig. 1. An example (in Spanish) illustrating simultaneous linking between the aligned text, the sound, an entry of the lexicon. The acoustic analysis (spectrogram, fundamental frequency curve, intensity, waveform) can also be displayed automatically (see figures below).

2. Building the database

Speech transcription is usually the first operation needed to analyze a corpus linguistically. In the old times, this operation was carried out (painfully) from tape (cassette) recordings, played back at fixed speed and with basic operations (rewind, fast forward, etc.) difficult to execute. Today's software tools allow simultaneous transcription and alignment, by establishing bidirectional pointers between text and sound according to the nature of the speech segments defined by the user. Alignment can be carried out on any kind of units, from phones to syllables, words, stress groups, syntactic units, sentences or speech turns. Correspondence between aligned units and sound is however necessarily approximate, as the aligned operation goes through some perception process, whether human or simulated by some speech recognition device.

After selection of speech material suitable for language teaching, the first step in the preparation of lessons consists in the transcription and alignment of the recorded sound. If no transcription is available, the selected speech must be transcribed and aligned in order to build a database linking appropriate segments of text to corresponding segments of speech. Segments can have various dimensions, and be related to syllables, words, syntagms, sentences, etc. Once alignment is completed, corresponding segments can be easily retrieved by selecting one of their counterparts: selecting text will playback and analyze the corresponding sound, and defining a speech segment will display the corresponding text. The transcription can be orthographic and/or phonetic, and labels (morphological, syntactic, semantic, etc.) can also be added to each segment.

Transcription of a given speech recording is frequently available (popular recordings of poems, songs, classical text, etc. can often be found on the web). In this case, only alignment of the text with the sound is necessary. WinPitch offers an easy-to-use function to align available text on the fly while listening to the recording.

2.1 Assisted transcription

A first example pertains to the case where only the speech recording of interest is available. Segments of speech must be defined according to some pedagogical aim. For instance, this could require examples with subordinate clauses, examples showing the importance of intonation in the organization of the partially well formed speech segments, etc. The program allows various modes of assisted transcription. The simplest consists in selecting graphically with the mouse a section of speech on the acoustic analysis window, and manually entering the corresponding text. In the second mode, the user defines speech segment boundaries while listening to the corresponding running speech by hitting a keyboard key (different keys may correspond to different speakers). The third mode proceeds automatically by detecting pauses (of user adjustable duration) to define segment boundaries. The last two modes automatically generate arbitrary text segments (e.g. "T0045"). By clicking on these text segments, the user can listen to the corresponding speech segment (at slower speed if desired) and directly edit the text.

One particular interesting feature is on the fly transcription. In this process, the user can assign on the fly the desired segment of speech to a specialized tier devoted to each speaker (or alternatively put all segments to the same tier and assign them to their proper tier later), while listening to recorded speech played back at any convenient speed and hitting a keyboard key at the appropriate instant (slowdown to 15 % real time can be achieved with very good quality, using a built-in Psola or phase vocoder engine). At a later stage, the text segments can be transcribed orthographically and reassigned to a specific tier if necessary.

Whatever the transcription mode chosen, WinPitch can handle the overlapping speech frequently found in spontaneous conversations. Fine adjustment of time segments is obtained by using intuitive mouse commands to align speech turn beginnings and ends for each speaker, and by adjustment of a cursor on a spectrogram for easy visual separation of the respective speakers' harmonics.

2.2 Assisted alignment

The three modes of transcription described above imply the alignment of each defined text string with the corresponding speech segment. But there can also be applications where the transcription is available without alignment. This is often the case for older elaborations of corpora, using tape recorders for instance, where only coarse alignment was possible. Rather than redoing the whole transcription from scratch with modern software tools, it is possible to align existing transcriptions with WinPitch without redoing them.

The process is simple: after the sound file has been loaded, the user displays the transcription text file on a window. The speech sound is then played back at the desired speed (usually a slowdown rate of 30 % to 50 % is adequate), and the user clicks on the text units (words, last word of syntactic units…) when they are perceived. The slow speech rate allows the coordination of the user eye, the mouse movement and the speech perception to achieve reasonable coordination. Every time the user clicks on a text unit in the transcription window, a speech segment boundary is defined with the appropriate text. Furthermore, in the case of conversations, if the transcription is properly formatted with every speech turn labeled with the string "*XYZ:" (Childes format), the segments are automatically assigned to their respective speaker tiers.

Alignment on the fly allows the user to perform a complete alignment in little more than the sound duration, and can thus be executed in real time for large segments (syntagms or sentences). To align smaller segments (words, syllables) slower playback speed should be used, down to a 30 % rate.

3. Pedagogical use of the program

3.1 Uses of aligned transcriptions

Any part of the data can be easily accessed and commented, and displayed automatically with its acoustic analysis (spectrogram, intensity and melodic curves). Access to the database is performed by selecting a section of interest in the text window (be it a word, phrase, or paragraph), or by selecting an entry in the lexicon (built automatically from the text entries, and linked to a complete dictionary in Excel format). The aligned text can also be based on learner-recorded performances, annotated by the instructor for further oral exercises. Complete text analysis based on speech recordings (recorded news, interviews, talk shows, etc.) can be elaborated for active use in the classroom, or in absentia on the learner's computer.

3.2 Prosodic morphing

Prosodic parameters, such as vowel duration, intensity and fundamental frequency, can be dynamically modified through the use of simple graphic commands. Intonational characteristics of the language can be illustrated by instructor or learner, either with the input material used for a particular lesson, or with learner performance data.

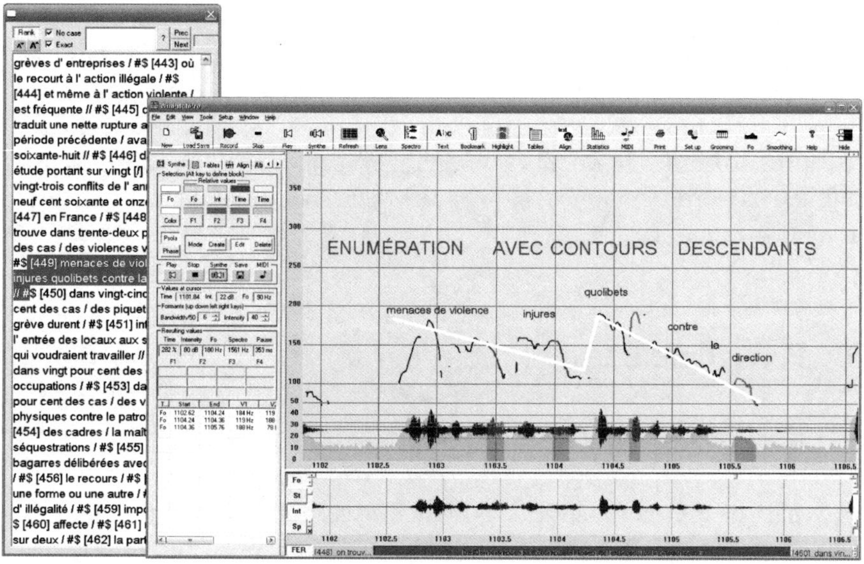

Fig. 2. Prosodic annotation and prosodic morphing showing the melodic variation in a sentence in French.

After selecting a section of the text (left window) the melodic (fundamental frequency) curve is automatically displayed (upper right window). Micromelodic variations are sketched by three lines which define the melodic variation of the synthesized speech (prosodic morphing).

3.3 Unicode compliance

As illustrated in Figs. 3–4 below, WinPitch is Unicode compliant. Any language whose writing is supported by the Unicode consortium can constitute the learning target. Transcription and alignment of right to left languages (such as Arabic or Hebrew) are completely supported, with a corresponding right to left display of acoustical data (spectrogram, intensity and melodic curves).

Fig. 3. A lesson developed in Mandarin. All functions of WinPitch are compliant with the use of Unicode or other fonts chosen by the instructor.

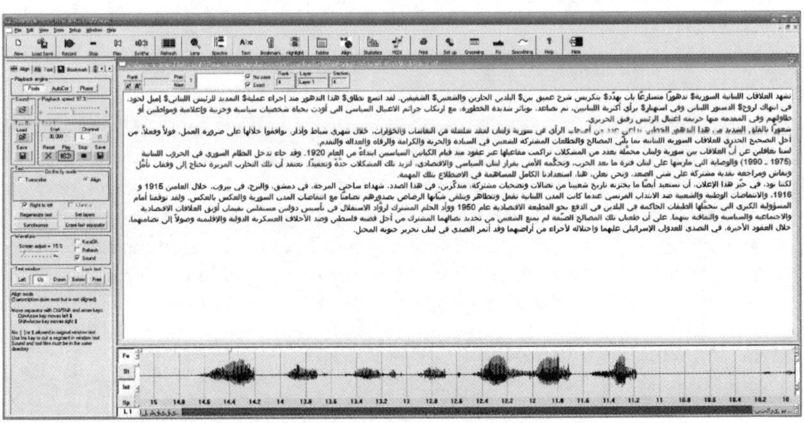

Fig. 4. A lesson in Arabic. Text and acoustic analysis are presented on a right to left layout.

3.4 Automatic lexicon

A lexicon is automatically generated from the transcribed text. A simple mouse click on any entry of this lexicon displays the corresponding entry of an Excel® format dictionary (including its translation, grammatical information, examples of use, etc.), as well as the playback and text display of the segments containing the entry. The dictionary can be edited at will, according to specific needs identified by the instructor.

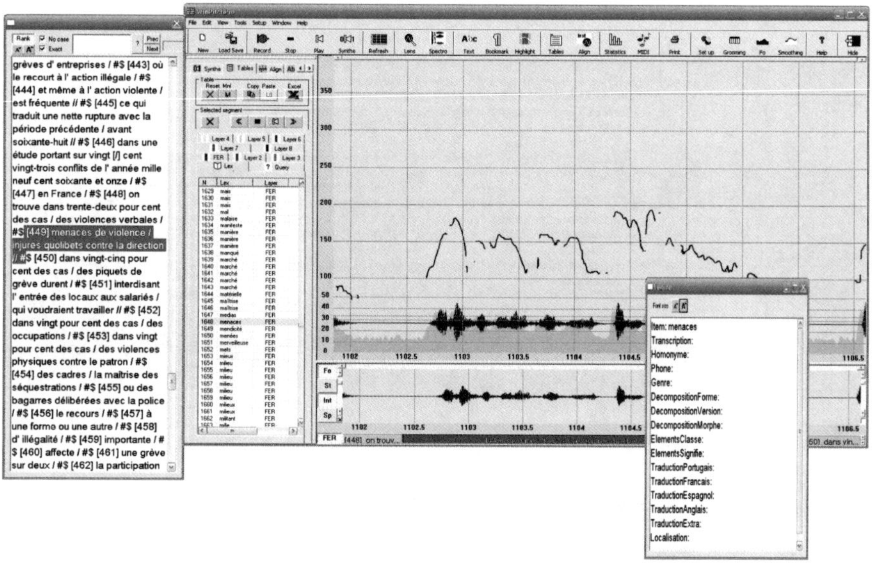

Fig. 5. A lesson dedicated to the analysis of a political debate in French. The left window displays the transcribed and aligned text. A portion of this text is selected and the corresponding segment of speech is played back and its acoustic analysis (spectrogram, intensity, wave form and fundamental frequency [melodic curve]) displayed on the upper right window (spectrogram, fundamental frequency curve, intensity, waveform). Any portion of the text can be selected to access the corresponding information from the automatically built database. Any portion of the speech sound can be played back at user selected speed (15 % to 200 % of real time). An Excel format dictionary is also displayed showing the entry corresponding to the word selected in the lexicon (*"j'espère"* in the example).

3.6 Data mining

A contextual search for textual data is possible, using various morphological criteria (for example by prefixes or suffixes), by segment duration, overlapping speakers, etc. It is thus possible to present a large number of examples extracted according to criteria, such as the rate/rhythm and the melody of noun phrases, prosodic factors associated with a change of turn, characteristics of overlapping speech, etc.

3.7 Real time acoustic analysis

Acoustic analysis, which can also be performed in real time during the recording of an audio file, displays spectrograms and curves of sound wave, intensity and fundamental frequency. This is particularly useful to provide a visual feedback to learners when they read aloud a portion of the text presented in a lesson. The instructor can, immediately or later, provide written or oral remarks related to student performance. These can also be sent by email to the learner.

Real time display is also available in playback mode, in order to help learners better grasp the relationship between auditory perception and acoustic display.

3.8 Instructor annotations

Any part of the audio data can be commented on the screen of acoustic analysis. It is possible to register comments on the model voice proposed, or on the learner's performance. Pictorial display of these comments joined to the analysis of the corresponding sound segments is similar to the annotations of a written diary. Parts calling for corrections can thus be commented on at will, either to indicate "faults" in pronunciation, or to draw attention to relevant details of the audio data. It is also possible to insert audio comments directly, for example phonetic corrections suggested by the teacher.

It is also possible to compare the acoustic analyses of models with those of learner imitations, eventually accompanied by teacher comments. The prosodic tool of morphing can then be used by learners to modify their realizations according to the model suggested.

3.9 Other features

WinPitch can read multimedia files with various input formats (wav, mp2.aiff, au, mpeg, mp2, mp4, avi, gsm 6.1, etc.). When the format corresponds to a multimedia file, the sound information is extracted and can be saved as a wav file, with a user-selected sampling frequency and mode (mono or stereo) if desired. Playback functions (variable speech) and data selection are preserved, while the multimedia content (movie, …) is displayed on a separate window.

The program handles stereo recordings by displaying acoustic analysis data in different (user selectable) colours. This is particularly useful for the study of simultaneous translation recordings for example, or for any other application where the two stereo channels correspond to different sources. The interaction between two speech events can then be studied easily.

WinPitch can directly read many popular input formats commonly used to encode text-speech alignment. The current input formats supported are: Praat textgrid files, trs Transcriber files, PFC (*Prononciation du français contemporain*) alignment files and CRFC (*Corpus de référence du français contemporain*) files. The program can also save the alignment data, together with any other information added by the instructor, in Excel or Ascii formats.

4. Conclusion

In summary, WinPitch is a tool for speech recordings which allows the same kind of indepth analysis classically performed on language texts in foreign language teaching classrooms. In analysing writing, the instructor scans the text translating unknown words and explaining difficult contexts, in order to deliver not only a satisfactory linguistic understanding but possibly also an in-depth comprehension of the historical and geographical context. WinPitch allows the same kind of deep analysis, not only at the comprehension level but also of the styles of the speakers studied. Details of pronunciation are easily highlighted and analyzed (by auditory perception and acoustic analysis if required), and can constitute the base for pronunciation exercises by learners at the word or sentence level. Provision to correct learner performance is also available, both by text and sound, through the use of prosodic morphing. Comprehension exercises are easily designed using variable speed playback, slower to facilitate auditory perception, faster to simulate real life auditory comprehension. Any language whose writing is supported by Unicode can be a target.

References

Germain A. & P. Martin (2000) Teaching oral production with computers. In Holland, M. and P. Delcloque (eds), *Speech technology in language teaching,* Zurich: Swets & Zeitlinger. PAGES??

Germain A. & P. Martin (2000) L'apport des technologies de visualisation et de synthèse dans l'enseignement des langues. In Raymond P. & C. Cornaire (eds) *Regards sur la didactique des langues*, Montréal: Editions Logiques, 105–131.

OLIVIER KRAIF & AGNÈS TUTIN

Using a bilingual annotated corpus as an academic writing aid: an application for EFL users[1]

Abstract

This paper describes the processing of a bilingual corpus for EFL learners. We focus on the identification of semi-frozen expressions specific to academic writing, using techniques such as POS tagging and finite states transducers: we show how, by coupling this identification with bilingual alignment, it is possible to develop interesting material that can be used as a writing aid and for corpus-based learning.

1. Introduction

Mastering Semi-Frozen Expressions (SFE), such as collocations, is one of the most difficult tasks in foreign language acquisition (Lewis 2000; Granger 1998). In the field of English for Scientific Purposes, and especially in writing activities, advanced learners need to have easy access to such lexical data. But to our knowledge, there are no existing dictionaries of collocations on this topic that are likely to meet these needs. In order to compensate for this lack of resources, we have proposed a corpus-based approach which makes it possible to observe collocations in their natural environment in corpora: this enables users to observe syntactic alternations, frequencies and collocations specific to particular subgenres or scientific fields. By using Natural Language Processing (NLP) techniques on English-French parallel annotated corpora at the semantic level, we aim to show how this material, implemented in a bilingual concordancer, can be used as a writing aid for French EFL writers of academic texts.

1 The research reported in this paper has been funded by the Région Rhône-Alpes (Projet Emergence).

First, we will explain how corpora can complement dictionaries and what kind of preprocessing is necessary to give learners easy access to corpora. Then we will describe the corpora of scientific writing and the various linguistic processes we have developed. We will finally show how a powerful concordancer designed for bilingual aligned text can be used as writing aid.

2. Using corpora as a writing aid

Dictionaries are essential to foreign language learners looking for the appropriate word in a writing task. But when it comes to collocations or idioms, dictionaries of collocations, even the most sophisticated ones, often fail to achieve their goals. Generally speaking, most dictionaries, due to lack of space, do not give a detailed account of syntactic alternations, frequencies, or register and domain variations. For example, in the *LTP Dictionary of Selected Collocations* (Hill & Lewis 2000), verbal collocates of the word *hypothesis* are just listed in alphabetical order (Fig. 1), without semantic treatment or exemplification.

HYPOTHESIS

V : accept, advance, agree with, bear out, challenge, confirm, construct, erect, favour, form, formulate, invalidate, oppose, propound, prove, put forward, raise objection to, refute, reject, rule out, set up, strengthen, support, test

Fig. 1. Verbal collocates of *hypothesis* (Hill & Lewis 2000).

Facing a set of this kind, how can the learner pick up the appropriate verb? What criteria should be used? While perhaps useful as a kind of "aide-mémoire" for learners with a very good command of the foreign language, it seems far less so for less advanced learners.

In the academic and scientific community, there is a real need for writing aids since many researchers have to publish results and ongoing studies in English. Using corpora could be especially appealing for academic and scientific language, which exhibits a rich phraseology, with many collocations and specific formulae (Gledhill 2000). An easy way to complement dictionaries could be to systematically look at examples in a bilingual aligned corpus in order to identify the most common translations and the most frequent collocations.

Several studies on corpus based-teaching have showed that corpora can make the writing task easier for foreign language learners (Chambers 2005; Caviglia 2004), helping them with syntax and word choice. But full text corpora used in basic concordancers are not really suitable for this task. First, as outlined by Caviglia (2004) corpora are more appropriate writing aids if they have been enriched with syntactic and semantic annotations. Annotation at the morpho-syntactic level enables users to look for all the inflected forms of a word and to select a specific part of speech for a given word, thus shortening the tedious process of sorting concordance results (Chambers 2005). Semantic annotation – e. g. the annotation of collocations in our project – permits the user to directly access word choice through a semantic query. Second, we think it essential that users are not technically challenged by software. A user-friendly interface has to be developed instead of complex query languages using tricky regular expressions. We think that the Alinea tool developed in our team, coupled with an annotated bilingual corpus of academic writing, can meet these needs.

3. Building a bilingual corpus annotated at the syntactic and semantic levels

3.1 Stages of corpus processing

For this project, a medium size corpus (400,000 words) of academic texts and their translations (French and English) was been collected. The corpus included research articles, reports, theses in linguistics, computational linguistics, and biology. Building such a corpus is a tedious and time-consuming process, due to the lack of freely available resources.

The corpus was then tagged at the morpho-syntactic level in both English and French. Collocations were then annotated in the French texts using finite state automata. Finally, the English and French texts were aligned at the sentence and the word level.

In the next two sections, we will detail the second and third stages of the annotation process.

3.2 Annotation of collocations

In order to deal with SFEs in French scientific texts, we studied the semantic properties of verb-noun combinations in our corpus of scientific writings. Our work (Bloquet 2003; Tutin 2007) showed that these associations are very often predictable given the semantic features of the nominal base and the verb collocate. For example, nouns which can be considered as "scientific objects" such as *paramètre* ('parameter'), *élément* ('element'), *données* ('data'), etc. are easily combined with verbs in the semantic field of "study": *étudier* ('to study'), *examiner* ('to examine'), *analyser* ('to analyse'), … In order to account for these regularities, we grouped a number of nouns and verbs into semantic categories, based on their linguistic properties, e.g. verbs of 'study', verbs of 'positive judgement', nouns of 'action', etc. These categories could be helpful to provide a semantic access to phraseology in a writing aid, and we assume that they could be easily translated into English. Beside semantic regularities, we noticed that SFEs often exhibit syntactic alternations: *the work presented below, we presented this work,* etc. The linguistic annotation of the corpus includes these two kinds of linguistic information which seem useful for EFL learners.

Once the corpus had been annotated at the morpho-syntactic level, the SFEs of the French corpus were analysed with transducers using lexicon-grammars implemented in Intex (Silberztein 1999). The XML annotation below gives examples of such annotated examples which include syntactic information regarding the construction (e.g. passive or active), the collocation (e.g. "*mener-étude*" [to perform studies]), the verb category ('make'), the noun category ('concept built by research activity'), the noun lemma (our description does not include the morpho-syntactic tags for the sake of readability).

La Bibliothèque du Congrès a elle aussi <colloc const="dir" colloc="mener-étude" type-verbe="faire.N"type-nom="n.fab.elab" lemme-nom="étude">mené</colloc> des études fondées sur la loi d' Arrhenius
[The Library of Congress (LOC) also performed Arrhenius studies]

Fig. 2. An annotated collocation.

The automated annotations were checked manually before the alignment process.

3.3 Bilingual alignment

Bilingual alignment aims at linking textual units (sections, paragraphs, sentences, phrases, words…) that are translational equivalents through a source text and its translation. It is not a trivial task, as there is no one-to-one matching between small textual units such as sentences, phrases or lexemes. Therefore, the automatic aligner has to determine *probable* groupings between units, in order to fit the translational equivalence, and these techniques usually give good results at sentence level, especially between related languages such as English and French (Langlais, 1998). For this task, we have used Alinea,[2] a software that implements techniques based on sentence length, identical chains and cognate words (Kraif 2001), and which yielded very good results during the Arcade 2 campaign (Chiao et al. 2006).

4. Corpus search

Using the Alinea bilingual interface makes it easy to retrieve sentence pairs in English and French which provide the requested SFE examples, and to observe the results in bilingual aligned text.

2 Freely distributed software available at: <http://w3.u-grenoble3.fr/kraif/>.

4.1 Bilingual interface

Alinea is a not only a bilingual alignment tool, but also a bilingual concordancer, which includes a powerful query language. Once the query has been submitted, Alinea displays the results in the bilingual concordancer, as shown in Fig. 3.

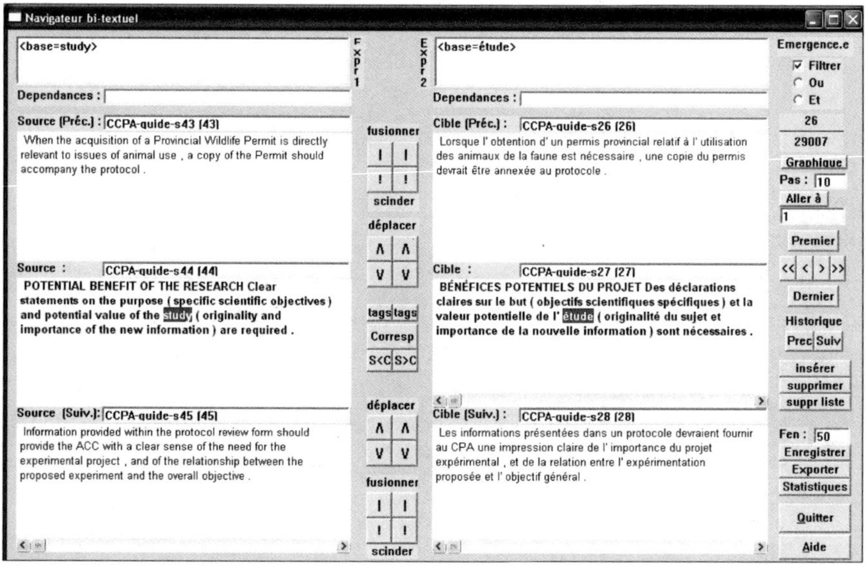

Fig. 3. The Alinea interface.

4.2 Query language

Alinea implements a query language that can mix forms, lemmas, morpho-syntactic features, collocation tags (actually, any XML tags that have been added to the tokens) using a formalism of regular expressions. This formalism can be invoked both at token and character level. For instance, the query

(<ctag=ver><ctag=adv>*<ctag=art>(<et>?<ctag=adv>?<ctag=adj>)*<base=étude>|<base=étude><>{0,4}<ctag=verb,msd=ppass>)

searches for two kinds of expression:

- a *verb*, followed by any number of *adverbs* (operator *), followed by an *article*, followed by any number of *adjectives* (which may be modified by an adverb and by coordination), followed by the lemma *étude*; OR (operator |)
- the lemma *étude*, followed by 0 to 4 tokens (operator {n,m}), followed by a *verb* tagged as *past participle*.

With this query, we may retrieve examples such as:

> [jimmu-s944] Nous avons **réalisé** la présente **étude** pour mettre au point , d'après une revue de la littérature , des critères capables de faciliter le diagnostic d' anaphylaxie .

> [CCPA-Manue-s1038] elle devrait plutôt être réservée à des **études sur le métabolisme approuvées** préalablement

Regular expressions may also be implemented at character level, to match any feature within a token. For instance, when using a corpus that has not been tagged and lemmatized, simple operators such as ^ (to express the beginning of a token), $ (to express the end of a token), ? (to express the optional presence of the preceding character) are useful to get the various inflected forms.

</^études?><>{3}</ées?$>

> [MAU_0203-s131] néanmoins , l' **étude devra être menée** sur un échantillon plus important pour confirmer une apparente supériorité de la photothérapie .

> [MAU_0203-s121] comparativement , il serait techniquement beaucoup plus difficile d' effectuer des **études centrées** sur les effets de la température que ceux de la lumière .

4.3 Different kinds of queries

4.3.1 Looking for a specific collocation

First, one may look for examples that illustrate a specific collocation, i.e. knowing both words of the collocation in the source language. To implement this search, the query may simply rely on the collocation tags that have been added to the corpus: for instance, <colloc=mener-étude> provides bilingual examples such as:

> [DAB_0203-s93] La Bibliothèque du Congrès a elle aussi **mené** des **études** fondées sur la loi d' Arrhenius (…) → The Library of Congress (LOC) also **performed** Arrhenius **studies** .

> [DAB_0203-s118] Comme pour le vieillissement à la chaleur , les **études** sur le vieillissement à la lumière ont été **menées** par deux laboratoires → As in the temperature-aging studies , the light **studies involved** the work of two laboratories .

These two extracts shows different ways of translating the same collocation: in the first, an equivalent collocation is involved (*to perform a study*), while the second uses a converse construction, where the base *study* becomes a subject. A quick look at other cases in the corpus shows that the passive construction of *mener-étude* is generally translated by the active voice, with no equivalent for the collocate *mener* (which is considered as a light verb, and as an "empty" word is not translated in some contexts).

4.3.2 Looking for verb collocates of a given noun

To widen the search scope, it is also possible to look for every collocation that involves the base *étude*. The query <colloc=/étude> gives many examples of constructions such as *publier une étude*, *proposer une étude*, *entreprendre une étude*, *poursuivre une étude*, *effectuer une étude*, with equivalent expressions such as *to conduct / to undertake / to carry out a study*, etc. Once again, the French collocate is hardly ever translated as such.

[CCPA-guide-s44] Le CPA peut recommander au chercheur de **faire** une **étude** pilote (…) → A pilot **study** may be recommended by the ACC (…)

[CCPA-Manue-s8844] C' est ainsi que les **études entreprises** au niveau pré-universitaire doivent être conçues de manière à developper le respect de la vie → **Studies** at the pre-university level should be designed to develop a respect for life

These examples reveal that the corpus not only provides potential equivalents for a given collocation, but also gives synonyms in the source and target languages. As a matter of fact, two expressions often translated in the same way are likely to be semantically related. The parallelism of the corpus makes it possible to observe these phenomena thoroughly.

4.3.3 Looking for expressions of a semantic type (for base or collocate or both)

As bases and collocates have a semantic tag, it is possible to look for any instance of an SFE related to a base in which the collocate belongs to a given category. Thus it is possible to reduce the scope of the previous search by focusing on the *'faire'* class of verbs: <colloc=/étude,type-verbe=faire.N>. The solutions contain such expressions as: *faire/conduire/mener/réaliser une étude (do/conduct/carry out achieve a study).*

Other semantic categories are linked to evaluative aspects, such as *to have a good or bad opinion of.* These may help to retrieve examples that illustrate enunciative features such as how to support/reject a point of view. Using <type-verbe=opinion.favorable.N>, we get:

[Citi1-s182] pourquoi et comment nous **préconisons** une **démarche** de design (…) → why and how we **promote** a design (…)

[jcardio-s265] En **soutenant** l' **idée** d' un essai contrôlé (…) → In **endorsing** the **idea** of a placebo-controlled …

[jimmu-s322] Kracke et Parker , aux Etats-Unis , ont **avancé** l' **hypothèse** que (…) → Kracke and Parker **argued** that (…)

[tao1-s18] Je veux **préconiser** une **approche** au problème (…) → I want to **advocate** a **view** of the problem (…)

These examples are interesting because although they concern different objects, they are *analogous*, and show different ways of supporting an idea/approach/hypothesis, using SFEs or just single words.

4.3.4 Checking a word-to-word translation

One of the most straightforward uses of a corpus is to check whether a given expression is actually used. For instance, various examples show that the verb *préconiser* may be translated by *promote*, and the noun *approche* by *approach*. But one may wonder whether the collocation *promote an approach* can be used in the same contexts as *préconiser une approche*.

Alinea's query language allows users to search for the cooccuring lemmas with the corresponding features (in the following case, separated by no more than 4 tokens):

> (<base=promote,ctag=verb><>{4}<base=approach,ctag=noun>|<base=approach, ctag=noun><>{4}<base=promote,ctag=verb,msd=/paprt>)

Our corpus gives a positive answer:

> [WHR95-s878] (…) l' OMS **préconise** une **approche** cohérente et intégrée de tous les aspects des soins aux enfants , y compris à la naissance → (…) WHO **promotes** a coherent , integrated **approach** to all aspects of child care including childbirth .

4.4 Building queries

As shown in the last example, building the appropriate query may appear to be tricky: it requires knowing how to use basic regular expressions, and how to handle morphosyntactic tags that have specific names (e.g. *paprt* for past participle) depending on the pos-tagger and lemmatizer. In order to cope with this, we are currently developing a graphical web-interface that allows step-by-step construction of the intended query without prior knowledge of this kind. Fig. 4 shows how the query of the last search is built.

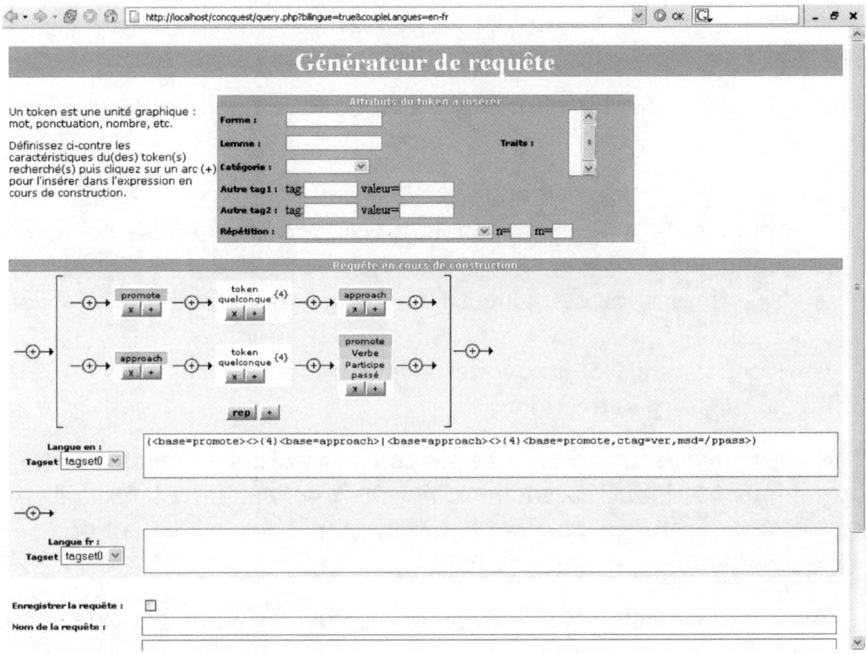

Fig. 4. Query building interface.

Every token is represented by a box, optionally containing data about the form, the lemma, the part-of-speech or grammatical features (that are translated into natural language). Subsequent tokens are linked by a horizontal arrow. Tokens, or expressions between squared brackets, may be repeated using + * or { } operators. The disjunction of two expressions (connected by *or*) is rendered by vertical superposition, with brackets around them. This representation is very close to the finite state automata definition, as used in the Intex software. Different tagsets may be chosen depending on the tagger that has been used.

5. Prospects: an experiment for academic writing

The web interface is not completely functional yet and needs to be improved with:

- a lemma index to speed up the search process;
- an option to browse the results in KWIC format in both source and target languages;
- highlighting of the equivalent forms when an expression has been selected;
- a wizard to easily build queries using collocation tags;

bilingual glossary extraction.

The query interface will then be tested as an aid for academic writing by a number of French academics. For this application, a subset of scientific texts on linguistics and computational linguistics could be selected. We will try to study:

- what types of queries are made, and particularly to what extent semantic queries are used;
- what kinds of additional commands and resources (linguistic annotations on source and target texts, graphical user interface, use of a thesaurus) could be integrated into a more comprehensive writing aid.

Then, we plan to investigate how to automatically construct formal queries starting from expressions written in a more "intuitive" language, such as: "V + étude" or "conduire + expérimentation".

References

Bloquet G. (2004) Vers une modélisation des collocations verbales du lexique méthodologique dans les écrits scientifiques: application au TAL, Mémoire de DEA, Université Grenoble 3-Stendhal.

Caviglia F. (2004) Students' diverse appreciation of text corpora as writing aids, In T. Cauderey (ed.), Proceedings of the Ninth Nordic Conference for English Studies (NAES 2004), Aarhus, Denmark, 27–29 May 2004.

Chambers A. (2005) Integrating corpus consultation in language studies, Language Learning and Technology, 9, 111–125.

Chiao Y.-C., O. Kraif, D. Laurent, T. M. H. Nguyen, N. Semmar, F. Stuck, J. Véronis, W. Zaghouani (2006) Evaluation of multilingual text alignment systems: the ARCADE II project, Proceedings of the fifth international conference on Language Resources and Evaluation, LREC 2006, Genova, May 2006.

Gledhill C. (2000) Collocations in science writing. Tübingen, Gunter Narr.

Kraif O. (2001) Exploitation des cognats dans les systèmes d'alignement bi-textuel: architecture et évaluation, TAL 42: 3, ATALA, Paris, 833–867.

Langlais P., M. Simard, J. Veronis, S. Armstrong, P. Bonhomme, F. Debili, P. Isabelle, E. Souissi & P. Théron (1998) ARCADE: A cooperative research project on parallel text alignment evaluation. Proceedings of First International Conference on Language Resources and Evaluation (LREC), Granada, 28–30 May, 289–292.

Lewis M. (2000) (ed.) Teaching collocations. Boston: LTP.

Hill J. & M. Lewis (1997) LTP Dictionary of selected collocations. Hove: LTP.

Silberztein M. (1999) INTEX: a Finite State Transducer toolbox, Theoretical Computer Science #231: 1, Elsevier Science.

Tutin A. (2007) Modélisation linguistique et annotation des collocations: une application au lexique transdiciplinaire des écrits scientifiques. Formaliser les langues avec l'ordinateur: de Intex à NooJ, S. Koeva, D. Maurel & M. Silberztein (eds), Besançon, Presses Universitaires de Franche Comté, 189–215.

Part four
Resources: Evaluation

Isabella Chiari

Teaching language variation using Italian corpora

Abstract

This paper aims at evaluating reference corpora of spoken and written Italian as tools for teaching variation to learners of Italian as a second language. Specifically, some of the main Italian reference corpora will be compared, focusing on their classification of varieties and their potential as sources of information on register, domains, genre, and text types.

1. Introduction

The aim of this paper is to evaluate reference corpora of spoken and written Italian as tools for teaching variation to learners of Italian as a second language. Language variation is traditionally one of the most crucial and complex abilities that learners are expected to acquire: aspects such as genre, register, text type, domain, topic, activity type, sublanguage and style are key in developing language awareness. In corpus design, there is a wide variety of approaches to capturing variation, a variety reflected in the possibilities offered by different query systems. What kind of information about linguistic varieties is encoded in Italian reference corpora? And how can learners acquire knowledge about variation from the available electronic resources, either autonomously or in guided classroom activities?

2. Language variation and corpora

The fruitfulness of corpora in language teaching has been widely stressed in the literature, be it in a general didactic environment (Sinclair 2004; Gavioli 2005; Scott & Tribble 2006), in translation studies (Bernardini & Zanettin 2000; Botley et al. 2000; Wang 2000; Zanettin et al. 2003), in classroom work (Johns 1991a; Partington 1998; Godwin-Jones 2001; Timmis 2003), and in learner corpus exploitation (Granger et al. 2000; Granger et al. 2002; Tono 2002). The advantages for the learner include easy access to authentic texts, autonomous management of the learning process in a data-driven framework (Johns 1991b, c; Wible et al. 2002), and stimulation of metalinguistic reflection. For the teacher they include the possibility to obtain real examples of language use, assistance in syllabus and materials design, and other functions (Kahn 1985; Szendeffy 2005).

The interaction between language teaching using corpora and the need to develop understanding of language variation has been addressed by a number of scholars. The general framework proposed by Biber (1988, 1995), being both theoretical and methodological, has led to considerable discussion of the relationship between language variation and corpora. Biber's attention has generally been focused on exploiting corpora for variation studies (Biber & Finegan 1991; Biber 1992, 1993a, b; Biber et al. 1998), and he attempts to clarify the terminological jungle that characterises this area by associating the term *genre* and *register* to "situationally defined text categories (such as fiction, sports, broadcasts, psychology articles)", and *text type* to "linguistically defined text categories" (1993a: 244–5).[1] Biber argues that precedence should be given to external criteria in corpus design, using genre and register as the main principles in distinguishing subcorpora.

But reference corpora of major languages have extremely dissimilar designs, and exhibit different capabilities for analysing language varieties. Not only are registers differently defined and represented (qualita-

1 While the term *register* is commonly used as a „general cover term associated with all aspects of variation in use" (Biber 1995: 9), it is most closely connected to linguistic patterns and choices instantiated by specific genres (Lee 2001).

tively and quantitatively), but the possibility to retrieve data about variation varies in different corpus querying systems.

Once the corpus has been designed and constructed, other questions arise as to the possibility of investigating different aspects of variation. Since corpora cannot be said to be representative of a single genre *tout court* – we can always think of features that are only marginally present in the corpus because they are rare, because they refer to a level of analysis which was not foreseen in the corpus design, or simply because they show marginal tendencies – we must always take into account the limits of data retrieval from different corpora, and from different subcorpora within a corpus. For the study of language variation, especially directed towards language learning, the obvious sources are reference corpora. A reference corpus has been defined as

> designed to provide comprehensive information about a language. It aims to be large enough to represent all the relevant varieties of the language, and the characteristic vocabulary, so that it can be used as a basis for reliable grammars, dictionaries, thesauri and other language reference materials. (Eagles 1996)

Reference corpora are not the only source of such data, but constitute, by definition, the most comprehensive portrait of a language's main varieties.

Variation must play a role in the language learning process, since it is a key aspect of communicative competence (Hymes 1971; Spolsky 1989) But a decision has to be made whether to adopt a genre-driven or a text-type-driven approach. If we accept Biber and Finegan's claim that *linguistic variation is generally conditioned by some combination of social, situational, discourse and processing characteristics* (1991: 216), then we will tend to prefer a functional approach that will give precedence to genre/register in presenting variation to language learners. This seems a sensible way to move if we wish to maintain a communicative methodology in teaching.

Whether we prefer a genre-driven or a text-type-driven approach, there remain practical problems related to corpus exploitation in classroom environments. When it comes to teaching such central aspects of variation as differences between spoken and written language, sociolinguistic variables, formal and informal registers, and language change, the need for explicitly coded information in corpora (as well as in dictionaries and other tools) becomes urgent: "language teachers and researchers need to know exactly what kind of language they are examining or describing" (Lee 2001: 37). But corpora encode aspects of language variation such as formal and informal styles (at phonological, morphological, syntactic and textual levels) and in general diaphasic variations (written vs. spoken, diatopic differences, speaker styles, genres, domains, sublanguages, etc.) differently. Furthermore, to investigate language variation, it is essential to have access to multiple linguistic sources, since it is only possible to detect variation through comparison. Features which are to be considered specific to a genre or a text type can only be detected through the observation of diversity or of different degrees of similarity. When it comes to analysing variation using corpora, the first condition is the possibility to keep different genre labels apart.

It is of course possible to investigate language variation by close analysis of textual material extracted from corpora. But it is not feasible to expect language learners to discover patterns of variation which have not been previously coded by the corpus designer or at least explored by the teacher in advance. The most obvious instruments for extracting information about variation are the retrieval tools associated with different corpora. These retrieval tools (mainly corpus querying systems) enable, to different extents, the user to mine a corpus for lexical, morphological, syntactic and pragmatic aspects of variation.

3. Exploiting available Italian corpora

Reference corpora are becoming widely used for teaching purposes and a number of theoretical investigations of their potential for teaching variation have been produced (Hunston 2002; Conrad 2004). Maximum coverage of variation is considered a prerequisite of reference corpora aiming at representativeness, register-diversity and balance among genres. So if we want to look at variation for teaching purposes, reference corpora should be the ideal tool. In this section I compare some of the main Italian reference corpora, focusing on their classification of varieties and their potential as sources of information on register, domains, genre, and text types. I will also look at examples of how variation can be observed, and how students can examine the main characteristics of register diversification identified by Biber (1993b: 221): "individual linguistic features are distributed differently across registers, and [...] the same (or similar) linguistic features can have different functions in different registers".

3.1 Written Reference Corpora

Among the corpora of written Italian developed during the past decades (Chiari 2005), some can be considered reference corpora in their design and scope. Excluding some which are no longer available, such as LIF (Bortolini et al. 1971), I will focus on two of these: the large 100-million word *COrpus di Riferimento dell'Italiano Scritto,* 1998–2001 (CORIS/CODIS: Rossini Favretti 2000; Rossini Favretti et al. 2002), and the smaller 4-million word *Corpus e Lessico di Frequenza dell'Italiano Scritto* (COLFIS: Laudanna et al. 1995).

3.1.1 CORIS/CODIS

Developed by the Centre for theoretical and applied linguistics of the University of Bologna (CILTA), this is currently the largest publicly available balanced corpus of written Italian. It exists in two forms: a static one (*COrpus di Riferimento dell'Italiano Scritto* (*CORIS*)), and a dynamic one (*COrpus Dinamico dell'Italiano Scritto* (*CODIS*)). The latter is a monitor corpus updated every two years, modelled on the Bank of English. The corpus is divided into subcorpora of traditional genres: press, fiction, administrative and legal prose, academic prose, miscellanea and ephemera. These subcorpora are divided into sections and subsections based on external parameters (see Table 1), including both national and local varieties of the language. The hierarchical structuring of sections and subsections involves a mixture of subgenres and domains. Thus the fiction subcorpus contains crime, adventure, and science-fiction, along with women's literature, literature for adults, and literature for children. Academic prose includes books, reviews, popular history, philosophy, arts, literary criticism, law, economy, biology, etc. Other subcorpora seem to be organized on the basis of differences in readers and purposes.

SUBCORPORA	*SECTIONS*	*SUB-SECTIONS*
FICTION *25 Mw*	*novels, short stories*	*Italian, foreign, for adults, for children, crime, adventure, science-fiction, women's literature*
PRESS *38 Mw*	*newspapers, periodic, supplement*	*national, local, specialist, non-specialist, connotated, non-connotated*
ACADEMIC PROSE *12 Mw*	*human sciences, natural sciences, physics, experimental sciences*	*books, reviews scientific, popular history, philosophy, arts, literary criticism, law, economy, biology, etc.*
LEGAL AND ADMIN. PROSE *10 Mw*	*legal, bureaucratic, administrative*	*books, reviews*
MISCELLANEA *10 Mw*	*books on religion, travel, cookery, hobbies, etc.*	*books, reviews*
EPHEMERA *5 Mw*	*letters, leaflets, instructions*	*private, public, printed, electronic*

Table 1. Design structure of CORIS/CODIS.

The only tool available to access the corpus is concordancing over the web (http://corpora.dslo.unibo.it). The dynamic version allows the user to choose which subcorpora to include, and how large each should be (seeFig. 1), adapting to different needs and working hypotheses The query interface admits single word forms, specific sequences of word forms (AND/OR logical operator), sequences at a distance (which retrieves two words with up to a given number of words in between), and returns the total number of hits satisfying the query, displaying a maximum of 300. Collocational values using mutual information, t-score or raw frequency are optionally shown. No grammatical annotation is provided to the end user, and at the moment the public online version of the corpus is not lemmatized (accessed May 2008). The extremely synthetic online help seems to suggest the presence of grammatical annotation, though no explanation of the tagset and query language is given. A major limitation is the impossibility of exploring entire texts (probably due to copyright issues), or of restricting queries to specific sections and subsections within the subcorpora. Distributions over subcorpora, sections and subsections are not given.

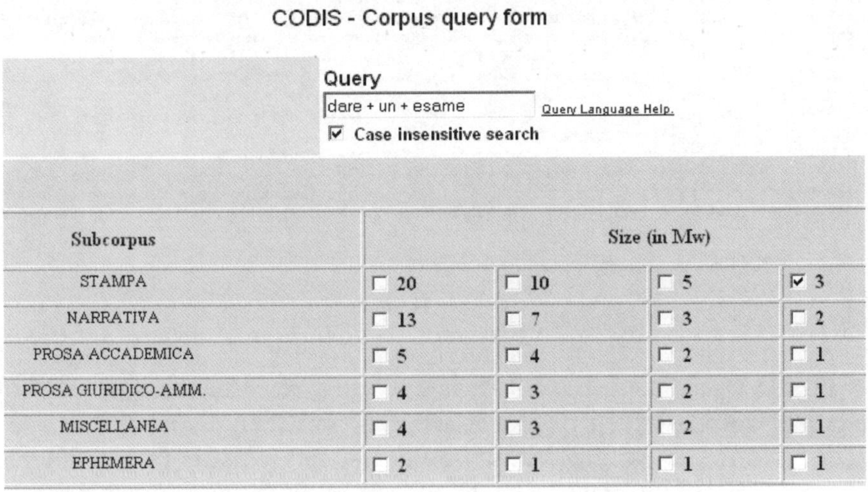

CODIS - Corpus query form

Query

dare + un + esame

Query Language Help.

Case insensitive search

Subcorpus	Size (in Mw)			
STAMPA	20	10	5	3
NARRATIVA	13	7	3	2
PROSA ACCADEMICA	5	4	2	1
PROSA GIURIDICO-AMM.	4	3	2	1
MISCELLANEA	4	3	2	1
EPHEMERA	2	1	1	1

Fig. 1. CODIS query form.

We can search for specific wordforms or sequences, such as *praticamente* or *a lui gli piace*, and obtain the actual number of hits found (309 and 2 respectively), a concordance display of up to 300 occurrences with a maximum of 160 characters of context, and an indication of which subcorpus each line comes from (see Fig. 2). If the total number of hits is over 300, but not too large, we can obtain all the concordance lines by doing separate queries for each subcorpus. But when faced, say, with the 2,232 hits for the form *diciamo (we say/let's say)*, we cannot analyse all the hits in order to distinguish uses as an ordinary verb from those as a discourse marker. No hints on the use of searches for lemmas are given in the help file or in the documentation. Information about register variation is only obtainable via separate queries in different subcorpora.

Number of concordances: 300/309

```
STAMPA_3  : e giorni dal fattaccio , il caso è praticamente chiuso . Un particolare : prima
STAMPA_3  : tando alla versione ufficiale , ha praticamente consegnato ai carabinieri il Cap
STAMPA_3  : ste dalla riforma Amato del ' 93 ( praticamente con i vecchi requisiti ) , ma ac
STAMPA_3  : tutte quelle riduzioni di pena che praticamente vanificano l ' effetto dissuasiv
STAMPA_3  : stato il giorno buono . La Roma ha praticamente chiuso l ' acquisto di Helguera
STAMPA_3  : icenne nel giardino condominiale , praticamente sotto gli occhi di alcuni compag
STAMPA_3  : " George " ? O quello che Teddy fa praticamente da sempre ? " Anche se l ' osses
STAMPA_3  :  " : in questa categoria includeva praticamente tutte le categorie sociali , dai
STAMPA_3  : della fabbrica " . Enzo Ferrari ha praticamente creato la pista di Imola : un am
STAMPA_3  : ace , amici che mi vogliono bene e praticamente tutto ciò che sognavo . Ma quest
STAMPA_3  : i sale cinematografiche a ingresso praticamente gratuito sono comunque ancora mo
STAMPA_3  :  connessioni ) facciano il mercato praticamente senza consultarli ( il caso - Ta
STAMPA_3  : nis , costretto dalla crisi a fare praticamente il custode , fa fatica a tirare
STAMPA_3  :  tornare indietro " dalla scelta , praticamente esclusiva , dell ' Assemblea Cos
STAMPA_3  : a laboratorio che girerà a Fiorano praticamente per tutto il mese a partire da m
STAMPA_3  : omenica l ' abbiamo a disposizione praticamente tutti . Ma possiede potenzialità
STAMPA_3  :  % rispetto a settembre ) . Prezzi praticamente fermi invece a Bari e Palermo (
STAMPA_3  : rtamente . Del resto l ' Africa ha praticamente sovvenzionato lo sviluppo dell '
STAMPA_3  : ungo telex in cui una nobildonna , praticamente , intima allo Stato di darle sub
STAMPA_3  : isticato sistema di trasmissione , praticamente esclusivo , che consente non sol
STAMPA_3  : o la squadra più forte del mondo , praticamente la stessa della passata stagione
STAMPA_3  : esta bambina , una famiglia l ' ha praticamente abbandonata e l ' altra se l ' è
STAMPA_3  : ntitativi venduti nel ' 96 si sono praticamente dimezzati . In realtà - spiega G
```

Fig. 2. CODIS concordance: *praticamente.*

3.1.2 Corpus e Lessico di Frequenza dell'Italiano Scritto (COLFIS)

COLFIS (Laudanna et al. 1995) is a recently released frequency list of Italian words derived from a 3,798,275 word corpus of written texts collected in the early '90s. While the frequency list is fully available (in a variety of different formats), the corpus at the moment is in prototype form, and queries can only be performed on those texts authorized by the copyright holders (<http://www.ge.ilc.cnr.it/strumenti.php>). COLFIS is an extremely interesting design, being based on reading statistics for a sample of the Italian population from 11 years of age, processed by the National Institute of Statistics (ISTAT). The relative proportions of texts included in the corpus were based on 1992–94 data for newspapers, magazines and books. In Biber's terms (1993a:245) the corpus is designed on *text reception* principles, aiming to represent language use from a demographic perspective.

SUBCORPORA	SECTIONS	SUBSECTIONS	
NEWSPAPERS 1,523,167	Corriere della Sera La Repubblica La Stampa	Business and economics Local news Gossip Crime Foreign affairs Home affairs Science	Arts and sport
MAGAZINES 1,084,574		Arts, science and technology Cars and boats Children and young people Home and hobbies Photo comics[2] General information Gossip	Radio and TV Sport Travel and ecology Women's Other
BOOKS 542,334		Art Children's Classic fiction Crime and espionage Drama and poetry Essays Hobbies and travel	Modern fiction Natural and exact sciences Romantic fiction Science fiction Other

Table 2. Design structure of COLFIS.

For each of the three national newspapers sampled, there are 9 canonical categories of texts (corresponding to sections in the newspapers). Magazines are divided into 12 categories using a mixture of genre, domain, and text-type criteria. Books are distributed into 13 categories, again with mixed genre and domain criteria.

2 A popular subgenre of comics in which the story is told not by drawings, but by photos.

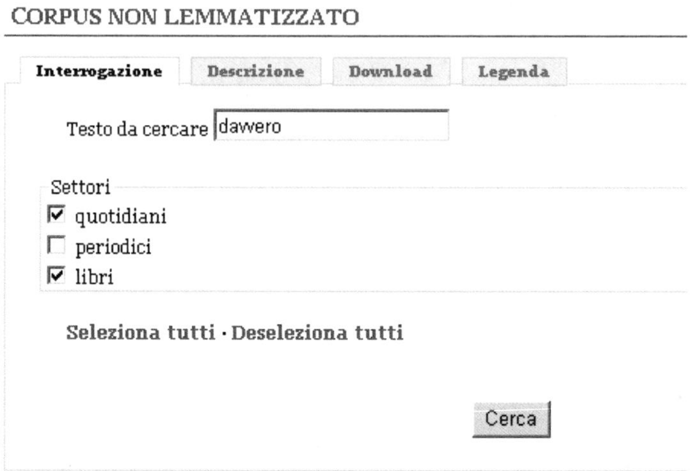

Fig. 3. COLFIS query form for the non lemmatized corpus.

The authorized portion of the corpus can be concordanced on the web, using either the raw text or the lemmatized version. The three subcorpora can be searched individually, but not subsections of these. The raw corpus has a very intuitive interface (see Fig. 3). As there is no query syntax, only word types and word sequences can be searched for. The output is a tabular concordance showing the hit paragraph with information on subcorpus, subsection, newspaper or magazine source, author, title, publisher, year, and date. Context length cannot be varied.

periodico	fotoromanzi	lancio-Lucky	Rienzi Alice	Immagini di una ragazza scomparsa		94-09-13	Janet è sempre piena di risorse, lo *sai*.
periodico	fotoromanzi	sogno	Mancuso Antonino	Sta suonando per me		92-12-01	Si sta divertendo, e poi lo *sai* che ci tiene alla tua presenza. Eppure, *sai*.
periodico	informazione general	epoca	Gnocchi Laura	Vi ricordate...Serena Cruz? ...Adesso è una bambina felice		92-09-16	Del resto, della sua vita passata ricorda poco, e soltanto ogni tanto dice: "Mamma *sai*.
periodico	informazione general	espresso	Siciliano Enzo	Il film: che profumo di Cechov!		92-09-13	Non *sai* se abbia letto più Cechov o Trifonov.

Fig. 4. COLFIS concordance of *sai*.

A similar query window is available for the lemmatized search, producing a similar output with POS tagging (12 categories) included, but only a sentence of context.

Most queries performed with CODIS can be performed in COLFIS, except that the latter does not support wildcards. Frequency information is not provided in the concordance tables, but can be obtained through a specific search mask giving frequencies, relative frequencies and dispersion values for all the wordforms and lemmas in the corpus. The general frequency lists can be downloaded, while results of single queries are not exportable. As with CODIS, access to the full text is not permitted.

If looking for specific words or sequences, COLFIS can be used to determine distribution across the main subcorpora, but morphological and syntactic patterns cannot be investigated. The impossibility of querying specific subsections significantly reduces the suitability of the corpus for studying variation.

3.2 Spoken Corpora

Many researchers have favoured the use of spoken language corpora in classroom work. Cresti (2007) notes how artificially constructed materials differ radically from natural conversations performed on the same tasks, and how the latter present far greater diaphasic variability. While for formal written language, real-life uses may be relatively similar to those presented to the learner in the classroom, the distance between the speech of teaching materials and that of real life communication is enormous, making the presentation of spoken language variation a key task for teaching.

If, as we have seen, written corpora can vary considerably in their coverage of language variation due to an ambiguous distinction between external and internal factors, for speech corpora the obstacles are multiplied by the absence of a shared classification of genres and registers.

Over the last fifteen years a number of Italian speech corpora have been created, starting with the pioneering *Lessico di frequenza dell'ita-*

liano parlato (LIP: De Mauro et al 1993). Some multilingual corpora also include spoken Italian components, such as C-ORAL-ROM, *Integrated reference corpora for spoken romance languages* (Cresti & Moneglia 2005). Other corpora have been designed to explore phonetic and phonological properties, such as *Archivio delle Varietà di Italiano Parlato* (AVIP: Pettorino & Giannini 2003), *Archivio di Parlato Italiano* (API), *Italiano Parlato* (IPar: Albano Leoni & Giordano 2005) e *Corpora e Lessici di Italiano Parlato e Scritto* (CLIPS: <http://www.clips.unina.it/>).[3] Here we will focus attention on two corpora that aim at representativeness of variation, namely LIP (500,000 words) and the Italian component of C-ORAL-ROM (300,000 words).

3.2.1 The LIP corpus

LIP was designed for use in the production of the first frequency list of spoken Italian (De Mauro et al. 1993). It was modelled on the corpus used for the first frequency list of written Italian (LIF: Bortolini et al. 1971). By current standards the corpus is rather small (500,000 words), consisting of 57 hours of speech recorded in the early '90s, transcribed and lemmatized. It was designed along two dimensions of variation: diatopic (4 cities: Rome, Florence, Milan and Naples) and interaction typology (5 classes: A: bidirectional, exchange, face to face, with free turn-taking; B: bi-directional exchange, not face to face, with free turn-taking; C: bi-directional exchange, face to face, with regulated turn-taking; D: unidirectional exchange, with the addressee being present; E: distanced unidirectional exchange). Criteria are thus mainly external ones (see Table 3).

The corpus can now be interrogated at the BADIP website (<http://languageserver.uni-graz.at/badip/>). The BADIP interface is a powerful one. The query syntax accepts wildcards, POS tags, lemma searches, gaps between sequences. Subcorpora can be queried separately. Simple statistics (frequency and subcorpora frequency) are given for each query.

3 The wide interest in spoken language corpora is testified by the Parlaritaliano project, directed by Miriam Voghera, aiming at the constitution of a web portal of electronic resources and bibliographies on Italian spoken language (<http://www.parlaritaliano.it/>).

TEXT TYPOLOGY	INCLUDED TEXTS
A: bidirectional, exchange, face to face, with free turn-taking	– conversations at home;
	– conversations at work;
	– conversations at school or at the university;
	– conversations during recreation or on means of transport.
B: bi-directional exchange, not face to face, with free turn-taking	– normal telephone conversations;
	– telephone conversations broadcasted on radio;
	– messages recorded by telephone answering machines.
C: bi-directional exchange, face to face, with regulated turn-taking	– legislative assemblies;
	– cultural discussions;
	– assemblies at school;
	– labor union assemblies;
	– meetings of workers;
	– oral exams in the elementary school;
	– oral exams in the secondary school;
	– oral exams at the university;
	– interrogations in the courtroom;
	– interviews on radio or television
D: unidirectional exchange, with the addressee being present	– lessons in the elementary school;
	– lessons in the secondary school;
	– university lectures;
	– speeches held during party conventions or labor union meetings;
	– presentations at scientific meetings;
	– speeches held during electoral campaigns;
	– sermons;
	– presentations at non-specialist meetings;
	– court pleadings.
E: distanced unidirectional exchange	– television programs; – radio programs.

Table 3. LIP text typology (from BADIP website).

A complete utterance is provided as context. Concordances can be exported in various formats (txt, xls, html; xml). As a simple search produces a concordance with statistics on dispersion in different text-types, it is immediately clear that *praticamente,* for example *t* occurs less frequently in unidirectional exchanges – type D, the most formal category – and is common in informal speech.

The strength of the LIP corpus lies in its coverage of different situational contexts. This avoids the vicious circle caused by designs based on internal criteria (the main problem with which is circularity in text selection and data retrieval). LIP's external classification seems particularly useful to investigate variation in language teaching contexts. Not only can expressions, tags, and syntactic patterns be queried over different situation-types, but access is available to the entire transcript, allowing the learner to explore this freely.

Among the disadvantages of LIP is its small size, which makes it unreliable for medium frequency words and patterns. A small scale investigation of the most frequent loan words in Italian (Chiari 2008) obtained sparse data, which was heavily influenced by single text domains. Another drawback is the inaccessibility of the original audio files, and the absence of phonetic and prosodic annotation. However it remains unrivalled for its balanced typology based exclusively on situational parameters.

3.2.2 C-ORAL-ROM

C-ORAL-ROM (*Integrated reference corpora for spoken romance languages*) includes a comparable set of spontaneous spoken language corpora for French, Italian, Portuguese and Spanish, each represented by 300,000 word samples (Cresti & Moneglia 2005a). The corpus was designed to focus on prosodic and pragmatic features (speech acts). The DVD includes the digitalized audio (in wav format), transcriptions (in CHAT format) and text analyses of the recordings, accessible in a simultaneous aligned format. The corpus is annotated prosodically and with action values. The Italian component comprises about 36 hours of speech.

Fig. 5. C-ORAL-ROM design scheme (from Cresti & Moneglia 2005).

The corpus design is specifically aimed at capturing variation, "covering a wide range of semantic and pragmatic domains of application" (Cresti & Moneglia 2005b, see *Fig. 23*). The highest level distinction is one of register, between formal and informal speech. The definition of these terms is rather peculiar, since *informal* is intended as an "un-scripted low variety of language, used for everyday interactive purposes", and the *formal* as a "partially-scripted task-oriented high variety of language" (Cresti & Moneglia 2005b). The second level takes into account the channel of communication for formal speech (face-to-face, broadcast and telephonic), and public versus private for informal speech. At the third level informal speech is divided into monologue, dialogue and (multi-party) conversation. For some formal speech categories a further distinction is made on the basis of domain: natural context (*political speech; political debate; preaching; teaching; professional explanation; conference; business; law*) and media (*news; sport; interviews; science; weather forecast; scientific press; reportage; talk sho*w). As Cresti notes, the criteria adopted for the formal and informal sections are rather different:

> The definition of a finite list of typical domains of use is the main criterion applied in documenting the formal uses of the four romance languages, while variations in dialogue structure and social context of use is the sampling criterion of the informal part. The choice of the specific semantic domain of use is left random in the informal sampling. (Cresti & Moneglia 2005b)

The architecture of the corpus is not consistent, including both internal and external criteria. In the domain distinction for formal natural contexts we can find topic-related categories (*preaching* "religion", *business, law*), but also ones that represent situational aspects and text-types (*teaching, professional explanation* and *conference*), as well as mixed topic- and activity-centered categories, such as *political speech* and *political debate*.

The quantitative balance of the different categories reflects a questionable principle:

> [...] while it can be assumed that in western societies the formal use of language is applied in a closed series of typical domains, the same does not hold for the informal use of language. The list of possible domains of use for informal language is by definition open, and no domain can in principle be considered more typical than others. (Cresti & Moneglia 2005b)

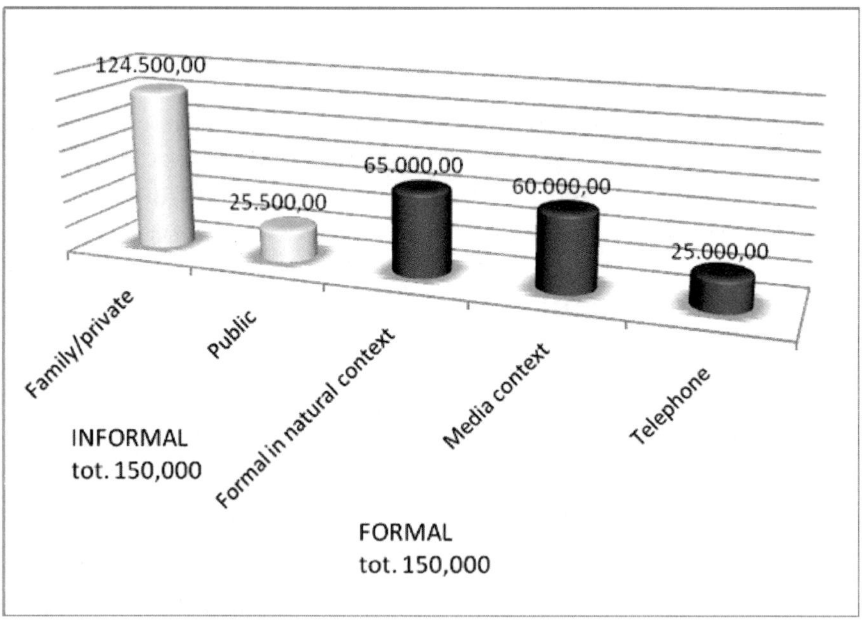

Fig. 6. Quantitative balance of C-ORAL-ROM (Italian component).

While the open nature of the domains of informal language use can be easily agreed with, the idea that formal language use is set in a predefined (or at least closed) set of domains is debatable. The formal-informal parameter seems a continuum rather than a clear-cut distinction, and hence theoretically weak. The sampling reflects these differences in the treatment of the formal and informal categories:

When it comes to the issue of language variation, it is extremely difficult to evaluate the project. On the one hand, if we suppose that the formal/informal distinction holds and has been applied consistently, it would be extremely practical to observe and compare the two sections in classroom work. On the other hand the different quantitative balance of the subsections makes it hard to go beyond this dichotomy.[4]

Turning to retrieval tools, C-ORAL-ROM is distributed with Véronis' *Contextes*. The query syntax accepts word types, lemmas, pos tagging, multiple word queries, and regular expressions, and the interface permits the export of concordances and frequency lists of selected words, as well as direct access to the full text. No general frequency and dispersion data is given for sections of the corpus, but a non-exportable frequency list for the whole corpus is provided (without dispersion and usage counts). Like the LIP corpus, C-ORAL-ROM is rather small and hence unreliable for medium frequency words.

4. Variation in Italian language teaching

Italian reference corpora treat language variation in very different ways, posing a number of problems for their exploitation in teaching. The speech corpora discussed have a number of features which are highly interesting from this point of view: access to both concordances and full text (the latter being essential to understand the speech acts involved), aligned audio, tagged versions for the investigation of grammatical patterns. Their disadvantages concern query limitations, their

4 The frame is of course different for research purposes, since it is always possible to evaluate representativeness related to single parameters (Biber 1993a; b).

small size, and design inconsistencies. If the learner wants to investigate similarities and differences between spoken and written Italian, she will encounter a number of obstacles (common in some cases to the language researcher): differences in size, design, and tools that do not permit statistical conclusions to be drawn from the different sources available. Italian corpus linguistics has been mainly concerned with the construction of balanced resources, and the debate over large vs. register-diversified balanced corpora (Biber 1993b) has barely touched the Italian scene, mainly because we do not have any very large corpora at the moment. But if we consider the problem from the language learner's perspective, it is obvious that a balanced diversified corpus will respond better to their needs.

Although language variation in all its aspects is at the centre of debate in corpus linguistics, there are still inconsistencies in the classification and labelling of variation, not only in reference to Italian. These lead to difficulties in managing corpus material, since text-types are grouped in different classes in unpredictable ways (a situation common to many English resources as well, as Lee 2001 has shown). At the level of query capabilities, there are severe limitations for Italian reference corpora (which have been largely overcome for English corpora like the BNC, with Dodd's Xaira (<http://www.oucs.ox.ac.uk/rts/xaira/>), Davies' View (<http://corpus.byu.edu/bnc/>), and Fletcher's Pie (<http://pie.usna.edu/>)). The flexibility of retrieval tools is indispensable for correct data extraction, and an interface offering accessibility, user-friendliness, clean and intuitive layout is a vital requirement from a teaching perspective, where aims potentially differ from those of linguistic research.

One of the main obstacles for teachers is the unpredictability of query results and thus a sense of unexpectedness, making them reluctant to use corpora extensively (it implies a lot of planning). A clear description of corpus features and the variation dimensions represented should be a priority in corpus distribution. Explicit evaluation of the main tasks that teachers and learners need to perform with single corpora should include: looking for patterns of variation from a lexical, syntactic, pragmatic, and sociolinguistic point of view; looking for specific features that characterize different genres, different domains and different text types; looking for textual specificity of sublanguages. For spoken corpora a requisite should be access to aligned audio, so that the user can examine spoken realisations of different registers (phonetic and prosodic features). C-ORAL-ROM and CLIPS (<www.clips.unina.it>) both go in this direction, albeit at different levels.

In order to explore such issues retrieval tools and documentation should provide:

– full classification of subcorpora and their subsections;
– querying in subsections;
– querying over POS tags, preferably using regular expressions or intuitive matching systems;
– explicit frequency data (including relative frequency and dispersion), perhaps indicated roughly with learner-friendly symbols like those in dictionaries);
– exact numbers of hits found and display of complete concordances with adjustable context length;
– full text access for traditional textual analysis and pragmatic observation.

Language teaching may benefit from the corpus-based study of linguistic variation in many ways: in the selection and grading of content for syllabus and materials design, in developing activities to enhance learner awareness and to help learners exploit resources, and in assessment procedures.

References

Albano Leoni F. & R. Giordano (eds.) (2005), *Italiano parlato. Analisi di un dialogo.* Napoli: Liguori.

Bernardini S. & F. Zanettin (eds) (2000) *I corpora nella didattica della traduzione.* Bologna: CLUEB.

Biber D. (1988) *Variation across speech and writing.* Cambridge: Cambridge University Press.

Biber D. (1992) The multi-dimensional approach to linguistic analyses of genre variation: an overview of methodology and findings. *Computers and the humanities,* 26, 331–345.

Biber D. (1993a) Representativeness in corpus design. *Literary and linguistic computing,* 8, 243–257.
Biber D. (1993b) Using register-diversified corpora for general language studies. *Computational Linguistics,* 19, 219–241.
Biber D. (1995) *Dimensions of register variation: a cross-linguistic comparison.* Cambridge: Cambridge University Press.
Biber D., S. Conrad & R. Reppen (1998) *Corpus linguistics: investigating language structure and use.* Cambridge: Cambridge University Press.
Biber D. & E. Finegan (1991) On the exploitation of computerized corpora in variation studies. In Aijmer K. & B. Altenberg (eds), *English corpus linguistics: studies in honour of Jan Svartvik.* London: Longman, 204–220.
Biber D. & E. Finegan (eds) (1994) *Sociolinguistic perspectives on register.* Oxford: Oxford University Press.
Bortolini U., C. Tagliavini & A. Zampolli (1971) *Lessico di frequenza della lingua italiana contemporanea.* Milano: IBM Italia.
Botley S., J. Glass, T. McEnery & A. Wilson (eds) (1996) *Proceedings of teaching and language corpora 1996.* Lancaster: UCREL.
Botley S., A. McEnery & A. Wilson (eds) (2000) *Multilingual corpora in teaching and research.* Amsterdam: Rodopi.
Burnard L. & T. McEnery (eds) (2000) *Rethinking language pedagogy from a corpus perspective.* Frankfurt am Main: Peter Lang.
Chiari I. (2005) Linguistica e informatica: la linguistica dei corpora in Italia. *Bollettino di Italianistica,* 4, 101–118.
Chiari I. (2008) Ingresso, uso, integrazione e produttività delle parole nuove in italiano. Metodi e problemi dell'indagine quantitativa sul lessico. In M. Pettorino, A. Giannini, M. Vallone & R. Savy (eds.) *Atti del Convegno internazionale sulla comunicazione parlata.* Napoli: Liguori, 402–421. Conrad S. (2004) Corpus linguistics, language variation and language teaching. In J.M. Sinclair (ed.), *How to use corpora in language teaching.* Amsterdam: John Benjamins, 67–85.
Cresti E. (2007) Some comparisons between UBLI and C-ORAL-ROM. In Zaima K. Y. S. & T. Takagaki (eds), *Spoken language corpus and linguistics informatics.* Amsterdam: John Benjamins, 125–115.
Cresti E. & M. Moneglia (2005a) *C-ORAL-ROM: integrated reference corpora for spoken Romance languages.* Amsterdam: John Benjamins.
Cresti E. & M. Moneglia (2005b) *C-ORAL-ROM: integrated reference corpora for spoken Romance languages.* URL: http://lablita.dit.unifi.it/corpora/descriptions/coralrom/ (date accessed May 15 2008).
De Mauro T., F. Mancini, M. Vedovelli & M. Voghera (1993) *Lessico di frequenza dell'italiano parlato (LIP).* Milano: Etaslibri.
Eagles (1996). Preliminary recommendations on Corpus Typology, EAG-TCWG-CTYP/P, <http://www.ilc.cnr.it/EAGLES96/corpustyp/corpustyp.html>. May, 1996. [Accessed April 2007].

Ellis R. (1987) *Second language acquisition in context*. Englewood Cliffs, NJ: Prentice-Hall.

Gavioli L. (2005) *Exploring corpora for ESP learning*. Amsterdam: John Benjamins.

Godwin-Jones B. (2001) Emerging technologies. tools and trends in corpora use for teaching and learning. *Language Learning & Technology,* 5(3), 7–12.

Granger S. & M. Wynne (2000) Optimising measures of lexical variation in EFL learner corpora. In Kirk J. M. (ed.) *Corpora galore: analyses and techniques in describing English*. Amsterdam: Rodopi, 249–257.

Hunston S. (2002) Pattern grammar, language teaching, and linguistic variation: applications of a corpus-driven grammar. In Reppen R., S.M. Fitzmaurice & D. Biber (eds) *Using corpora to explore linguistic variation*. Amsterdam: John Benjamins, 167–183.

Hymes D. (1971) *On communicative competence*. Philadelphia: University of Pennsylvania Press.

Johns T. (1991a) *Classroom concordancing*: University of Birmingham, Centre for English Studies.

Johns T. (1991b) From printout to handout: grammar and vocabulary learning in the context of data-driven learning. *English Language Research Journal,* 4, 27–45.

Johns T. (1991c) Should you be persuaded – two examples of data-driven learning materials. *English Language Research Journal,* 4, 1–16.

Johns T. (2002) Data-driven learning: the perpetual challenge. In Kettemann B. & G. Marko (eds) *Teaching and learning by doing corpus analysis*. Amsterdam: Rodopi, 107–117.

Kahn B. (1985) *Computers in science: using computers for learning and teaching*. Cambridge: Cambridge University Press.

Laudanna A., A. M. Thornton, G. Brown, C. Burani & L. Marconi (1995) Un corpus dell'italiano scritto contemporaneo dalla parte del ricevente. In Bolasco S., L. Lebart & A. Salem (eds), *III Giornate internazionali di analisi statistica dei dati testuali*. Roma: CISU, 103–109.

Lee, D. Y. (2001) Genres, registers, text types, domains, and styles: clarifying the concepts and navigating a path through the BNC jungle. *Language Learning & Technology*, 5(3), 37–72.

Lewandowska-Tomaszczyk B. (ed.) (2003) *PALC 2001: practical applications in language corpora*. Frankfurt am Main: Peter Lang.

Lewandowska-Tomaszczyk B. (ed.) (2004) *Practical applications in language and computers: PALC 2003*. Frankfurt am Main: Peter Lang.

Lewandowska-Tomaszczyk B. & P.J. Melia (eds) (1997) *International conference on practical applications in language corpora*. Lodz: Lodz University Press.

Lewandowska-Tomaszczyk B. & P. J. Melia (eds) (2000) *PALC'99 – Practical applications in language corpora*. Frankfurt am Main: Peter Lang.

Meyer C. F. (2004) Can you really study language variation in linguistic corpora? *American Speech,* 79, 339–355.

Paltridge B. (1996) Genre, text type, and the language learning classroom. *ELT Journal,* 50, 237–243.

Partington A. (1998) *Patterns and meanings: using corpora for English language research and teaching*. Amsterdam: John Benjamins.

Pettorino M. & A. Giannini (2003) Progetti AVIP e API-unità di ricerca dell'Università degli Studi di Napoli l'Orientale. In Albano Leoni F., Cutugno F., Pettorino M., Savy R (eds.), *Il parlato italiano Atti del Convegno Nazionale*, D'Auria, Napoli, N06.

Rossini Favretti R. (2000) Progettazione e costruzione di un corpus di italiano scritto: CORIS/CODIS. In Rossini Favretti R. (ed.), *Linguistica e informatica. Multimedialità, corpora e percorsi di apprendimento*. Roma: Bulzoni, 39–56.

Rossini Favretti R., F. Tamburini & C. De Santis (2002) A corpus of written Italian: a defined and a dynamic model. In Wilson A., P. Rayson & T. McEnery (eds), *A rainbow of corpora: corpus linguistics and the languages of the world.* Munich: Lincom-Europa, 27–38.

Scott M. & C. Tribble (eds) (2006) *Textual patterns: key words and corpus analysis in language education*. Amsterdam: John Benjamins.

Sinclair J.M. (ed.) (2004) *How to use corpora in language teaching*. Amsterdam: John Benjamins.

Spolsky B. (1989) Communicative competence, language proficiency, and beyond. *Applied Linguistics,* 10, 138–156.

Szendeffy J. (2005) *A practical guide to using computers in language teaching*. Ann Arbor: University of Michigan Press.

Timmis I. (2003) *Corpora, classroom and context: the place of spoken grammar in English language teaching.* Ph.D. Thesis, University of Nottingham.

Tono Y. (2002) *The role of learner corpora in SLA research and foreign language teaching: the multiple comparison approach.* Ph.D Thesis, University of Lancaster

Wang L. (2000) *The use of parallel texts in language learning: computer software and teaching materials for English and Chinese.* Birmingham: University of Birmingham.

Wible D., F.-y. Chien, C.-H. Kuo & C.C. Wang (2002) Toward automating a personalized concordancer for data-driven learning: a lexical difficulty filter for language learners. In Ketteman B. & G. Marko (eds) *Teaching and learning by doing corpus analysis*. Amsterdam: Rodopi, 147–154.

Wichmann, A., S. Fligelstone, T. McEnery & G. Knowles (eds) (1997) *Teaching and language corpora*. London: Longman.

Zanettin F., S. Bernardini & D. Stewart (eds) (2003) *Corpora in translator education.* Manchester: St. Jerome.

GEOFFREY WILLIAMS

The Learner's Dictionary and the Sciences: Mismatch or no match?

Abstract

Learner's dictionaries are at the forefront of lexicographical practice; it is through them that corpora have become standard practice, through them that the most dynamic electronic dictionaries have come onto the market. The market for such dictionaries is enormous with the big five working hard to keep and increase their share of the market. However, it may well be that they are failing to take into account the needs of a particular user group; the ESP/EAP learner. This communication looks at how scientific usage is shown in three major learner's dictionaries and proposes a corpus-based solution using prototype theory.

1. Introduction

"In praise of dictionaries" was the title of John Sinclair's 2004 Euralex plenary (Sinclair 2004). As he pointed out, there is much to be praised. Dictionaries have evolved over centuries to become the major reference works that we rely on today. In the second half of the 20th century, computer technology ensured a revolution in the publishing world in general, but in the world of lexicography in particular by opening up new systems for the analysis and management of data, but above all new sources. The world of electronic resources was opened in the late fifties and sixties with projects such as Frantext, the Brown and the OSTI corpora, but the great revolution came about in the eighties with the COBUILD project in Birmingham and the development of a brand new advanced learner's dictionary (Sinclair 1987).

Learner's dictionaries are at the forefront of lexicographical practice; it is through them that corpora have become standard practice, through them that the most dynamic electronic dictionaries have come onto the market. The market for such dictionaries is enormous with the big five working hard to keep and increase their share of the market. However, it may well be that they are failing to take into account the needs of a particular user group; the ESP/EAP learner.

All depends on the definition one gives to learner. In France, at least, this is often restricted to those studying English as a language; at least as far as dictionary acquisition is concerned. Students in ESP/EAP tend to rely heavily on bilingual dictionaries and often have poor dictionary skills. However, some of these students go on to become fully fledged research scientist, for whom publication in English is a necessity, but whose dictionary skills will still be minimal. In ESP/EAP, lexical acquisition has tended towards the terminology that a specialist must master, but, as a discipline, terminology has only recently moved towards consideration of collocational and sociolinguistic context (L'Homme 2003, Temmerman 2000) and the job of a terminologist is not to help with language production; that is the role of the lexicographer.

This text then looks at two aspects of special language lexicography: the use of a corpus to adapt learner's dictionaries to the needs of the non-language specialist and the possibility of going beyond the general learner's dictionary to a corpus-based dictionary of subject specialists.

2. From general word list to the Oxford 3000

The OALD is the father of learner's dictionaries having grown out of the pioneering work of Palmer and Hornby in the 1920's and 30's. Palmer was concerned with the teaching of English as a foreign language. His work in applied linguistics was central in the definition of a basic vocabulary for learners (Palmer 1930, 1931, Palmer & West 1936), work which ultimately lead to the "General Service List" (West 1953) which provided the underpinning of most post-war language teaching methods. Palmer was not just concerned with words as isolated items as it was he who first introduced the notion of collocation into English language teaching in a revolutionary document that, unfortunately, is still not widely available (Palmer 1933). It is but a small step from a contextualized list to a true learner's dictionary. Palmer's collaboration with Hornby led to new lexicographical practices, and, in 1948, to the publication of Hornby's "Advanced Learner's Dictionary". The latter became the "Oxford Advanced Learner's Dictionary" (OALD), the father of the now vibrant and dynamic world of learners' dictionaries for English.

Writing a dictionary requires the establishing of a list of headwords and also of a defining vocabulary in that the words used to define should not, in theory, be more complicated than those that are being defined. Such lists are accumulative and were not seriously challenged until the COBUILD revolution in the nineteen eighties that brought corpora into the dictionary making picture (Sinclair, ed. 1987). The most recent version of the OALD makes use of corpora, but also the knowledge of ELT research to set out a basic vocabulary for the use of Advanced Learners: the Oxford 3000. This list has been established taking into account the frequency factor, but also those of range and familiarity (OALD 7th edition R99). In addition to this list, Oxford also has a list of specialist words in fields such as the sciences; it is this last list that is the start point for the current research.

3. The Oxford Scientific list

The Oxford Scientific list consists of 250 headwords; in fact 265 word-forms once spelling variations are taken into account. The aim of this list, according to the blurb is to "help you understand texts about these subjects more easily" (OALD 7, R115). The question as to who is concerned by "you" is not addressed. Are these general readers who wish to read more widely or ESP science students? The answer can only lie in a very broad definition of the language learner at upper school and university levels as much depends on the attitude of the teaching to the use of dictionaries. The issue that is addressed here is not so much of the general language user, but that of the non-English specialists. In other words, do the scientific 250, and by extension the other specialized word lists, address the needs of these specific learners, or simply widen the vocabulary available to a more general audience. Part of the answer will be found in looking at these words in the OALD.

To carry out this study, the list has been analyzed to address a number of factors. Are all these words headwords within the dictionary? Are they signaled as being scientific by a general or domain-specific label? Is the scientific aspect explicit or implicit in the definition and the example? Which words have a label and which do not? Finally, the presence of this specialized vocabulary has been checked against a very specialized corpus – the Parasitic Plant Corpus (Williams 1998) – to see whether this language could represent a very widely available core of scientific usage.

The findings of the study reveal a remarkable degree of inconsistency with some other words being clearly signaled with subject field labels, whilst in others the 'scientific' aspect is simply implicit in the definition or example. In some cases there is no indication of any specialized usage whatsoever.

One word 'rat' has an unclear status. It could be the fact that this mammal is used in experiments, although 'mouse' is what most people would associate with laboratory work, and also in computing. The dictionary does not show any particular scientific status which may mean that a typographical error has given 'rat' rather than the noun 'rate'. In only one case is the word-form actually missing from the dictionary, this is 'cloning' which is present in the list as being a derived form from 'clone'. The adjectival form is not given even in the examples, which makes its presence in a list of knowable forms surprising given that in the BNC it is present 143 times for 45 texts, whereas 'cloned' is more frequent (174 for 39), but not in the list. Another surprising feature is to be found in the names of disciplines that the learner should 'know'. 'Geology' needs to be listed, but 'biology', chemistry' and 'physics' do not. The derived adjective 'biological' is listed, but not 'chemical'. The reasoning behind the choice of derived forms selected is far from clear. All of this is, however, relatively anecdotal, what is more important is the presentation of words from the list in dictionary entries.

The dictionary uses a series of labels to designate more specialized usage. These range from the very general, such as *technical*, to specific disciplines as in *biology*, *physics*, *computing*. In fact, only 25% of the words from the list carry a usage label. In this case the usage label will be between brackets and may be found in single sense entries, as for 'chromosome', or to differentiate between several senses as with the verb 'evolve'.

- chromosome
- (biology) one of the very small structures like threads in the nuclei (= central parts) of animal and plant cells, that carry the genes
- evolve
- 2 evolve (from sth) (biology) (of plants, animals, etc.) to develop over time, often many generations, into forms that are better adapted to survive changes in their environment:
- The three species evolved from a single ancestor.
- The dolphin has evolved a highly developed jaw.

If the scientific aspect is not given in the label, the learner has to rely on the definition or example in order to see why they need to 'know' these words as can be seen with the 'activate' where the terms 'chemical process' and 'germ' show the scientific aspect.

- ac·ti·vate [vn] to make sth such as a device or chemical process start working:
  The burglar alarm is activated by movement.
  The gene is activated by a specific protein.

In 30% of the cases there is nothing in the definition to show a scientific aspect. In 60%, it is the example that implicitly shows some specialized usage, although in 18 cases this example follows a definition that has no specialized aspect. This is the case for 'undertake' which is implicitly shown to collocate with 'research'.

- 1[vn] to make yourself responsible for sth and start doing it: to undertake a task / project – University professors both teach and undertake research. – The company has announced that it will undertake a full investigation into the accident.

In 45 cases (17%) there is a scientifically-oriented definition, but no example, which implies that the user is expected to need assistance with decoding, but not be expected to encode. 'Chromosome' (above) is a good example of such a practice and corpus evidence confirms that such words often form complex terminological groups that are beyond the needs of the general user.

In other cases the reader is left to his or her own devices to find the scientific aspect

- assess 1. sb/sth (as sth) to make a judgement about the nature or quality of sb/sth:[vn] It's difficult to assess the effects of these changes. – *to assess a patient's needs – The young men were assessed as either safe or unsafe drivers. – I'd assess your chances as low. – [v wh-] – The committee assesses whether a building is worth preserving. – We are trying to assess how well the system works.*
- as·sess·ment
  1[C] an opinion or a judgement about sb/sth that has been thought about very carefully SYN evaluation: *a detailed assessment of the risks involved – his assessment of the situation*

All in all, it remains difficult to see who exactly is being addressed. Definitions should help with decoding, but when they are missing what status does the word have? When examples are present, they may help with either encoding or decoding, but only in very general usage as a learner's dictionary cannot be expected to cater for the needs of the scientific research article.

4. From corpus to corpus: a question of readership

In order to look at the question of readership, the next stage has been to look at how the dictionary meanings compare to those found in a specialized corpus. The dictionary has been built using a corpus, but a general reference corpus rather than its specialized subdivisions. It is most probable that the more general meanings have been privileged rather than those found in more specialized sub-corpora. This is perfectly normal as a reference corpus as a whole is representative of a language, whilst the degree of true representativity lessens with the subcorpora which are present to demonstrate a generic tendency, but not necessarily a sub-field. On the other hand, a specialized corpus based on research articles demonstrates a type of lexical usage and a terminological density that is way beyond the needs of a general language user. However, it is worthwhile looking at more specialized corpora for three reasons: to see to what extent the words in this vocabulary list are to be found in all scientific texts, and to see whether it is possible to improve the dictionary to demonstrate general scientific usage, or to use the dictionary as a model to build a tool for use within a more specialized environment. Two corpora have been used: the scientific section of the British National Corpus (BNC) to look at general scientific usage and a highly specialized one on parasitic plant biology (Williams 1998). If a majority of words from the Oxford 250 list are present in the specialized corpus one of two conclusions may be reached; the list gives a very good coverage of scientific specificities, or these are very general words.

A close study of these specialized contexts has shown that while many of the Oxford 250 scientific words are present, their nature is not necessarily even semi-technical. Some 76% of the words are present; of these a mixed bag of 48 entries includes adverbs, adjectives and one abbreviation. The adverbs such as 'consequently' and 'furthermore' are used in scientific texts, but can also be used to organize any text. The only scientific adverb is 'genetically' which brings us back to the question posed earlier as to why certain derived forms have been selected and not others. Most of the adverbs can be seen as having a specific scientific usage, but this is hardly truc of 'respective', 'subsequent' and 'widespread'. The one word marked as being an abbreviation 'et al.' is not specific to science. Other abbreviations are included in the list, nut these are classed as being nouns, as in 'DNA' and 'PC'.

5. Dictionary tweaking

It is all too easy to criticize, it is better to attempt a solution. The following stage in this research is to look closely at the words in the context of a specialized corpus to see what sort of changes would be necessary to improve coverage. For this, corpus-driven studies on a wide variety of specialized corpora are necessary so as to help fill in the gaps and enable adjustments in the definitions. The current research is far too limited, but does allow an insight into what might be done. The aim is simply to use corpus data to slightly alter the dictionary definition in order to improve or adapt its scientific coverage. This is illustrated below with examples of what might be proposed

In the list, 128 entries have a nominal form and 30 have a verbal form. We shall first look at two of the verb forms that also occur in the parasitic plant corpus; 'probe' and 'differ'. The two former are classed as being verbs first, nouns after. In the corpus it is the noun form that dominates in both cases. If we look at the entry for the verb form for 'probe' in the dictionary we find:

> 2[vn] to touch, examine or look for sth, especially with a long thin instrument: *The doctor probed the wound for signs of infection. Searchlights probed the night sky.*

The nouns form of 'probe' is neatly introduced by repeating the definitional statement of 'long thin instrument'. The corpus examples do not necessarily show the use of a probe as can be seen in the following examples taken from the BNC and the PPC corpora

> Electrochemistry is also being used to probe the electronic structure of the fullerenes.
> By observation we can probe this world and attempt to discern the laws which regulate it.
>
> BNC
>
> the subclones were labelled with 32P and used to probe gel blots of Conopholis total cellular RNA
> coding region of tobacco ABP1, was used to probe a Southern blot of tobacco genomic DNA (Figure 5)
>
> PPC

This is allowed for in the OALD definition, the problem is more with the examples in this case which both give an active use. In the PPC the verb is mostly used in the infinitive, a choice confirmed by the natural and pure sciences section of the BNC where for 67 concordancer lines for the lemma 'probe', 27 (40%) use the infinitive. It would take just a small change to make the text scientist-friendly.

In the case of 'differ' the situation is different. This word is to be found in the science list, but in the dictionary neither the definition nor the examples show any particular scientific usage, unless of course if 'medical opinion' can be considered relevant.

- 1A and B ~ (from each other) | A ~s from B to be different from sb/sth: They hold differing views. – French differs from English in this respect. – French and English differ in this respect. – Ideas on childcare may differ considerably between the parents.
- 2differ (with sb) (about / on / over sth) to disagree with sb: I have to differ with you on that. – Medical opinion differs as to how to treat the disease.

Differ is a relatively frequent verb in the PPC occurring 132 times (0.03 %). In all cases the sense used is that 'A' differs from 'B', the first sense in the OALD. Examples from the BNC and PPC show the following:

> Spines differ from spine-like setae in being produced by undifferentiated epidermal cells.
> Their methods differed accordingly [Shonfield, 1965].
> BNC
> These invertases differ in pH and tempera optima.
> The tRNALeu/2 gene from maize (20) differs from the bean tRNALeu/2.
> The two biotypes differed in both the amount and depth of rhizome production.
> PPC

In this case, the examples given with sense 1 of the OALD confirm the usage found on the corpora. In the BNC, we also find the second sense which does collocate with 'opinion', but not prototypically with 'medical'. This shows thus a predominance of the first sense, but whilst a scientist might appreciate a more specific example, but it is hard to see how the word can really be considered 'scientific'.

If we now turn to semi-technical and 'lightly' technical words as 'control', we find that the dictionary entries give little help as to encoding.

- IN EXPERIMENT
- 5[C] (technical) a person, thing or group used as a standard of comparison for checking the results of a scientific experiment; an experiment whose result is known, used for checking working methods: *One group was treated with the new drug, and the control group was given a sugar pill.*

This is quite adequate for general uses, but a detailed study of the PPC corpus has shown that, in practice, the word enters into a number of relationships. This is illustrated in appendix 1, which will be discussed in more detail later

Sometimes it may be necessary to widen slightly the prototype on which the word is based. This will be illustrated with a word that is not on the list, but which does have a particular scientific usage – bank.

6. Adapting the prototype: Bank

Improving coverage does not necessarily mean changing the content in the general language learner's dictionary, but widening the reference of the underlying definitional prototypes. The notion of corpus-driven prototypes has been introduced by Hanks (1994, 2000) in order to overcome the problem of polysemy in corpus data. In Hanks (2000), the theory is developed with a prototype for "bank" which is deemed to have the following characteristics:

- is an institution
- is a large building
- for storage
- for safekeeping
- of finance/money
- carries out transactions
- consists of a staff of people

This covers the many meanings of bank and allows for meaning extension through the characteristic of storing and safeguarding for future use. An extended meaning can be seen with the blood and sperm banks mentioned in the OALD.

- STH COLLECTED / STORED
- 3an amount of sth that is collected; a place where sth is stored ready for use: *a bank of knowledge – a blood / sperm bank – see also databank*

A close look at the PPC data shows (appendix 1.) a further use, that of clone bank and seed bank. Whilst the former enters into the same group as sperm bank, the latter is more problematic in that a seed bank is not voluntarily stored but something that accumulates naturally. In this case the data in the parasitic plant corpus shows that the prototype needs enlarging to take into account the notion of non man-made reserve of something, which is necessary to understand the notion of "seed bank". Again, this is not a radical change, just a small updating to take into account more specialized usage.

7. Not 'learner', but 'user'

Throughout, we have insisted on the fact that close study might show inconsistencies in the OALD as concerns its scientific list, but that overall the remedy is only a slight alteration of the content to make it useful to a much wider audience. A learner's dictionary is not the place for specialized terminology, but in so far as the dictionary successfully enables advanced learners to improve encoding skills, could the same model not be adapted for a specialized learner's dictionary?

Widening the reference of definitional prototypes would clear the way for the creation of special language production dictionaries that would go beyond the needs of the 'advanced learner' to become tools in the production of publishable scientific papers. Such dictionaries would be aimed at scientists, who would benefit from the clarity of learner's dictionaries, but who do not necessarily see themselves as learners, but as specialized users. This population knows its terminology in English but requires help in production. This is what is amply provided in the learner's dictionary model with its emphasis on clear example and information on collocation and syntactic patterns; what is needed is to apply this model to material drawn from a special language corpus as, for example, in the dictionary proposed in Williams (2002).

The Parasitic Plant Dictionary is purely experimental and designed to show what can be done using a specialized corpus and a model based on a learner's dictionary. The dictionary is corpus-based and is being developed using the Tshwanelex[1] database system. The dictionary could

1 <http://tshwanedje.com>.

be printed, but the amount of data makes a hyper text format preferable. The type of entry foreseen can be illustrated with two examples: 'control' and 'haustorium' (appendices 2 and 3). The former is simply a detailed analysis of a semi-technical word in a specialized context; the latter is a domain specific word. What is being built is a dictionary, not a terminology. The difference is crucial as the aim is to empower the user, not to standardize. This example is a case in point as the *haustorium* is the defining element of parasitic plants. However, the scientific community involved does not agree on the extracted terminological definition, much argument turns around prepositions. The definition seeks thus to summarize the corpus data and show how the word is used. No attempt is made to formalize a concept as this would be presumptuous on the part of the lexicographer.

8. Conclusion

This article has set out to show that whilst a learner's dictionary such as the OALD does not apparently set out to deal with the needs of the ESP user, it could be adapted to such use. It also shows that in looking at specialized corpora it will be possible to remove some of the inconsistencies found in the dictionary and especially in its specialized word lists. The examples given do not take away from the value of the dictionary, but do aim to show that some adjustments are necessary to adapt them to the needs of the EAP/EAP user in scientific studies. By adapting a dictionary the path is opening to dictionaries for specialized users.

To achieve such dictionaries two strategies are possible: entirely reinventing the wheel by creating a dictionary from zero or adapting and adding to an existing dictionary. The former will require a great deal of works hardly feasible as the work load and technical needs go beyond the scope of the corpus linguist and dictionary analyst; their role is to propose solutions and demonstrate what can be done. The second is the ideal solution, but this requires collaboration in building a broad based corpus, or corpora in specialized usage, and a desire on the behalf of the major publishing houses to open towards the market of the ESP/EAP user.

This study has concentrated on the OALD because it supplies a clear list of scientific words. This is just a beginning as further research is looking at the other major learners' dictionaries and also studying their CD-ROMS to see how complex searches can show scientific data in the dictionary.

This is a very rapid overview of a much larger research project into dictionary, as opposed to terminology, creation for ESP/EAP users. What it reveals however is that scientific usage is handled in a very inconsistent manner in the learner's dictionaries, but that in many cases a very small modification of the definitional prototype would render them usable in specialist contents. It also reveals that the well tested format used in learner's dictionaries could be easily adapted to corpus-based specialized dictionaries, provided the big dictionary houses agree to collaborate in what could be a very fruitful partnership for them.

References

Hanks P. (2000) 'Do word meanings exist?'. In Kilgarriff A. and M. Palmer (eds) 2000. Senseval: Evaluating Word Sense Disambiguation Programmes. *Computers and the Humanities*. 34/1–2. 205–215.

Hanks P. (1994) 'Linguistic norms and pragmatic exploitations or, why lexicographers need prototype theory, and vice versa.' *Papers in Computational Lexicography: Complex 94*, 89–113.

L'Homme M.-C. (2003) 'Les combinaisons lexicales spécialisée (CLS): Description lexicographique et intégration aux banques de terminologie. In Grossman, F and A. Tutin 2003. *Les Collocations: Analyse et traitement.* Travaux et Recherches en Linguistique Appliquée. Amsterdam: Editions De Werelt. 89–104.

Palmer H.E. (1930) IRET *First interim report on vocabulary selection*, Tokyo, IRET.

Palmer H.E. (1931) *Second interim report on vocabulary selection*, Tokyo, IRET.

Palmer H.E. (1933) Second Interim Report on English Collocations. Tokyo: Kaitakusha.

Palmer H.E., West M.P., Faucett, L. (1936), *Interim report on vocabulary selection for the teaching of English as a foreign language, London, P.S King & Son.*

Sinclair J. McH. (ed.) (1987) Looking up: an account of the COBUILD Project in Lexical Computing. London: Collins.

Sinclair J. McH. (2004) 'In praise of the dictionary'. In Williams, G. and S. Vessier (eds) 2004. Proceedings of the Eleventh EURALEX International Congress. 1–12.

Temmerman R. (2000) Towards new ways of terminology description: the sociocognitive approach. Amsterdam: John Benjamin's.

West M.P. (1953) *A general service list of English words, with semantic frequencies and a supplementary word-list for the writing of popular science and technology*. London: Longman, Green.

Williams G. (1998) 'Collocational networks :interlocking patterns of lexis in a corpus of plant biology research articles'. *International Journal of Corpus Linguistics*. Vol. 3/1. pp. 151–171.

Williams G. (2006) 'Advanced ESP and the learner's dictionary: tools for the non-language specialist'. Proceedings of the Twelth EURALEX International Congress, Turin 6th–9th September 2006.

Williams G. (2002) 'Corpus-driven lexicography and the specialised dictionary: headword extraction for the Parasitic Plant Research Dictionary.' In Braasch A. and C. Povlsen (eds) 2002. Proceedings of the Tenth EURALEX International Congress. 859–864.

Dictionaries consulted

OALD - Oxford Advanced Learner's Dictionary. 7th Edition 2005.

Appendix 1. Concordance for 'bank'

</P><P>A data	bank	search revealed no significant similarit
imilarities between that region and data	bank	sequences, suggests a different evolutio
ain degree of similarity with other data	bank	sequences.
d the <TERM TYPE="pp">Striga</TERM> seed	bank	while improving grain yield (Fig 2).
d the <TERM TYPE="pp">Striga</TERM> seed	bank	by about 30% annually through inducing i
d the <TERM TYPE="pp">Striga</TERM> seed	bank	by 300% on average.
e the <TERM TYPE="pp">Striga</TERM> seed	bank	significantly (Table 2).
e the <TERM TYPE="pp">Striga</TERM> seed	bank	in the soil and to assess the suitabilit
e the <TERM TYPE="pp">Striga</TERM> seed	bank	, no single methodology will be complete
f the <TERM TYPE="pp">Striga</TERM> seed	bank	in the soil is reduced.
n the <TERM TYPE="pp">Striga</TERM> seed	bank	(!
both <TERM TYPE="pp">Striga</TERM> seed	bank	reduction and enhanced host productivity
scussed in terms of controlling the seed	bank	of <TERM TYPE="pp">Striga</TERM> in the
varying management practices on the seed	bank	of land that was heavily infested with <
been aimed at reducing the parasite seed	bank	in the soil of infested fields and have
as a trap crop helps to reduce soil seed	bank	and increases soil fertility.
bioherbicides could reduce the soil seed	bank	of this noxious parasitic weed.
nd one picture illustrates the soil seed	bank	.
flowering, then certainly the soil seed	bank	would be completely depleted over severa
ome and the availability of a ctDNA gene	bank	in <REG ORIG="S.
A clone	bank	of EcoRI-digested light band DNA was est
ents in mind we have established a clone	bank	and show the construction of the physica
ailability of a physical map and a clone	bank	of potato ctDNA in conjunction with chlo
gest of potato ctDNA to generate a clone	bank	, since the number of different fragment
was established with the help of a clone	bank	and molecular hybridization to <TERM TYP
</P><P>Using a clone	bank	of twelve restriction fragments covering
"><HEAD>Hybridizations </HEAD><P>A clone	bank	of the entire <TERM TYPE="hp"> tobacco <
ell as the availability of a ctDNA clone	bank	.

Appendix 2. Provisonal entry for 'control' (output TshwaneLex)

Forms: **control**[1] **(= controls, controlling, controlled)** *(verb transitive)* **1** To limit. To control something is to restrain or limit the capacity of something to act. In the case of parasitic plant biology it means to limit the spread or degree of infestation of the parasites. : ***Most farmers in Gambia control Striga by weeding.*** Other example. : ***The tree canopy completely controlled Striga infestation.*** Other example. : ***Orobanche aegyptiaca was controlled by all chemigated treatments.*** **a** MODAL VERBS. The verb is often modified by a modal verb such as can or may to show possibilty or probability. : ***Pot experiments had shown that chlorosulphuron can control Broomrape in tomato.*** Other example. : ***Ethylene may control the growth of dodder.*** **b** PHRASAL PATTERNS. The present participle "controlling" is often used in the pattern of adjective/noun + in + controlling + noun or noun + for + controlling + noun. : ***The herbicide was found effective in controlling the parasite.*** Other example. : ***The semi-arid zone of West Africa holds a great potential in controlling Striga hermonthica.*** Other example. : ***They could provide a potential for controlling parasites.*** Collocate Infestation, Treatment, Dodder, See control[2], Compare Striga **2** To manage. to control is to manage something. : ***Ethylene negatively controls the growth of dodder.***

Forms: **control**[2] *(noun)* **1** A control is a comparative sample used in an experiment. , It consists of an uncontaminated sample or population used as a standard against which the infected sample can be compared. : ***A set of uncovered plants was used as a control.*** **a** Collocation: The noun control is frequently found in the singular, where it is referred to as "a control" (general) or "the control" (specific). The singular form may be used as a modifier as in "control plants" or be modified as in the "untreated control". The plural form cannot modify another noun, but can be modified as in "uninfected controls". **i** Control can modify nouns. **control lane**, **control plant**, **control tissue** Equivalence Control lane, Control plant, Control tissue **ii** Control can be modified by adjectives. : ***negative control.*** Other example. : ***positive control*** Other example. : ***Susceptible control.*** Other example. : ***untreated control.*** Other example. : ***uninfected control*** Collocate susceptible, uninfected, untreated **b** PHRASAL PATTERNS. Control is often used in comparative phrases. Different patterns require different prepositions. : ***Height was lower than that of control plants.*** Other example. : ***Dry mass was slightly modified in comparison with the control.*** Other example. : ***The number of striga plants was significantly lower than in the control.*** Other example. : ***A higher number of Striga plants compared to the control.*** See compare **2** Restraint or limitation, generally used in the singular. , Control in this sense is the action taken to prevent spreading or propogation of a parasite as opposed to its elimination. Control in this case concerns parasitic plants as weeds rather than botanical specimens. **3** Management., Control in this sense is the action of managing something. It is often expressed using the pattern "to be under the control of something or someone".

Forms: **Control lane** *(noun)*
Forms: **controlled** *(adjective)* Controlled refers to the fact that the noun object is limited or restrained in some way. : ***The experiments were carried out under controlled conditions.*** See control**[1]**:1
Forms: **controlling** *(adjective)* Controlling refers to something that controls or limits the capacity of something else. : ***This could be the controlling factor.*** See control**[1]**:1
Forms: **Control plant** *(noun)* Plant or plants used as a standard group for comparison with the plants under study. Equivalence control**[2]**:1
Forms: **Control tissue** *(noun)*

Appendix 3. Provisonal entry for 'haustorium' (output TshwaneLex)

Forms: **haustorium (=haustoria)** *(noun)* **1** A parasite attaches itself to a host plant by means of a haustorium which penetrates the host conductive tissues. The haustorium forms a physiological bridge through which nutrients pass from the host to the parasite. It is the defining feature of parasitic plants. Haustoria may be either a primary or a secondary haustorium. : ***The sieve tube connection from the haustorium of the holoparasite.*** Other example. : ***This paper discusses the mechanisms of haustorium penetration.*** Other example. : ***Evidence of pectinase activity released by Orobanche haustorium in host tissues.*** Other example. : ***The intrusion of the haustorium inside host tissues.*** Other example. : ***Haustorium development is also under control of biological molecular signals.*** **Primary haustorium** The primary haustorium develops at the apex of the young root that emerges from the parasite seed. It attaches itself to the host root before penetrating the host tissues and seeking the conductive elements located inside the host root . : ***Striga penetrates the host tissue by developing primary and secondary haustoria.***, **Secondary haustorium** Secondary haustoria may develop laterally from the primary root system of the parasite or on adventitious roots developing from parasite shoots. These provide further contact between the host roots, or branches in the case of aerial parasites such as mistletoe, and the parasite. This is particularly true in facultative parasites that do not have a primary haustorium. In some cases secondary haustoria allow the parasite to be attached to more than one host. : ***Secondary haustoria develop from the primary root system of the parasite*** Other example. : ***The secondary haustoria are borne on the adventitious root system of Alectra vogelli.*** **a** Collocations: Haustorium occurs with a variety of other words. **i** Haustorium may be used to modify another noun. **Haustorium development.**, **Haustorium penetration.**, **Haustorium size.** **ii** Haustorium is often modified by another word. : ***Resistance occurred during the establishment of a functional haustorium.*** Other example. : ***Secretion was found along the abortive haustorium*** Other example. : ***The transformation of a young haustorium into a functional haustorium*** Other example. : ***The mature haustorium of***

Scleropyrum. **iii** Haustorium is often associated with certain verbs. : ***The haustorium develops when intrusive cells of the parasite penetrate host tissues.*** Other example. : ***The germ tube develops and forms a haustorium.*** Other example. : ***The changes in cell wall composition persist long after the haustorium has penetrated.*** Other example. : ***Haustoria penetrate host tissues.*** Other example. : ***The host stem where the dodder haustoria are attached.***

Etudes contrastives

Vol. 1 Anne-Marie Laurian & Thomas Szende (Eds):
Les mots du rire, comment les traduire? • Essais de lexicologie contrastive
VIII, 391 pages. 2001. ISBN 3-906758-54-0

Vol. 2 Thomas Szende & Györgyi Máté (Eds):
Frontières et passages • Actes du colloque franco-hongrois sur la traduction
VIII, 357 pages. 2003. ISBN 3-906768-92-9

Vol. 3 Anne-Marie Laurian (Ed.):
La langue libérée • Etudes de socio-lexicologie
VI, 244 pages. 2003. ISBN 3-906769-05-4

Vol. 4 Françoise Bidaud:
Structures figées de la conversation • Analyse contrastive français-italien
X, 350 pages. 2002. ISBN 3-906769-06 2

Vol. 5 Anne-Marie Laurian (Ed.):
Dictionnaires bilingues et interculturalité
XII, 258 pages. 2004. ISBN 3-03910-334-2

Vol. 6 Florentina Fredet & Anne-Marie Laurian (Eds):
Linguistique contrastive, linguistique appliquée, sociolinguistique • Hommage à Etienne Petri
XXIV; 286 pages. 2006. ISBN 3-03910-498-5

Vol. 7 Agnès Celle:
Temps et modalité • L'anglais, le français et l'allemand en contraste
VIII, 200 pages. 2006. ISBN 3-03910-759-3

Vol. 8 Anne-Marie Laurian (Ed.):
Les cinq sens et les sensations • Lexicographie contrastive
XIV, 294 pages. 2007. ISBN 978-3-03911-198-5

Vol. 9 Anna Sőrés:
Typologie et linguistique contrastive • Théories et applications dans la comparaison des langues
XVI, 212 pages. 2008. ISBN 978-3-03911-518-1

Vol. 10 Jean-Philippe Claver Zouogbo:
Le proverbe entre langues et cultures • Une étude de linguistique confrontative allemand/français/bété
361 pages. 2009. ISBN 978-3-03911-667-6

Vol. 11 Mirella Conenna
La salle de cours • Questions/réponses sur la grammaire française
XII, 195 pages. 2010. ISBN 978-3-03911-786-4

Vol. 12 Natalie Kübler (ed.)
Corpora, Language, Teaching, and Resources: From Theory to Practice
340 pages. 2011. ISBN 978-3-0343-0054-4